Doing Business in Cameroon

From the mid-1980s to the early 2000s, images of crisis and reform dominated talk of Cameroon's economy. *Doing Business in Cameroon* examines the aftermath of that period of turbulence and unpredictability in the northern city of Ngaoundéré. Taking the everyday encounters between business actors and state bureaucrats as its point of departure, the book vividly illustrates the backstage and interconnected dynamics of four different sectors (cattle trade, trucking, public contracting, and NGO work). Drawing on his training in law and social anthropology as well as his fine-grained ethnography, the author shows how developments in government policies and business regulation have played out in practice, often in ways quite removed from their original intentions. A widespread picture emerges of actors grappling with the long-term implications of selective or suspended enforcement of legal rules. The book deftly illuminates a set of shifting configurations in which economic outcomes such as monetary gains or the circulation of goods are achieved by forgoing the possibility of relying on or complying with the law.

José-María Muñoz is a lecturer in African Studies and International Development at the University of Edinburgh. Muñoz trained as a lawyer in Spain, his home country, before pursuing degrees in Social Anthropology at University College London and Northwestern University, Illinois. He held a postdoctoral fellowship with Emory University's Program in Global Development Studies before relocating to the UK.

THE INTERNATIONAL AFRICAN LIBRARY

General Editors
LESLIE BANK, *Human Sciences Research Council, South Africa*
HARRI ENGLUND, *University of Cambridge*
ADELINE MASQUELIER, *Tulane University, Louisiana*
BENJAMIN SOARES, *University of Florida, Gainesville*

The International African Library is a major monograph series from the International African Institute. Theoretically informed ethnographies, and studies of social relations 'on the ground' which are sensitive to local cultural forms, have long been central to the Institute's publications programme. The IAL maintains this strength and extends it into new areas of contemporary concern, both practical and intellectual. It includes works focused on the linkages between local, national and global levels of society; writings on political economy and power; studies at the interface of the socio-cultural and the environmental; analyses of the roles of religion, cosmology and ritual in social organisation; and historical studies, especially those of a social, cultural or interdisciplinary character.

For a list of titles published in the series, please see the end of the book.

Doing Business in Cameroon
An Anatomy of Economic Governance

José-María Muñoz
University of Edinburgh

International African Institute, London
and

CAMBRIDGE UNIVERSITY PRESS

CAMBRIDGE
UNIVERSITY PRESS

University Printing House, Cambridge CB2 8BS, United Kingdom

One Liberty Plaza, 20th Floor, New York, NY 10006, USA

477 Williamstown Road, Port Melbourne, VIC 3207, Australia

314–321, 3rd Floor, Plot 3, Splendor Forum, Jasola District Centre, New Delhi – 110025, India

79 Anson Road, #06–04/06, Singapore 079906

Cambridge University Press is part of the University of Cambridge.

It furthers the University's mission by disseminating knowledge in the pursuit of education, learning, and research at the highest international levels of excellence.

www.cambridge.org
Information on this title: www.cambridge.org/9781108428996
DOI: 10.1017/9781108684477

© José-María Muñoz 2018

This publication is in copyright. Subject to statutory exception and to the provisions of relevant collective licensing agreements, no reproduction of any part may take place without the written permission of Cambridge University Press.

First published 2018

Printed and bound in Great Britain by Clays Ltd, Elcograf S.p.A.

A catalogue record for this publication is available from the British Library.

Library of Congress Cataloging-in-Publication Data
Names: Muñoz, José María (Anthropologist), author.
Title: Doing business in Cameroon : an anatomy of economic governance / José María Muñoz, University of Edinburgh.
Description: Cambridge, United Kingdom ; New York, NY : Cambridge University Press, 2018. | Series: The international African library | Includes bibliographical references.
Identifiers: LCCN 2018021302 | ISBN 9781108428996 (hardback : alk. paper)
Subjects: LCSH: Business enterprises–Cameroon. | Trade regulation–Cameroon. | Industrial policy–Cameroon. | Cameroon–Commerce. | Cameroon–Economic policy.
Classification: LCC HD2925.7 M86 2018 | DDC 330.96711–dc23
LC record available at https://lccn.loc.gov/2018021302

ISBN 978-1-108-42899-6 Hardback

Cambridge University Press has no responsibility for the persistence or accuracy of URLs for external or third-party internet websites referred to in this publication and does not guarantee that any content on such websites is, or will remain, accurate or appropriate.

Contents

	List of figures	*page* vi
	List of maps	vii
	Acknowledgements	viii
	List of abbreviations and acronyms	xi
	Introduction	1
1	Making a living in Ngaoundéré	26
2	The ordering of public things	64
3	'Cattle saves the day'	93
4	On and off the road	131
5	Under the NGO label	166
	Conclusion: letting pass, letting go	197
	Bibliography	205
	Index	219

Figures

1.1 Shops in the commercial district undergoing reconstruction,
    Ngaoundéré, May 2004 *page* 33
1.2 The view from the VIP seats, Roumdé Adjia stadium,
    Garoua, May 2011 37
1.3 Parking yard, Ngaoundéré cargo terminal, June 2011 51
3.1 Weekly distribution of freight car space among cattle traders,
    Ngaoundéré railway station, October 2004 98
3.2 Cattle market, Tello, August 2005 108
4.1 The blackboard used in the SNTRC's attempt to revive the
    tour de rôle in 2010, Ngaoundéré cargo terminal, July 2014 150
5.1 Sydev members with the author at the NGO's office in
    Ngaoundéré's Tongo-Bali neighbourhood, June 2011 185

Maps

1 Cameroon *page* 21
2 Adamaoua 22

Acknowledgements

Many friends and colleagues in Cameroon and elsewhere have accompanied the research and writing that has led to the publication of this book. Intellectual, logistical, and financial support has come from a variety of people and institutions, for which I remain profoundly grateful.

Initial fieldwork and archival research in Cameroon was funded by a British Economic and Social Research Council research grant (R000-23-9960). My gratitude extends to the other three members of the project's research team: Philip Burnham, Saïdou Abdoullaï Bobboy, and Martial Massike Loke. Northwestern University's Program of African Studies (Hans Panofsky Award), Emory University's Program in Development Studies, Universidad Autónoma de Madrid's African Studies Group (AECI grant), and University of Edinburgh's School of Social and Political Science supported additional field trips in 2005, 2010, 2011, and 2014.

These pages owe their greatest debt to two people whose acquaintance over the years has offered me countless lessons in academic and non-academic life. From the earliest stages of my endeavours in this project, Philip Burnham has offered indefatigable support. His lifelong commitment to ethnographic research in Cameroon opened professional and personal horizons that would otherwise have remained out of reach. His intellectual honesty, encyclopaedic knowledge, sense of humour, and generosity have been a constant source of encouragement and inspiration. Mohamadou Abbo Fodoué has also been an extremely influential presence within and without the confines of this book. *Beero* is the term most often used by people in the city of Ngaoundéré to talk about our ties. This Fulfulde word refers to both host and guest: he is my *beero*, and I am his. *Beero* connotes the customary practices of extending hospitality to strangers. Abbo, however, has gone far beyond a host's customary duties. His widespread reputation for intellectual prowess and independent-minded character, which he earned in his youth, meant that the mere mention of his name opened all kinds of doors for me in Adamaoua and beyond. I have also lost count of the times I benefited from his truly pedagogic disposition, his endless patience, his hands-on approach to problem solving, and his courage.

Acknowledgements

Many business operators and state officials shared with me their time and views on various issues. Although they remain anonymous in these pages, I do not want to miss the opportunity to express my gratitude for their openness and their willingness to reflect critically on things close to their heart. Many other Cameroonians from all walks of life took me in and helped me out. Particular thanks go to Hamza Abdelmadjid, Abdourhamane Moodibo, Sandra Nyambara, and Aboubakar Ousmanou. At the University of Ngaoundéré, I benefited greatly from getting to know Saïbou Issa, Adama Hamadou, Gilbert Taguem Fah, Alexis Avom, and Oumarou Issa. They combined encouragement and practical advice with a rare readiness to engage in different sorts of intellectual exchanges. In Abbo Fodoué's household in Ngaoundéré I have always felt like a spoilt member of the family. Hajja Koulou's common sense and savoir faire made all the difference. I will never be able to thank her and her children for their generosity. Djenabou Guimbel always made a point of treating me like a son whenever I stayed with her in Ngaoundal. Alberto Cerezo and Fatima Godinez at the Spanish Embassy in Yaoundé went out of their way numerous times to accommodate my extravagant requests for logistic support.

My reinvention as a social anthropologist after an uninspiring career in law would not have been possible without mentors and colleagues in the three universities where I spent my formative years: Alicia Campos, Juan Carlos Gimeno, Enrique Luque, Olga Mancha, Victoria Martín, Belen Molinuevo, Gema Robledo, and Ana Toledo at Universidad Autónoma de Madrid; Mukulika Banerjee, Philip Burnham, Tomoko Hayakawa, Ioannis Kyriakakis, Murray Last, Costantino Pes, Nanneke Redclift, Barrie Sharpe, Deborah Soothill, and Jorge Varanda at University College London; and Tatiana Andronova, Caroline Bledsoe, Noah Butler, Tim Earle, Niki Fabricant, Jane Guyer, Karen Tranberg Hansen, Robert Launay, Bishupal Limbu, Aurélien Mauxion, Bill Murphy, Dawn Pankonien, Sam Weber, and Mary Weismantel at Northwestern University.

Robert Launay, Karen Tranberg Hansen, Jane Guyer, and Timothy Earle (the members of my committee at Northwestern University) provided invaluable feedback on the doctoral thesis from which this book originated. LeRay Denzer helped me polish that text. The book's long writing process has been enriched by exchanges with Peter Little, Clifton Crais, David Nugent, and Sita Ranchod-Nilsson at Emory University, and my colleagues and students at the University of Edinburgh. In Madrid, Pedro Díaz-del-Río and, most especially, Sergio Suarez Blanco have never shied away from indulging me in all kinds of intellectual excursions. Always willing to go beyond the call of duty, Stephanie Kitchen at the International African Institute did everything in her power to help the final version of this book live up to its potential.

Philip Burnham, Elaine Peña, and Peter Geschiere read different versions of the full manuscript and gave me advice that was both sensible and stimulating. The excesses and flaws are mine.

Sections of Chapter 2 appeared in 'Making contracts public in Ngaoundere, Cameroon', an article published in *City and Society* (26 [2]: 175–95) in 2014. Materials in Chapter 3 were previously published in article format: 'Business visibility and taxation in northern Cameroon' (*African Studies Review* 53 (2): 149–75) and 'Talking law in times of reform: paradoxes of legal entitlement in Cameroon' (*Law and Society Review* 45 (4): 893–922).

The book is dedicated to my family and friends in Ngaoundéré, San Antonio, and Madrid, and to my wife Elena.

Abbreviations and acronyms

AJLC	Association des Jeunes de Ngaoundéré pour la Lutte contre le SIDA / Association of Ngaoundéré Youth for the Fight against AIDS
ANCBC	Association Nationale des Commerçants à Bétail du Cameroun / Cameroon's National Association of Cattle Traders
ANY	Archives Nationaux de Yaoundé / National Archives, Yaoundé
APROSPEN	Action pour la Promotion de la Santé et la Protection de l'Environnement / Action for Health Promotion and Environmental Protection
ARA	Association des Ressortissants de l'Adamaoua / Association of Citizens from Adamaoua
ARMP	Agence de Régulation des Marchés Publics / Public Contracts Regulatory Board
BARC	Bureau d'Affrètement de la Centrafrique / Central African Freight Bureau
BEAC	Banque des États de l'Afrique Centrale / Bank of Central African States
BGFT	Bureau de Gestion du Fret Terrestre / Road Freight Management Bureau
BNF	Bureau National de Fret / National Freight Bureau (Chad)
CAR	Central African Republic
CBF	Cameroon Business Forum
CCI	*Chef de centre (départemental) des impôts* / MINEFI's head of (district) centre for taxes
CEMAC	Central African Economic and Monetary Community
CFAF	CFA franc
CLSS	*Comité local pour la lutte contre le SIDA* / local committee for the fight against AIDS

Abbreviations and acronyms

CNJD	Coalition Nationale des Jeunes pour le Développement / National Youth Coalition for Development
CNLS	Comité National de Lutte contre le SIDA / National Committee for the Fight against AIDS
CODASC	Coordination Diocésaine de Développement et des Activités Sociales – Caritas / Diocesan Coordination for Development and Social Activities – Caritas
CONSUPE	Contrôle Supérieur de l'État / National Audit Office
CORDAID	Catholic Organisation for Relief and Development Aid
COSCA	Collectif des Organisations de la Société Civile de l'Adamaoua / Coalition of Adamaoua's Civil Society Organisations
COTCO	Cameroon Oil Transportation Company
CPAR	Country Procurement Assessment Report (World Bank)
CTT	Coopération des Transporteurs Tchadiens / Chadian Transporters' Cooperative
DB	'Doing Business'
DGI	*Directeur Général des Impôts* / MINEFI's General Manager of Taxes
DGTC	Direction Générale des Grands Travaux du Cameroun / Cameroon Directorate General of Public Works
DSF	Développement sans Frontières / Development without Borders
ELCOBCAM	Éleveurs et Commerçants à Bétail de Cameroun / Cameroon Cattle Farmers and Traders
FEICOM	Fonds Spécial d'Équipement et d'Intervention Intercommunale / Special Council Support Fund for Mutual Assistance
FIMAC	Fonds d'Investissement des Micro-réalisations Agricoles et Communautaires / Investment Funds for Agricultural and Community Micro-projects
GDP	Gross domestic product
GIC	*Groupe d'initiative commune* / community initiative group
GIE	*Groupement d'intérêt économique* / economic interest group

GTC	Groupe Technique Central / Central Technical Group
GTP	Groupe Technique Provinciale / Provincial Technical Group
HIPC	Heavily Indebted Poor Countries
IMF	International Monetary Fund
INS	Institut National de la Statistique / National Institute of Statistics
LCC	Local community contact (COTCO)
LDP	Livestock Development Project
MINEFI	Ministry of Economy and Finance (now MINFI)
MINEPAT	Ministry of Economic Planning and Regional Development
MINEPIA	Ministry of Livestock, Fisheries, and Animal Industries
MINFI	Ministry of Finance
MINT	Ministry of Transport
MINTAD	Ministry of Territorial Administration and Decentralisation
NGO	Non-governmental organisation
OHADA	Organisation for the Harmonisation of African Business Law
OTTC	Organisation des Transporteurs Terrestres du Cameroun / Cameroon's Ground Transporters' Organisation
PACDDU	Programme d'Appui aux Capacités Décentralisées de Développement Urbain / Support Programme for Decentralised Capacity Building for Urban Development
PADI	Programme d'Appui au Développement Integré / Programme for the Support of Integrated Development
PARFAR	Programme d'Amélioration du Revenu Familial Rural / Project for the Improvement of Rural Households' Income
PASC	Programme d'Appui à la Société Civil / Civil Society Support Programme
PASOC	Programme d'Appui à la Structuration de la Société Civile / Support Programme for the Structuring of Civil Society
PCPA	Programme Concerté Pluri-Acteurs / Consultative Multi-Actor Programme

PIAASI	Projet Intégré d'Appui aux Acteurs du Secteur Informel / Integrated Project for the Support of Informal Sector Operators
PNDP	Programme National de Développement Participatif / National Programme for Participatory Development
PNG	Progamme National de Gouvernance / National Governance Programme
PPRT	Project for the Preparation of the Transport Reform
PSREP	Programme de Sécurisation des Recettes de l'Élevage et la Pêche / Programme for Enhanced Revenue Reliability in Animal Husbandry and Fisheries
RDPC	Rassemblement Démocratique du Peuple Camerounais / Cameroon People's Democratic Movement
RELUFA	Réseau de Lutte contre la Faim / Network for the Fight against Hunger
SETRACAUCAM	Syndicat de Transporteurs par Car et Autobus de Cameroon / Cameroon's Union of Passenger Transporters
SMP	Simplified management programme
SNTRC	Syndicat National des Transporteurs Routiers du Cameroun / Cameroon's National Union of Road Transporters
SOCOOPED	*Société cooperative pour la production et le développement* / cooperative society for production and development
SP	Société de Prévoyance / Provident Society
Sydev	Synergies de Devéloppement / Development Synergies
TCL	Tchad-Cameroun Logistique
TPG	*Trésorier-payeur général* / paymaster general
UNDP	Union Nationale pour la Démocratie et le Progrès / National Union for Democracy and Progress
UNDP	United Nations Development Programme
UPC	Union du Peuple Camerounais
UTA	United Transport Africa

Introduction

The world's emergent political economies include many regions where multiple organisational forms, pathways, and temporalities meet and intersect. By bringing ethnographic attention to experiential dynamics in the lives of participants in these economies, and politico-legal attention to different groups and their material and ideological bases in changing economic sectors, we can track organisational emergence. Northern Cameroon in the 1990s and 2000s witnessed many innovations, including those resulting from the construction of the Chad–Cameroon oil pipeline, while the region's agropastoral and trading economy retained its vitality. The chapters of this book explore these processes. I start this Introduction with an example of a person and an organisation of the kind that I will draw on later. The chapters then trace in detail the many intersecting dynamics, concluding with inferences about the place of vulnerable economic actors within the framework of legality. I introduce the reader, first of all, to one of the actors, or analysts, in this scenario.

Dressed in an immaculate khaki suit, Sanda Maliki spoke with the confidence of a seasoned professional. Over the more than three decades that had followed his return from studies in Belgium, he had undertaken many roles in the transport business. On this occasion, he had chosen to introduce himself as president of the North Province chapter of the national truckers' association. Yet most of his energy was in fact spent working for an international freight forwarder, a job he made compatible with the management of his own small trucking firm. Sanda was addressing participants in a seminar on the formal and informal dimensions of business activities in Cameroon.[1] As his remarks came to an end and he delivered his punchline, his studied seriousness gave way to a playful grin: 'They are unavoidable. It is them who try to regulate transport. Without the safe conduct they issue, no loaded truck can go anywhere.

---

[1] 'Le Formel et l'Informel dans les Activités des Opérateurs Economiques Camerounais', a seminar sponsored by the Economic and Social Research Council at the University of Ngaoundéré, 24 September 2004. As a rule, proper names of my interlocutors have been changed to pseudonyms.

You will find they have offices everywhere. They are the informal arm of the state.' He was talking about the Cameroonian Bureau de Gestion du Fret Terrestre (Road Freight Management Bureau or BGFT). The notion that the state apparatus might be actively engaged in maintaining informality struck a chord with the audience.

The BGFT is indeed a formidable actor. It presides over a sector that in 2004, the year the seminar took place, handled more than 6 million tons of freight that went through the port of Douala. That year, however, trucking firms began to feel a drop in turnover as the boost generated by the Chad–Cameroon oil pipeline project fizzled out with the completion of the construction phase. In spite of encouraging growth figures, the country's broader economic outlook was not particularly bright either. Only three weeks before Sanda uttered those words, the International Monetary Fund (IMF), on whose assistance Cameroon had depended since 1988, had declared the country 'off-track' in its implementation of the *Poverty Reduction Strategy Paper*. This meant that the substantial debt relief expected under the Heavily Indebted Poor Countries (HIPC) initiative would have to wait another two years. Among other factors, this decision had been justified by the lack of fiscal discipline shown by the government in the run-up to the presidential elections of October 2004. With the elections less than a month away, the chances of a change in power were broadly seen as very slim. The united front of opposition parties had just collapsed, thus paving the way for another victory for Paul Biya, who had been head of state since 1982. Another seven years of governmental inertia seemed to lie ahead.[2]

Established in 1993 in the context of what for about two decades was known as *la crise* (the crisis), the BGFT's beginnings had been characterised by instability. In the 1980s, Cameroon had gone from oil euphoria to enduring recession. Between 1986 and 1993, the country's real gross domestic product (GDP) per capita was estimated to have fallen by 42 per cent. In this period, the regime was unable to quell popular unrest. In 1991, it faced the challenge of a series of nationwide general strikes known as the *villes mortes* (ghost towns). The regime weathered these massive protests with a combination of repression, liberal rhetoric, and control of the electoral timetable leading to multiparty politics. In the

---

[2] For recent official statistics on transport and on the port of Douala specifically, see INS (2013: 288). The country's official GDP growth rate for 2004 was 4.8 per cent. The *Poverty Reduction Strategy Paper* was approved and published in 2003 (Republic of Cameroon 2003). On the delay of the HIPC initiative's completion point, see Batongué et al. (2004) and Charlier and N'Cho-Oguie (2009: 58–9). For an interpretation of the collapse of the opposition front focused on party finances, see Arriola (2013: 187–94). Inertia was singled out by President Biya as 'our main enemy' in his New Year's speech for 2004. For a journalistic example of the centrality of inertia in representations of the country's public administration, see Monda Bakoa (2008).

ensuing legislative and presidential elections of 1992, which were marked by widespread irregularities and fraud, Biya and his party managed to hold on to power. A year later, in the context of the regime's reassertion of authority, the Ministry of Transport gave its stamp of approval to the creation of the BGFT. This was an attempt to bring under control the *désordre inventif* (inventive disorder) that had taken hold of freight transport as well as many other sectors after the economic slump of 1987. In June 1992, the World Bank conducted an evaluation of road transport in Cameroon aimed at advancing a liberalising agenda. The establishment of a freight bureau was a way of foreclosing some of the most drastic implications of the Bank's designs.[3]

The BGFT offers an apt illustration of the complexities and ambiguities of economic governance that are the focus of this book. For all its power, the bureau was created (and has since been ruled) by a minister's decision, the flimsiest of legal bases. Although formally included in the Ministry of Transport's organigram, it operates with considerable autonomy. Only one of the five members of its management committee represents the government. The other four are representatives of the railway company, shippers, truckers, and forwarding agents. Neither its accounts nor its statistics on transport are publicly available. It was probably the combination of the bureau's questionable legal status, its autonomy, and its opacity that Sanda Maliki wanted to underscore with his remark about it being an informal arm of the state. The round-table conversation that followed Sanda's presentation triggered an intriguing response from another of the seminar participants, a representative of the country's Chamber of Commerce: 'Then, the BGFT is truly *une organisation patronale* [an employers' organisation].' 'Yes, of course!,' replied Sanda, embracing the paradox with apparent glee. This was more than the idiosyncratic position of a veteran trucker; it is a position that the bureau itself has advanced repeatedly. In 2012, its *coordinateur général* (managing director) was categorical in this regard: 'The BGFT has never been a

---

[3] On the onset of the Cameroonian crisis as a macro-economic phenomenon, see Hugon (1996) and Aerts et al. (2000). On crisis as a structuring idiom in the country, see Mbembe and Roitman (1995), Johnson-Hanks (2005), and Roitman (2016). The World Bank's country assistance evaluation of 2001 contains the GDP figures relating to the reversal of the country's fortunes. Equally significant is the document's critical assessment of the World Bank's programme, which is deemed 'uneven and poorly adapted to changing needs and sharp policy turning points' (World Bank 2001: 1). On the *villes mortes* and their aftermath, see Courade and Sindjoun (1996), Takougang and Krieger (1998), Saïbou Issa (2006), and Roitman (2005). 'Désordre inventif' is part of the title of an article by Luc Sindjoun (1996a) on the political transformations of the 1990s. 'Le désarroi camerounais' (Cameroonian disarray) is the title of another academic volume on the economic transformations of this period (Courade 2000). Disorder and disarray are prominent words in my interlocutors' accounts of the transport sector in the late 1980s and the 1990s. For a chronicle of the World Bank's attempts to reshape this sector in the 1990s, see Meyo-Soua (1999).

governmental structure. There is neither an act of parliament nor a decree that creates the bureau. We created the bureau and its internal management is our responsibility' (CONAC 2013: 129).

To any informed observer of political and economic processes in West and Central Africa, this is in many ways a familiar story. Organisations that straddle the public–private divide and whose informal dimensions are decisive in shaping the range of what is possible offer illustrations of what Jean-François Bayart famously termed the 'rhizome state'. Indeed, inspired by the elaboration of the rhizome that frames Deleuze and Guattari's 'infectious' *A Thousand Plateaus* (1987), Bayart's notion grew out of his earlier account of state formation in Cameroon. The creation of the BGFT could thus be seen as a moment in the state's 'infinitely variable multiplicity of networks whose underground branches join together the scattered points of society' (Bayart 1993: 218). Similarly, the proliferation of organisations such as the BGFT with vague but expansive mandates that overlap and compete with those of other authorities resonates with the insights of a number of authors who have underscored the fragmented, plural, and composite nature of public authority in different African contexts.[4]

This book goes beyond those characterisations by drawing readers' attention to the specific practices through which the economy is governed. How does the BGFT regulate international freight transport? Exploring this sort of question involves stepping away from round-table discussions, legal texts, and policy reports. For one thing, it calls for venturing into places such as the BGFT offices, where on an everyday basis *offres de fret* (freight offers) from forwarding agents are received, national quotas are calculated and assigned, documents are issued to truckers, fees are collected, and statistics are compiled. For document verification purposes, the BGFT also makes its presence felt at designated checkpoints along international transport corridors. In any case, the interactions that take place at those offices and checkpoints are only part of a broader configuration that creates the conditions under which trucks and goods circulate.

Thus, no matter how influential it might be, an organisation such as the BGFT cannot be the end point for an analysis of economic governance. The task of governing transport is shared with a constellation of other actors and its analysis involves considering a range of interactions (with sundry entangled objects) on and off the road. Offices and checkpoints other than those of the bureau, cargo terminals and parking lots,

---

[4] See Bayart (1985; 1993) and Deleuze and Guattari (1987). The claim that the work of Deleuze and Guattari infected contemporary social thought is John Urry's (2000: 27). On the fragmentation of public authority, see Lund (2006), Mbembe (2001), and Roitman (2005).

garages and petrol stations are some of the arenas in which key relationships are constituted, reproduced, and transformed. In them, trucking companies' owners and employees routinely engage with colleagues and intermediaries, with freight forwarders' staff, with trucking associations' representatives and the delegates of drivers' unions, with customs officials, gendarmes, and police. Those ties, which can be cultivated, eroded, reactivated, or severed at any point in the process, loom large in the minds of those active in the trucking business.

An anatomy of economic governance

A word about the book's title. It deliberately echoes 'Doing Business' (DB), a long-term benchmarking exercise launched by the World Bank Group soon after I began conducting fieldwork in Cameroon. Relying on a bold communication strategy, DB developed a set of influential indicators designed to measure the quality of regulatory environments across the world. Invoking Hernando de Soto as a tutelary spirit, its first annual report made two of its key tenets explicit from the outset: 'heavier regulation brings bad outcomes' and 'when it comes to the manner of regulation, one size often fits all' (World Bank 2004: xiv, xviii, 17). Over the years, in response to widespread criticism of the soundness and relevance of its data and tools of analysis, DB has become more explicit about its limitations and more cautious about its claims. Despite this, the World Bank still considers DB one of its flagship 'knowledge products' and its reports and data continue to attract considerable attention from government officials and business leaders across the world. In Cameroon, for example, the national platform for dialogue between the government and the private sector, which has been institutionalised as the Cameroon Business Forum (CBF) since 2009, monitors the country's performance in DB indicators periodically. Many of the CBF recommendations to the government are in fact explicitly aimed at improving the country's DB rankings (with modest success thus far).[5]

---

[5] Hernando de Soto is a Peruvian economist turned policy entrepreneur who gained international prominence with the publication of the bestseller *The Other Path* (1989), where he sets out to test empirically the thesis that enterprises choose to comply with the regulatory framework once they reach a point where the costs of informality outweigh their benefits. For a scathing critique of de Soto's work, see Mitchell (2007). Critical responses to DB have included a report from the World Bank's own Independent Evaluation Group (2008), which triggered numerous changes to the initiative. DB also features prominently in the recent wave of research on governance by indicators. Merry, Davis, and Kingsbury (2015) is a good example of this. It is worth pointing out that the CBF's permanent secretary is a representative of the International Financial Corporation. For the CBF's six-month reports assessing the progress made by the government in implementing its recommendations, see www.cbfcameroun.org. Cameroon's rankings have not suffered substantial changes since the DB indicators were launched in 2004.

That *Doing Business in Cameroon* and the DB project bear little resemblance will hardly come as a surprise, but the contrast will allow me to emphasise this book's intended contribution to scholarship. DB primarily approaches laws and regulations as they are written and not as they are applied. This book pays attention to both law on the books and law in action and explores the relationship between the two. DB is designed to capture information on resorting to or complying with laws and regulations and not on practices that entail only partial reliance on or compliance with those laws and regulations. This book is as interested in partial compliance and non-compliance as it is in compliance. By focusing on hypothetical scenarios that businesses may experience, DB can generate comparable data across all the countries it covers – and it does this affordably, as it relies on local experts to provide answers to questions based on such scenarios. Its much humbler scope allows this book to focus on actual rather than stylised practices. More fundamentally, as lucid analyses of the DB initiative have pointed out (Davis and Kruse 2007: 1104–8), the project's indicators are a poor match for the inherent complexity and uncertainty of legal norms and practices. Shedding light on how both authorities and business actors handle complexity and uncertainty is one of this book's concerns. This is only fitting, as most of the people I met in 2003 when I began my fieldwork were still contending with the ramifications of the turbulent 1990s.

In contrast to the DB's concentration on the cost and time required to perform ordinary tasks when running a business, I have a less constricted focus on the everyday encounters of a varied range of business actors with public bureaucracies and their agents. Those encounters and the performances that accompany them – great and small, publicly accessible and restricted in various ways – are at the core of what socio-legal scholars would call legality. This term is meant to convey the 'meanings, sources of authority, and cultural practices that are commonly recognized as legal, regardless of who employs them or for what ends' (Ewick and Silbey 1998: 22). From such a perspective, the shape that law takes results not so much from 'an authoritative rule-producing voice' as from 'a multiplicity of voices and dialogues within and outside the state' (Channock 2001: 12). Such voices and dialogues are framed within specific registers that feature prominently in the production of legalities (and illegalities) in the economic sphere. To refer to those encounters, dialogues, and registers that are integral to economic activities anywhere, I use the capacious term 'economic governance'.

For instance, in terms of 'ease of doing business' (the DB's aggregate indicator), the country has gone from 130 out of 155 countries in the 2006 report to 166 out of 190 countries in the 2017 one.

Governance emerged in the late 1980s as a new field of analysis in sociology and political science. The proliferation of the term owed much to its espousal in the 1990s by international and national policymakers. Cameroon, for instance, announced the adoption of a National Governance Programme in 1996. The usage of the term in policy circles was overtly normative, calling for the promotion of good governance, which was largely understood in terms of minimising the role of the state, downsizing the civil service, and supporting non-state mechanisms of regulation. The DB initiative itself is in many regards part of the long-term legacy of this good governance agenda. In explicit contrast to this normative usage, academic work on governance tended to approach it as an emergent pattern arising out of complex interactions between actors, groups, and organisations; of these, state institutions were only one example, and not necessarily the most significant, among many others. While anthropology was slower than other disciplines to address academic and policy debates around governance, recognition of the whole variety of authorities that govern in different sites, in relation to different objectives, and with recourse to different techniques has in many ways been one of its long-standing characteristics.[6]

Anatomy, a trope with a long and venerable history, refers to 'the dissection ... of anything material or immaterial for the purpose of examining its parts', or, more simply, a 'detailed examination' (OED). I have been inspired in my choice of 'anatomy' in the subtitle of my book by Béatrice Hibou's advocacy of a political anatomy of economic detail (2011: 17). The economic field whose governance is dissected in these pages refers to several types of economic activity. Freight transport is only one of them. Cattle trade, public contracting, and work by non-governmental organisations (NGOs) are the other three. The focus on four sectors is partly a matter of design. I set out to explore who governed what in diverse settings. Different types of activity occupied distinct places in popular hierarchies of value (e.g. the precedence of cattle wealth) or in widespread topographies of power (e.g. the mobility of truckers, which makes them distant, elusive targets for some state

---

[6] Gerhard Anders (2010) and Brenda Chalfin (2010) have approached ethnographically what being 'in the shadow of good governance' meant respectively for the Malawian civil service and the Ghanaian customs authority. Critics of the new sociology of governance of the 1990s underscored its largely descriptive thrust and how it neglected the assumptions and blind spots of existing strategies for governing (e.g. Rose 1999: 19). In turn, scholars inspired by Foucault, who favour analyses of power in terms of governmentality, have conceded that within their approach to the blueprints and programmes of government there is limited scope for studying how those blueprints and programmes are implemented and adopted (Rose, O'Malley, and Valverde 2006: 100). For an Africa-focused anthropological intervention that tries to strike a balance between a governmentality approach and an exploratory, descriptive notion of governance, see Blundo and LeMeur (2009).

bureaucracies, compared with the proximity of public contractors to those bureaucracies). I also wanted to explore how the shape of the economic itself was interrogated, as is the case with NGO work and the debate over whether it should be considered an economic activity. Nonetheless, these choices were also a function of the relationships that I could forge during my fieldwork.

Although my interlocutors and I use the notion of 'sector' as shorthand for the worlds that hinge around these different types of activity, it is important to avoid any temptation to conceive of them as compartmentalised. The same can be said about occupational categories. Commonly used labels to designate cattle traders in the places where I conducted research (the Fulfulde *filooɓe na'i*, the Hausa *falke*, or the French *commerçants à bétail*), for example, carry with them a set of distinct albeit changing connotations. These tend to permeate the identity of those involved in the trade in ways that obfuscate their engagement in other activities, from livestock husbandry and butchery to other commercial enterprises and transport. The chapters that follow feature numerous people who engage in different activities either simultaneously or successively. Financial resources derived from one line of business are also frequently used to help sustain other activities. Words such as 'sectors' and 'professions' are thus useful in tidying up a messy world for the sake of clarity, but it is important to see them for what they are: widely used categories that may serve as heuristic devices but should not blind us to what happens between, across, and beyond them.

The work of the state in times of crisis and reform

How has the Cameroonian government gone about its mission of governing the economy in an era marked by contestation over what that mission should consist of and by severe, albeit fluctuating, financial constraints? The myriad periodic reports of ministerial departments are a good starting point to explore this question. Consider the Ministry of Economic Planning and Regional Development report (MINEPAT 2003) on the Adamaoua Province's economy and society for the fiscal year 2001–2. The report opens with a disclaimer. The author, a young official who had spent only a couple of years in the north of the country and whose only previous professional experience had been in the capital Yaoundé, explains how the provincial offices of many ministries had simply stopped producing the annual reports on which MINEPAT's own reports relied. Moreover, the ministries that still bothered to write those reports had to be hounded to share them with MINEPAT. If such a situation had become the norm in recent times, readers are informed, it had been made worse by the 'specific circumstances' of 2002. What made that year different from others? The legislative and municipal elections in June and the cabinet reshuffle in August 2002 had created 'a distinct wait-and-see attitude' among the staff of many provincial offices. In a climate marked by 'the popular fever' of electoral periods and 'the uncertain days ahead' of government rearrangements, many of those in charge 'simply forgot to compile their annual reports'. The MINEPAT report was prepared without any contribution from nine ministerial departments. As a result, it lacked 'statistical data about vital sectors' of Adamaoua's economy, such as agriculture and livestock (MINEPAT 2003).

In recent decades, routines such as the production of periodic reports, which were established in the colonial era and reinstated in the early years after independence, have become obsolete in many islands of the Cameroonian 'administrative archipelago'. Such bureaucratic practices tend to generate effects that have been dissected by the anthropology of the state in recent decades. This type of report is premised on the 'taken-for-granted spatial and scalar image of a state that both sits above and contains its localities, regions and communities' (Ferguson and Gupta 2002: 982). Reports offer synoptic views of economic activity at the district, provincial, and national levels, those at higher scales subsuming reports produced at lower scales. When these routines of official document production are upset, claims of vertical encompassment are weakened. A report with glaring gaps in what it covered was an admission of sorts of the long-term decline of MINEPAT, which, like other planning departments in the 1990s and 2000s, was starved of support and resources by international financial organisations that privileged finance ministries instead. In such situations, when state agencies falter in their task of constructing the economy as 'an object of knowledge through an extensive process of statistical representation', the idea of the economy itself as a totality 'subject to intervention, adjustment, and management by an externally situated state' (Mitchell 1999: 94) seems to be in jeopardy.[7]

It would seem disingenuous, however, to give much importance to the periodic activity reports coming out of ministerial offices across the country. After all, these reports might be thought of as the 'empty

---

[7] Jean Copans (2001) proposed the image of the archipelago to capture the unevenness of the state apparatus in sub-Saharan Africa. A prime minister's instruction of 1968 establishes an explicit link between periodic reporting and the efficiency of government departments (National Archives, Yaoundé (ANY) 1AA 1381, 'Cameroun Francophone, Administration, Efficacité, Rapport Annuel, Instruction Premier Ministre'). On anthropology and state effects, see Trouillot (2001). Thomas Bierschenk (2014: 232) points out that the decline of planning ministries is an outcome of structural adjustment and its aftermath. However, the reactivation of infrastructural investment in the late 2000s has reversed this trend in many countries.

calories' of economic governance. The day-to-day operations of these ministries do not depend on such reports in any meaningful way. In terms of documentation, decisions and activities are amply covered in copious official minutes and correspondence. In fact, this is a common justification among civil servants for the current rarity of reports. The usefulness of periodic reports has always been limited, some argue. This sort of document hardly ever constitutes a lever of control by superiors and, given its restricted circulation, the opportunities it opens up for meaningful public scrutiny are meagre. The reports are riddled with formulaic, vacuous turns of phrase. Their authors do not hesitate to draw a veil over any developments that could cause controversy or contestation. Beneath the ready-made formulas, the reports contain scant information, and the little information they do provide in terms of statistics is often unreliable.

If activity reports are not the most consequential instance of the Cameroonian state failing to live up to its ambitions, there is no lack of other examples. The last national census to be completed is a case in point. It was ordered by presidential decree in 2001, well past the ten-year periodicity recommended by international bodies – the previous census dated from 1987. As international financial support took several years to materialise, the census operations were only completed by the end of 2005. The data gathered suffered from numerous technical deficiencies, which were blamed for successive postponements of the publication date. The political sensitivity of census data was broadly seen as an equally important delaying factor. In 2010, when the results were finally made public, they came in the form of projections of the 2005 data to 2010 and generated much controversy. The whole lengthy saga, which received extensive media attention, does not speak of a state invested in generating statistical knowledge about its population.[8] As in the case of activity reports, the importance of the census could be questioned. Although it can certainly affect the territorial distribution of resources, the absence of an updated, reliable census is not something that in itself hinders the operations of public offices representing different ministries at the district and provincial levels.

Nonetheless, the civil servants I encountered were not inclined to dismiss as trivial the interruption of activity reports or the failure to produce a census worthy of the name. Many saw these as symptoms of the demotivated, under-resourced, and politicised bureaucracies that make up the Cameroonian state. The late 1980s and early 1990s are

---

[8] Presidential decree no. 2001/251 of 13 September 2001 ordered a national census to be conducted. The previous 1987 census was itself marred by irregularities and its results were never fully published. For a sample of press coverage of the 2005 census, see Foute (2005), Nkonlak (2008), and Guichi (2010).

seen by most as having marked a clear downward trend. During this period, the civil service, which canonical analyses of Cameroon's political system had seen as the 'main social force in the country' (Bayart 1985: 216), saw its position eroded. International donors made their support contingent on cuts in public spending. An early product of this period was Opération ANTILOPE. Launched in 1987, this was aimed at unifying the management of the state payroll and cleansing it of 'ghost' employees. By 1990 ANTILOPE had become a *gouffre à sous* (money pit), enabling the embezzlement of significant funds within the Ministry of Finance, according to the retrospective assessment by the head of the civil service of the time. As he put it in 2005, with the humour that distance from both those events and his government position afforded him, that antelope had shown itself to be 'out of breath' early on.[9]

The Cameroonian regime dragged its heels with the *dégraissage* (slimming down) treatment prescribed by its international funders. Plans to reduce the state payroll through layoffs and salary cuts were postponed in the troubled years of transition to multiparty politics. Finally, in January 1993, salaries were reduced by 15 per cent on average, excluding the police and military personnel. Later that year, in November, there was an additional reduction of 32 per cent. The 1994 CFA franc (CFAF) devaluation further eroded their economic position. Senior civil servants, for example, saw their real wages fall by 75 to 80 per cent from 1992 to 1995. As the limitations of approaches to civil service reform that focused almost exclusively on the containment of costs became apparent, international funders sponsored so-called 'second-generation' reforms across Africa. In Cameroon, the first reflection of this shift was the 1994 Statut Général de la Fonction Publique de l'État (Civil Service General Statute), which was drafted with the participation of the United Nations Development Programme (UNDP), with the intention of creating a legal framework conducive to improving civil service efficiency. Despite its ostensible aims, and although it listed devotion to the service as a fundamental obligation (Article 15), the new statute explicitly accepted civil servants' parallel involvement in private activities (Article 37). This unprecedented formal sanction of the widespread practice of 'straddling' (seeking economic advantage by simultaneous involvement in state employment and private business) did not pass unnoticed by critics. In the 1990s, straddling continued unabated and extended to the lower ranks of the civil service. The 1994 statute also opened the door for

---

[9] '*L'antilope se montrait essoufflée*' (Deutchoua 2005). Operation ANTILOPE's exuberant acronym stood for Application Nationale des Traitements Informatiques et Logistiques des Personnels de l'État (National Implementation of Computerised Management and Logistics of State Personnel). With time, the operation became a point of reference for national public opinion on the ease with which reforming measures could be hijacked.

a reduction in the number of civil servants by 30,000 through voluntary departure and early retirement, in fulfilment of conditions imposed by the IMF and the World Bank.[10]

On the ground, different ministries followed distinct trajectories. The Ministry of Livestock, Fisheries, and Animal Industries (MINEPIA), which readers will encounter again in Chapter 3, offers a fitting example. The injunction to downsize and liberalise had a clearly identifiable origin as a donor imposition, but the government enjoyed considerable room for manoeuvre in deciding the modalities and the pace of reform. Moreover, liberalising measures were foreshadowed in many respects by the liberalising effects of diminished capacity and commitment to enforce regulations. MINEPIA was indeed one of the ministries used by donors as a showcase to test the willingness of the Cameroonian government to implement the larger adjustment package. In exchange for a World Bank-funded Livestock Development Project (LDP), the government committed in 1988 to a restructuring programme aimed at ending the state monopoly of veterinary services. This was not unlike programmes adopted in other countries around this time at the behest of international lenders (Leonard 1993). The idea was to bring about private service delivery by encouraging veterinary professionals to leave the civil service. Financial and in-kind support was to be given to departing officials. Yet, the mechanisms to make this happen took years to materialise and the incentives turned out to be meagre. Officially, the sales of veterinary products were not liberalised until 2000, although numerous veterinarians set up private practice with the help of foreign pharmaceutical companies much earlier. In the end, MINEPIA saw a significant reduction in personnel only when its staff were able to access the post-1994 early retirement and voluntary departure options available across all ministerial departments and parastatals. Lack of continuity in key senior positions fuelled uncertainty in this period of radical reorientation of MINEPIA's role – in the three years that followed the 1988 agreement with the World Bank, the ministry had a succession of three secretary

---

[10] On *dégraissage* in Cameroon, see Mbonji (1999). The source for the figures on the decreased real wages of civil servants is a World Bank's country assistance evaluation (World Bank 2001: 4). On the contrast between first- and second-generation civil service reforms in Africa, see Lienert and Modi (1997). On the broadening scope of civil service reform beyond spending cuts in Cameroon, see Ngouo (1997). The Civil Service General Statute is contained in decree no. 1994/117 of 7 October 1994. On the UNDP's involvement in the drafting of the statute, see Bruneau and Abouem (2004: 7). On straddling in Cameroon, see Bayart (1993), Geschiere and Konings (1993), and Roitman (1990). On the statute's explicit acknowledgement of straddling, see Sindjoun (1996a: 64) and Nanga (2000: 5). Mbonji (1999: 3) elaborates an emic distinction between straddlers in the high ranks (*cumulards*, or accumulators) and those in the low ranks of the civil service (*débrouillards*, or small-timers). Bayie Kamanda (1999) discusses the post-1994 programmes for so-called *deflatés* (departing civil servants).

generals. To this uncertainty were added the pay cuts of 1993 and the effects of the currency devaluation on purchasing power in 1994. The authority, prestige, and rewards that state veterinarians had enjoyed in the 1970s and 1980s seemed to belong to a bygone era. MINEPIA 'old-timers' in the mid-2000s spoke of the early 1990s as a period marked not only by the open defiance of the *villes mortes* strikes but also by the disaffection of government officials. Low morale within their ranks weighed as heavily as social contestation on the loosening of their grip on livestock-related economic activities.[11]

Since the mid-1990s, numerous initiatives tackling different aspects of state organisation in order to increase its efficiency and integrity have come to light, many of them drawing on the private sector management recipes advocated by the New Public Management school of public administration and placed under the mantle of good governance. These include an overarching National Governance Programme (PNG), which has undergone two phases (2000–4 and 2006–10), and a myriad of other programmes and projects. Learning to live with reforms has become part of the social condition of Cameroonian civil servants. Reforms have accentuated the image of the state as 'an unfinished, apparently perpetual building site where construction, repair, abandonment and re-purposing proceed simultaneously' (Bierschenk and Olivier de Sardan 2014: 8). As Thomas Cantens (2007) has shown in his pioneering research on customs reform at the port of Douala, responses have varied widely depending on factors ranging from the reforms' substance, sponsors, resources, and timescales to the concerned officials' connections, ranking, and educational capital. Those well placed to position themselves as reform champions often try to turn these programmes and projects into platforms for career advancement or personal enrichment. Others endure them as threats to their position, rights, and privileges. These reforms often also trigger conflicts between senior officials, who do not hesitate to fight it out by enlisting rival press outlets. In the last decades, such recurrent conflicts have taken their toll on 'the myth of *l'Etat structurant* (the state organiser) that speaks with one voice' (Sindjoun 1996a: 58). Not surprisingly, many officials share a deep scepticism about the reforms' transformative potential. Overall, the reforms

---

[11] In the mid-2000s, the administrative record of Adamaoua Province's MINEPIA office reflected this state of affairs. Its annual reports went only from 1984–5, their first year in operation after Adamaoua became a separate province, to 1990–1, which marked the turmoil of the *villes mortes*. In the next 15 years, nobody bothered to revive the practice of producing annual reports. Jean-Germain Gros's doctoral thesis offers a detailed account of the negotiations between the World Bank and the Cameroonian government over the LDP and the programme's tortuous implementation (Gros 1993). The 1988 reform led to the enactment of law 1990/033 of 10 August 1990, which contained the new organisation of the veterinary profession. New regulations on veterinary pharmaceutical products had to wait until the passing of law 2000/018 of 19 December 2000 (Messomo Ndjana 2006).

of the last two decades have done little to curb the sense of decline and instability that set in within the ranks of the civil service in the late 1980s.[12]

Over more recent years, the reduction in the size of the civil service that took place in the second half of the 1990s has been reversed. Data on the state's monthly wage bill indicate that it went from CFAF 17 billion in 1992 to 37 billion in 2005. In that year, the government reached an unprecedented 65 ministerial posts, a number it has since kept. On the lower rungs of the civil service, the reversal of staff reductions took place largely through the employment of temporary agents. In 2011, the approaching presidential elections pushed President Biya to break with a two-decade-long taboo and announce the recruitment of 25,000 youth into government jobs. This new growth in personnel has not attenuated the insecurity or precariousness that permeates the daily experience of many government employees. From officials well past retirement age whose retirement never seems to materialise to new ministerial organigrams that take years to translate into nominations, interim situations can be maintained indefinitely. New recruits typically have to wait months and even years before they receive their first salary. Officials in most ministries and parastatals experience substantial salary arrears periodically. Elections bring about months of administrative paralysis on account of the campaigning commitments of most senior officials. Cabinet reshuffles and rearrangements of administrative units entail lengthy readjustment processes in terms of nominations and transfers. These are all important considerations for any analysis interested in treating state bureaucrats 'as active human beings rather than as ciphers of a state machine' (Herzfeld 2004: 5).[13]

The passages of economic governance

If structural adjustment and the good governance agenda have entailed drastic changes in the terms, conditions, and expectations of work for the civil service, is it possible to identify parallel shifts in the registers mobilised to frame relations between state bureaucracies and business actors? A register that has proved particularly enduring in Cameroon has been that of *la tutelle* (trusteeship), a term with a long lineage in French

---

[12] On the influence of New Public Management ideas in Cameroon, see Ngouo (2000), Tamekou (2008), and Muñoz (2013). As mentioned earlier, the PNG was first announced by President Biya in his 1996 New Year's Eve speech but not approved by him until 2000. A 2004 critical evaluation (Bruneau and Abouem 2004) gave the impetus for a reformulation of the programme in 2005. The UNDP participated in the programme's conception at both stages.

[13] Garga Haman Adji, former minister in charge of the civil service, is the source for the increase in the state wage bill (Deutchoua 2005). On the number of ministerial posts, see Mbog (2015). On the decision to recruit 25,000 youth in 2011, see Pigeaud (2011: 91).

administrative law. It has been used to characterise both external and internal relations, both relations between the state and its citizens and, for example, those between the central government and municipalities. In this legal tradition, *tutelle* entails a relationship of control that, in contrast with hierarchical controls, is premised on the autonomy of those being controlled. In Cameroon, as required by the United Nations in 1945, *tutelle* was also the term that came to define the relationship between France and French Cameroon – a change that, significantly, took place in the same context in which the *indigénat* (the set of rules that permitted colonial officials to impose penalties and even short prison terms on 'natives' who had not been explicitly granted citizen rights) was formally abrogated. After independence, the one-party state's vision dissected by Bayart (1985: 216) of Cameroonians as a *peuple-enfant* (infant people) to be guided and disciplined often found its expression in the language of *tutelle*. Not surprisingly, the effects of the regime's hegemonic quest could vary considerably across the country. As Peter Geschiere (1987) showed in an early response to Bayart's account of the Cameroonian political system, which drew on ethnographic materials from the Haut-Nyong District (East Province), in some places the state and party officials' work of *encadrement* (supervising and managing people) largely amounted to the surveillance of subversive remarks and the sale of party member cards.

When, in the 1990s, the brand of paternalistic authoritarianism that had prevailed in the three decades following independence became less palatable, economic governance began to be couched in different terms. Yet, notions such as *tutelle* or *encadrement* have not disappeared from the country's administrative lexicon. *Tutelle* is used to frame relations between governmental departments and the organisations to which they have delegated powers. The BGFT, for example, is said to be under the *tutelle* of the Ministry of Transport (MINT). *Tutelle* is also used in depictions of the authority of ministries over those operating within relevant sectors. Thus MINT is the truckers' *ministère de tutelle*, and the same can said about MINEPIA and cattle traders.[14]

Tutelle and *encadrement* incorporate ideas of verticality and encompassment that naturalise the missions and powers of different government departments. This is perhaps most apparent in references to *descentes sur le terrain*, the phrase that is still most often used to refer to state agents' incursions in the world outside their offices for purposes of control. While an idiomatic translation would render it as 'inspection visits', that would mean leaving out the connotations of the more literal 'descent into

---

[14] On the legal theory of administrative *tutelle*, see Hariou (1903: 236). For a discussion of the impact of the French legal tradition on Cameroonian administrative law, see Sindjoun (1993).

16   Introduction

the field'. In this framing, the journey from public offices to business premises, shops, markets, cargo yards, and other arenas of economic activity is a downward journey. It is often seen by officials themselves as laborious and fraught. A senior tax official, for example, complained about the countless *descentes sur le terrain* involved in the remaking in 2002 of the 'practically useless' directory of businesses on which the tax authorities in Adamaoua had been relying for over a decade. These *descentes* are moments for officials to reckon not only with recalcitrance on the part of economic actors but also with the limits of their own resources and gaps in cooperation between different authorities. It is thus not surprising that the practices of *la tutelle* and *l'encadrement* involve some interiorisation of the values of those being overseen on the part of supervising officials and acknowledgement of the mutual dependencies that exist between them.

This sense of a patchy, flawed *tutelle* has as its counterpart a certain topography of the economic field in which large sections are imagined as being beyond the reach of state institutions. In much government-authorised discourse, these domains are referred to as 'the informal economy', 'the informal sector', or, simply, 'the informal'. This confirms the policy success of the notion that grew out of Keith Hart's ethnographic research in Accra in the early 1970s, a success that, in Hart's own view, has entailed an erosion of the notion's analytical usefulness. Even when such conceptions of informality may be argued to obscure rich and complex engagements with bureaucratic forms and procedures, the fact that they feature so prominently in my interlocutors' own understandings cannot be ignored. In such discourses, the informal is commonly framed as actively produced by economic actors through strategies and tactics of avoidance, concealment, and evasion. Spaces of informality are thus stigmatised as indocile.[15]

I have come across a rich vocabulary to designate what lies beyond the reach of the state. Terms such as *ladde* (bush in Fulfulde), *la brousse* (bush in French), or *le maquis* (scrubland or brushwood in French) are often used colloquially. The latter, for example, may more generally refer to an inaccessible area used as a refuge, whose meaning extends metonymically to resistance movements. In Cameroon, *le maquis* is inextricably associated with the guerrilla war fought by the Union du Peuple Camerounais (UPC) against the French authorities and their postcolonial heirs

---

[15] For Hart's initial take on the informal economy, see Hart (1973). In one of several recent publications that revisit the question, he has argued that by lending 'an appearance of conceptual unity to whatever goes on outside the bureaucracy', the concept of informal economy has allowed scholars and practitioners alike 'to incorporate the teeming street life of exotic cities into their abstract models without having to confront the specificity of what people were really up to' (Hart 2006: 28). On indocility, see Mbembe (1988) and Guyer (2004: 155).

between 1957 and 1971. When *le maquis* is used to refer to domains of ungoverned, unregulated economic activity, the undertone is therefore not simply of indocility or recalcitrance but of outright subversion. Not surprisingly, this usage proliferated in the period when the governmental imaginary of *incivisme fiscal* (fiscal disobedience in the translation of Janet Roitman (2005), whose work has turned it into a scholarly point of reference) crystallised around the social contestation of the *villes mortes*. From such a standpoint, therefore, those who are said to inhabit *le maquis* are being accused of being bad citizens. Yet, it is important not to lose sight of the fact that the layered structures of feeling within which these words are deployed can have ambivalent resonances. Lynn Schler, for example, has admirably captured how the discursive construction of New Bell, the 'strangers' quarter' of colonial Douala, as 'the bush' in the interwar period was 'a local innovation, and an important step in the process of placemaking among immigrants' (2003: 66). Similarly, in certain contexts, *le maquis* may be vindicated as a legitimate place of refuge from the excesses of obstructive or venal officials.[16]

La tutelle and *l'encadrement* are not the only registers that frame encounters through which economic governance is made. A different register that has acquired salience in recent decades is that of *la concertation*, whose associated values are dialogue, consultation, participation, and partnership. The genealogy of *concertation* sends us back to specific developments in francophone administrative sciences in the 1960s. The proponents of *l'économie concertée* saw in it the promise of participatory forms of government at a time when there was a growing awareness of a widening gap between policies designed by technocrats and the felt needs of citizens generally and of employers and workers specifically. Significantly, those advocating *concertation* were explicit in positing it as a democratic alternative to *tutelle*, the earlier paradigm of state–citizen relationships that conceived the state as a trustee or guardian. In Cameroon, as in most of francophone Africa, talk of *concertation* gained wide currency only in the era of multiparty politics. Its emergence was also closely tied to the dominance of the idea of participation in international development. Today, *concertation* is invoked as a remedy to all kinds of problems, including difficulties and conflicts that arise in the process of governing economic activities. It has become a label attached to a domain of fluid engagement between government officials and a

---

[16] On the UPC rebellion, see Joseph (1977), Mbembe (1996), and Terretta (2013). *Fiscal Disobedience* is the title of Roitman's monograph on economic regulation in the Lake Chad Basin (Roitman 2005). 'Structures of feeling' is a concept coined by Raymond Williams, whose *The Country and the City* (1975) is a seminal text on the construction of relations between town and country, which, as the semantic field evoked by *ladde*, *brousse* and *maquis* makes apparent, is central to the topography of economic governance sketched here.

constellation of other actors. *La concertation* stages with varying degrees of conviction and success a state that listens to its citizens and is open to negotiated solutions to their problems. It explicitly calls for state and non-state actors to facilitate the task of economic governance through deliberation and the co-production of truths about economic activity. For all its discursive prominence, and in spite of frequent calls for it to be 'permanent', *la concertation* tends to take place in response to extraordinary circumstances, when accumulated tensions and conflicts pose serious, urgent problems that call for exceptional measures.[17]

Much of the work involved in governing the economy thus comes in the form of more ordinary encounters outside the confines of *concertation* meetings or sporadic *descentes sur le terrain*. Taking inspiration from Jane Guyer's reading of the historical and ethnographic record on asymmetrical transactions in West and Central Africa (Guyer 2004), this book proposes to approach these encounters as crossings of boundaries or thresholds. Indeed, as can be gleaned from Sanda Maliki's reference to the BGFT's safe conduct, many of these encounters between business actors and state bureaucrats are explicitly framed as moments of passage. What are at stake in this type of interaction are the terms of passage of people and goods. This explains the prominence of *laissez-passer* (let pass), the French injunction that has been incorporated into most Cameroonian vernaculars since the colonial era (Kaptué 1980). As well as the passes introduced by the colonial authorities to control population flows and the veterinary certificates authorising the movement of cattle across national and subnational boundaries, *laissez-passer* has also come to designate the documents that allow circulation. The fact that the injunction to 'let pass' is equated to the document authorising passage in all sorts of interactions goes to show how central formalities can be to economic governance. Yet, the powers of the bureaucratic form are highly variable. Lynn Schler's discussion of the *laissez-passers* that were required to travel between different administrative units during the colonial era in Cameroon is illuminating in this regard. Until 1941, there was no sustained effort to make these passes uniform in terms of the information they contained, their format, or their validation. This opened the way for counterfeiting. Moreover, the enforcement of the pass system itself, particularly in Cameroonian cities, was anything but systematic (Schler 2003: 67–9). Louisa Lombard offers an equally suggestive analysis of more recent social dynamics around another type of document designed to afford unimpeded passage. What in the Central African Republic (CAR) are known as *services* are papers that important people (usually civil servants) prepare to extend to the bearer the freedom from

---

[17] On *concertation*, see Bloch-Lainé (1964). For a contrast between *tutelle* and *concertation*, see Grémion (1974).

searches at roadblocks that they enjoy. In the roads from the north-east of the country to the capital Bangui, such documents provide convenient protection from the confiscation of game meat (or requests for payments to let it pass) by anti-poaching guards. Crucially, however, the effects of *services* are far from automatic. While they can provide useful 'tools for roadblock navigation', their effectiveness is contingent on the enactment of relationships and alliances (Lombard 2013: 163–4).

Similarly, this book considers how an array of formalities (including documents such as the BGFT's safe conduct) on which the circulation of goods and people depend are used. Across the board, business actors and state bureaucrats engage with formalities creatively and tactically. Following Guyer, my analysis of the range of engagement with formalities pays attention to repertoire and performance. In these interactions, human identities and things are transacted as value is created in what Michel Callon has conceptualised as a constant movement of disentanglement and entanglement.[18] From this perspective, the disentangling effects of documents and other formalities are not to be taken for granted. Often, as Guyer has stated, what actors are faced with is 'a coral reef of separate formalities that coexist with – and shade into – conversionary modes of exchange' (2004: 159). How are modes of valuation combined, tinkered with, and reinvented in these encounters? How do documents – whose issuing, verification, and validation may be at stake – and other formalities feature? When and how does money change hands and what are the effects of those payments when they take place? How are laws and regulations brought to bear? What dynamics are generated by the modulation or suspension of the enforcement of legal rules? This book explores these questions at length. It argues that 'letting pass' often entails a letting go.

The research and the book

The book draws on fieldwork and archival research conducted in Cameroon between 2003 and 2014. I lived in Ngaoundéré for most of my fieldwork but I often joined the people whose activities I followed on their business trips to other parts of Cameroon and Nigeria. Ngaoundéré was one of the main precolonial urban centres of what is today northern Cameroon. It emerged in the 1830s as a result of the movement of

---

[18] Michel Callon's programme for 'an anthropology of entanglement' is spelled out in the introduction to the edited collection *Laws of Markets* (Callon 1998). More recently, alongside Koray Çalışkan, Callon has celebrated the contribution of Guyer and other anthropologists to 'a pragmatics of valuation' (Çalışkan and Callon 2009). Guyer (2016) has recently discussed her own position with regards to Callon and his colleagues' research agenda.

conquest triggered by the jihad declared by Usman dan Fodio in faraway Gobir in 1804. The city is today the capital of Adamaoua, one of Cameroon's ten *régions* (provinces).[19] The province itself takes its name from a nineteenth-century emirate of the Sokoto caliphate. Ngaoundéré is located on a high plateau that separates the tropical forests to the south from the savannah plains to the north (Maps 1 and 2). It hosts a multi-ethnic population, which in 2005 was estimated at 153,000 and whose diversity increased considerably with the completion in the early 1970s of the railroad linking it with Yaoundé and Douala, which caused a massive influx of people from other parts of Cameroon as well as from neighbouring countries.

My initial 14 months of fieldwork took place between June 2003 and November 2004 within the framework of a research project funded by the Economic and Social Research Council. Entitled 'An Ethnographic Study of Recent Trends in Business Activity in Northern Cameroon', the project had Philip Burnham as principal investigator.[20] The research team also included Martial Massike Loke, then a postgraduate student at the University of Ngaoundéré, and Saïdou Abdoulaï Bobboy, secretary general of the Chamber of Commerce at the time. Further research trips in August and September 2005, August 2010, May and June 2011, and June and July 2014 have helped me track my interlocutors' trajectories in the long term. I conducted research in French and in Fulfulde, the vehicular language of northern Cameroon. From February to September 2004, Massike Loke and I surveyed a purposive sample of 98 business owners and employees. While this allowed us to get a sense of the broad range of backgrounds and experiences of men and women based in Ngaoundéré trying to make a living in different lines of business and of the opportunities and constraints they faced, by far the most prolific source of research insights was my routine presence in spaces that my interlocutors inhabited. These were as diverse as markets, cargo yards, building sites, public offices, and several *faadaji* (meeting points where people with time to spare stopped by daily for a chat with friends and acquaintances). I also had extensive access to many of my interlocutors' households, which are often the favoured arenas in which to cultivate commercial ties.

---

[19] In this book, I have used the spelling Adamaoua to refer to the present-day *Région de l'Adamaoua* in Cameroon. In the first decades of the postcolonial period, this administrative unit had the status of a *département* (district) within a vast North Province but Adamaoua became a province of its own in 1983. In 2008, Cameroon adopted *régions* as the official designation for what had until then been called provinces. I retain province as the preferred translation throughout in order to avoid confusion. I use the spelling Adamawa to refer either to the Adamawa plateau as a geographical feature or to the precolonial political domain established during the nineteenth century, whose capital was Yola.

[20] ESRC's Research Grants Scheme, award ref. R000 23 9960.

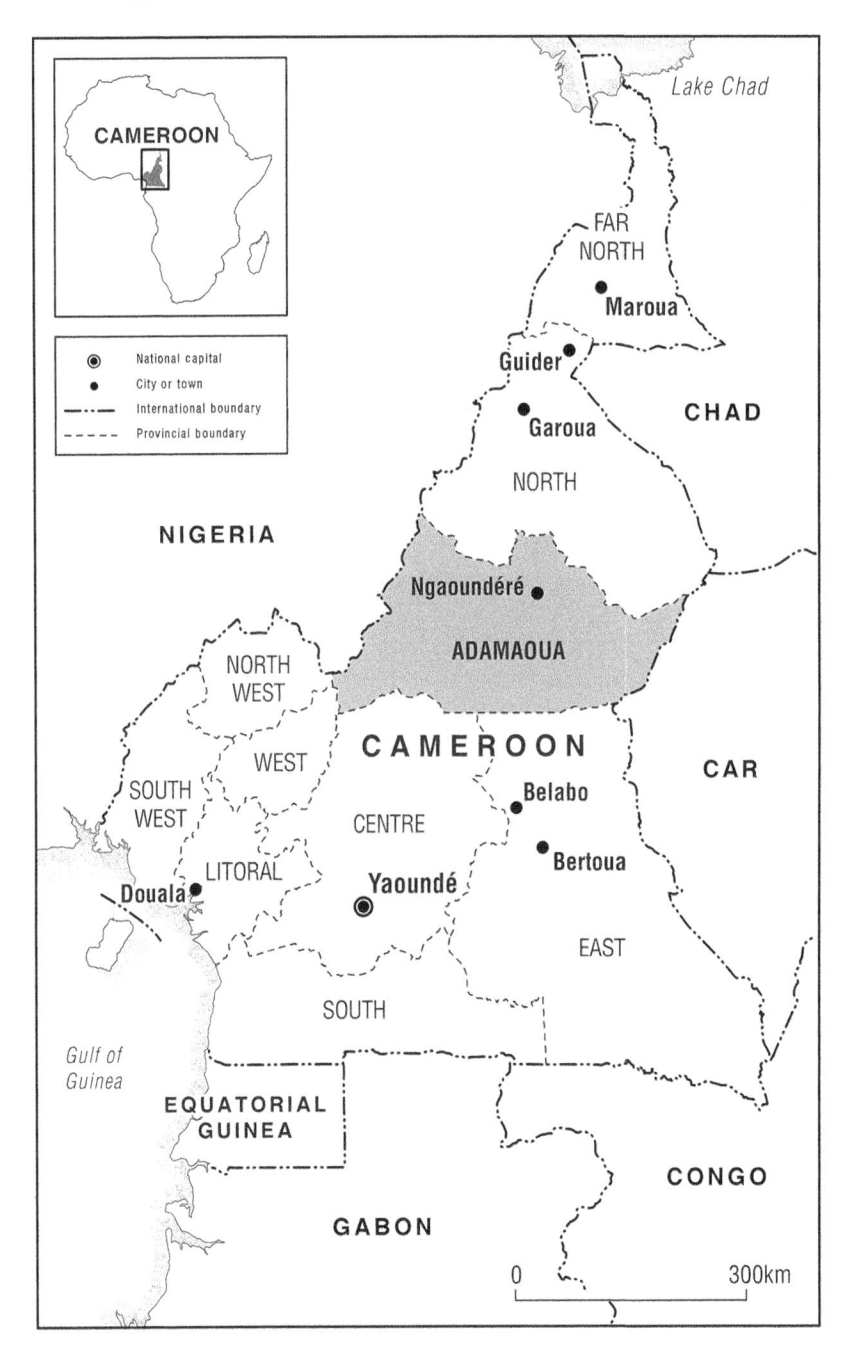

Map 1 Cameroon

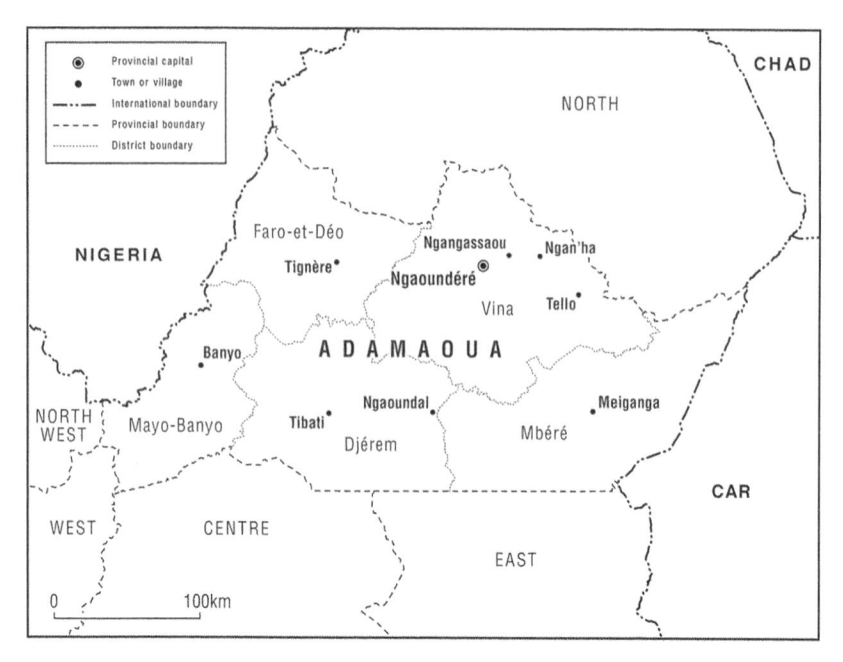

Map 2 Adamaoua

Given the many sensitive issues surrounding established business practices, my overtures to both business actors and state bureaucrats were met with scepticism and rejection on numerous occasions. Most of my interlocutors had the social skills and material resources to deflect unwanted attention from a foreign researcher whenever they felt like it. In fact, one of the underlying arguments of this book is that economic success is premised on the selective projection of business visibility attuned to varying audiences and circumstances. However, more often than not, people were quite happy to tolerate my presence without much protocol or fuss. My introduction to Ngaoundéré's main cattle merchants, for example, took place by the rail tracks in the midst of one of the most acrimonious and tense cattle-loading sessions I ever witnessed. It was only the day after I had moved in with my host family, and my bookish, tentative Fulfulde left me completely unprepared to make sense of what was happening. It was a first experience of people's readiness to help me better understand their world, as much to ingratiate themselves with me as to make sure I did justice to that world. One of many misunderstandings originated on that day in those first conversations with some of the people I would accompany for months. A passing reference to my erratic academic itinerary before studying anthropology impressed one of the traders enough to begin calling me *l'avocat* (the lawyer) thereafter. No matter how hard I tried to lay to rest this misleading identification in the coming weeks, I was stuck with it. As my attempts to undo the confusion failed to bear fruit, I consoled myself with the fact that the lawyering role was frequently further elaborated to make me an *avocat defenseur* (defence counsellor) and not just a simple lawyer. With time, the epithet was to acquire an unequivocal ring of mockery that reassured me that it had become a playful nickname. This goes to show the extent to which ethnography is made of misunderstanding and obfuscation as much as enlightenment.

The mode of writing I employ in many sections of this book relies on inscribing the actions and words of my interlocutors within their social backgrounds and business trajectories. While trying to avoid self-absorption, my writing also makes explicit the position of the ethnographer in different research situations. Although I have made a point of not providing information that would unnecessarily expose the individuals discussed in the following chapters, the identity of a number of them could be found out by anyone with a good knowledge of the sectors of economic activity in which they operate. As the book makes apparent, although many of the business practices documented depart from existing laws and regulations, they are hardly exceptional. This protects most of the individuals involved from unwanted exposure. Alhadji Djibrilla, for example, was adamant about this after he read the section that contains a portrait of him. He has no qualms in discussing the business practices prevalent in public contracting. As far as he is concerned, he is a good professional who has simply adapted to the way in which this sector works. In his view, only contractors who deliver deficient work have anything to regret. All the same, in the cases where there is sustained focus on a person (as happens with Badjo, Yero, Djibrilla, and Bello), I have avoided providing details that would expose them unnecessarily. As a rule, the names of individuals used are pseudonyms. The main exceptions occur in references to media coverage of events relating to public figures and the analysis of meetings I attended that were open to the public, where participants are quoted as representatives of state agencies, professional groups, or other organisations.

The book is organised into an Introduction, five chapters, and a Conclusion. Chapter 1 contains a condensed history of political and economic life in Ngaoundéré and the portraits of four people whose careers I have followed for more than a decade: Badjo, Yero, Djibrilla, and Bello. The portraits are intended to illuminate the ways in which specific trajectories are inscribed in distinct socio-economic backgrounds. Details of these portraits are taken up in subsequent chapters.

Chapter 2 zooms in on public contractors based in Ngaoundéré. Public contractors have government authorities as their clients. This lends a level of bureaucratisation to their activities unknown in other domains. After the 1990s, a decade marked by depleted state coffers and the emergence of corruption as a global policy challenge, the bureaucratic apparatus and the procedures governing public contracts have become targets of protracted reform efforts. The chapter tracks the work of contractors in this period of reforms. It argues that their business is premised both on the mastery of shifting bureaucratic formalities and on the assiduous cultivation of personal ties with relevant officials. While fuelled by monetary payments and embedded in gender and ethnoreligious hierarchies, the ensuing relationships can attain high levels of intimacy and fluidity. A documentary trail backing the integrity of the contractual process and its satisfactory completion thus tends to go hand in hand with adherence to parallel agreements reached by contractors and officials. This combination, which the reforms have done little to disrupt, systematically results in economic transactions to which the authorities are party but that violate existing legal rules.

Chapter 3 takes an attempt of the authorities to change the modes and amounts of tax paid by cattle traders as a lens through which to examine the ways in which the cattle economy, a line of business with a long pedigree in Ngaoundéré, is organised and governed. The circulation and commercialisation of cattle are regulatory targets for an array of government departments and agencies, which traders as well as farmers, butchers, and numerous other actors who make a living around cattle encounter in their daily work. Such encounters belie widespread accounts of helpless authorities confronted with a set of singularly elusive economic actors. In practice, officials in charge of regulating this trade display a tenuous commitment to bureaucratic rigour and little inclination to cooperate with colleagues from other government departments. The terms of compliance with the law are negotiated locally with traders and enforcement is assisted (and modulated) by the helping hand of traders' associations and large firms such as the railway company.

Chapter 4 explores the governance of freight transport, one of the pillars of Ngaoundéré's economy since the arrival of the railway in the 1970s turned the city into a regional hub. This chapter chronicles the highs and lows of the trucking business, from its prosperous early years, through the downturn of the late 1980s and 1990s, to the boom of the early 2000s caused by the Chad–Cameroon oil pipeline project. It is a trajectory of contrasting policy visions and more muted institutional continuity. Law enforcement on the road appears as a crucial dimension in shaping truckers' prospects. Checkpoint dynamics illuminate the practical significance of documents and the potential and limits of prevailing forms of economic governance. They are occasions for the mobilisation of repertoires and the enactment of resolutions that decide the terms of passage and the gains or losses to be made. Less eye-catching but just as decisive as law enforcement on the road are the mechanisms through which who accesses freight (and on what terms) is decided.

Chapter 5 focuses on NGO work. An NGO scene coalesced in Ngaoundéré in the late 1990s and early 2000s around the widening of the struggle against HIV/AIDS and the Chad–Cameroon pipeline project's regional compensation package for Adamaoua. Under such stimuli, the NGO label spread rapidly, even though, under Cameroonian law, no organisation based in the city was entitled to use it. More consequential than these organisations' legal standing were the terms set by funders offering them contract work. The chapter dissects the strategies and tactics deployed to obtain contracts and the effects that they have on these organisations and their work. It also analyses the ambiguities surrounding profits within organisations that are supposed to be non-profit. It argues for the need to understand NGO work in light of the shifting expectations that underwrite cycles of contracts between funders and NGOs.

The concluding chapter recapitulates the insights contained in earlier chapters and summarises the book's distinct contribution to a more sophisticated understanding of the task of governing the economy in Cameroon and beyond.

1 Making a living in Ngaoundéré

In 1950, transport activities were not significant enough to merit a specific discussion in Jean-Claude Froelich's meticulous portrayal of Ngaoundéré's economy (1954a). Things would change in the following years. In November 2004, in the company of two other transport veterans, Mohamadou Wakiili recalled his involvement in the early development of the city's transport sector.[1] In his twenties, Mohamadou had become the right-hand man of Bakary Bandjou, a trader with privileged connections to Ngaoundéré's chieftaincy. In 1956, Bakary sent him to Douala to purchase his first small truck, a Renault *mille-kilos* (one ton). Mohamadou gave the following account of the difficulties he had faced in fulfilling his boss's wishes:

> I arrived in Douala and placed an order at the dealership. God be my witness, I spent almost six months there waiting for a truck. When I found out that the fair was due to start in Maroua, I got a plane – 11,000 [francs for a] return [ticket]. At the fair, I bought tablemats and other artisanal housewares. Back in Douala, I took them to the wife of the Renault dealership's manager. When she saw them, she asked for the price. 'Ah, Madame, this is a gift!' The manager then told me: 'Today is Thursday. On Monday, three trucks will arrive in the port. One is for Serret [a French transporter based in Ngaoundéré from 1953], one is for a white man in Nkongsamba, the last one is for another white man in Bangui.' The trucks that were reserved for clients in Cameroon, he told me, he could not touch. But, as far as the white man in Bangui was concerned, if he did not show up, he would give that truck to me. I was lucky enough [he did not show up] and I got a truck.

Once he got the vehicle's papers in order, he returned to Ngaoundéré. His travails, however, did not end there. They were able to use the truck for only a few days.

> We did not have an ordinance [authorising Bakary as a licensed transporter]. Serret denounced us [to the subdivision authorities]. They took instant action and had the truck stopped indefinitely ... We then went to Yaoundé, where [a northern civil servant at the] Political Affairs Bureau offered to help us. It was thus that we were able to unblock the ordinance for my boss. The file was

---

[1] Mohamadou Wakiili objected to the idea of using pseudonyms for actual names in my account of these events. I have respected his wishes.

immediately sent to Douala, where the Transport Bureau processed it in due form. 1956 was nearing its end.

As his nickname indicates (Bandjoun is an important Bamileke chieftaincy), Bakary had started out as a trader bringing kola nuts from West Cameroon to Ngaoundéré. In 1946, Mohamadou Abbo, newly restored as *laamiɗo* (ruler) of Ngaoundéré by the French administration after a seven-year exile, had turned Bakary into his main commercial agent.[2] When the *laamiɗo* died in January 1957, Bakary was able to strike out on his own with the capital he had accumulated from his lucrative position.[3] Only a few months after Mohamadou Wakiili's laborious purchase, Bakary bought a two-ton truck. During the next decade, he managed a fleet of some 15 trucks and minibuses, which he entrusted to people such as Mohamadou. Bakary Bandjou thus joined the ranks of a generation of merchants who pioneered transport in the area. Alhadji Nana Hamadjoda, the son of an old dignitary of the Ngaoundéré court and one of the leaders of the 'internal opposition' to the *laamiɗo*'s authority, was the most prominent among them. He had made his fortune in the cattle trade and had gone on to invest in transport in the late 1940s. At the height of his political ambitions in the run-up to the elections for the Assemblée Territoriale du Cameroun (ATCAM, Cameroon's Territorial Assembly) in December 1956, Nana was described by the *chef de subdivision* as leading 'the merchant bourgeoisie of Ngaoundéré, *une caste remuante d'esprit frondeur* [a restless caste of rebellious spirit]'.[4]

In their own different ways, Nana Hamadjoda and Bakary Bandjou are examples of the generation of 'self-made men' whom Jean-Pierre Warnier (1994) identified as distinctive figures of the late colonial era. They had

---

[2] *Laamiɗo* comes from the Fulfulde verbal root *laam-* (to rule). The plural form is *laamiɓe*. Lamidates is the established scholarly term to refer to the polities that were formally subject to the authority of the Emir of Adamawa in the nineteenth century. In the precolonial era, the title of *laamiɗo* was reserved for the Emir in Yola, while the leaders of these polities were instead referred to as *arɗo'en* (from the verbal root *art-* [to walk at the head, to lead], which comes from the lexicon of migration that was so central to the Fulbe jihad).

[3] Mohamadou Abbo's inheritance provides an idea of the amounts involved in supplying Ngaoundéré's ceremonial machinery with all it required. At the time of his death, his monetary assets, which included a pending percentage of colonial taxes collected the previous year, were 2,284,000 francs. His debts, recorded in both cattle and money, amounted to 5,780,000 francs (ANY 2AC 4337, 'Procès verbal, Réunion des créanciers du Lamido Mohamadou Abbo', 9 February 1957). In 1958, French officials calculated his successor's annual income at 14 million francs (ANY 2AC 8559).

[4] ANY 2AC 8570, 'Rapport Annuel 1956, Partie Première Adamaoua'. The report was written in the aftermath of the elections, in which Alhadji Nana was part of the local opposition to the *laamiɗo*. The elections involved a newly expanded electoral body, which in Ngaoundéré's lamidate included around 44,000 people. Nana was one of the most prominent Fulbe figures in the city who had made their affinity with the nationalist UPC public. The UPC had been banned in 1955. On the UPC in Ngaoundéré, see Taguem (1997), Hansen (2000: 201–3), and Mokam (2006: 83–5).

received no formal schooling, they managed their affairs in highly personalised ways, and they were firmly rooted in the local society of the city where they were based (although their connections outside Ngaoundéré were just as decisive). In the years that followed Mohamadou's acquisition of the Renault truck, the competition that expatriate transporters so much regretted only increased.[5] The authorities changed their restrictive, obstructionist approach towards new 'native' entrants, which, until the late 1950s, had been the norm throughout French Cameroon (Joseph 1977: 117, 334). At a meeting in March 1957, M. Lemain, the adjunct to the *chef de région* in Adamaoua, explained to a group of transporters that included Serret, Nana Hamadjoda, and Bakary Bandjou that the administration could no longer continue to 'oppos[e] the establishment of new transport firms'.[6] Thus, on the eve of independence, expatriates such as Serret were forced to quit and leave the country. Nana Hamadjoda, his political career blocked for good by the French authorities and by rivals within Ngaoundéré's chieftaincy, found little support for his commercial ventures from the northern political elites in the newly independent country. His business suffered as a result. Bakary Bandjou died prematurely in the late 1960s, leaving two young children. Few traces of his prosperity remained after his death, but many of his former employees became local figures in the transport business in the following decades.

Through four portraits, this chapter will introduce readers to the world inhabited by business actors based in Ngaoundéré. The portraits are preceded by a brief introduction to the history of the city. It is important to emphasise that the four protagonists described in the remainder of the chapter do not offer a representative sample of Ngaoundéré society. Even if we were to consider only its business circles, the city is much richer in its diversity. Nor do these four individuals neatly fit with the stock characters of what Warnier (1994) called *la bigarrure* (the kaleidoscope) of Cameroonian business owners: the self-made men who had to overcome all sorts of odds, those of a later generation whose careers were built on privileged positions made available to them through connections with state bureaucrats, and the technocrats whose passage through the university system translated into an adoption of professional management styles. In many ways, the 1990s disrupted the teleology of progress built into Warnier's typology. The snippets of the four lives described in this chapter are meant to illustrate the impact of the disruption, turbulence, and uncertainty of those years.

---

[5] ANY 2AC 4108, 'Adamaoua, Transport, Lettre de 25 Mai 1954, Serret au Chef de Région de l'Adamaoua'; ANY 3AC 2308, 'Adamaoua, Transport, Reglementation 1956, Correspondance concurrence déloyale'.
[6] ANY 2AC 4108, 'Adamaoua, Transport, Procès verbal réunion des transporteurs', 8 March 1957.

None of these four business actors have had direct experience of the colonial era. Only one of them, Yero, was born before Cameroon became independent, and then only by less than two years. Yet, in their own ways, they all relate to several aspects of Nana Hamadjoda's and Bakary Bandjou's trajectories, including the centrality of cattle holdings as both durable reservoirs of wealth and springboards for other business ventures; contentious relations with foreign competitors; and the gains to be made by mediating exchanges between the north (the savannah) and the south (the equatorial forest and the coast) or by providing for (and funding) the many needs of cash-strapped public authorities. The four portraits in this chapter relate to Muslim men with a deep sense of belonging to the societies that emerged in the nineteenth century in northern Cameroon. Except for Yero, who considers himself Kanuri but learned Fulfulde as his native tongue, they see themselves as Fulbe.[7] The historical account that follows matters to them in distinct ways.

Ngaoundéré in historical perspective

The Ngaoundéré of the 1950s that saw Mohamadou Wakiili venture into the world of transport and become the head of a household was very different from the city of a century earlier. Ngaoundéré was founded in the 1830s, in the aftermath of the Fulbe conquest of most of what is today northern Nigeria and northern Cameroon. In the mid-nineteenth century, the city grew as the centre of a prosperous lamidate under the nominal authority of the Emir of Adamawa, and thus fell within the Sokoto Caliphate's orbit. The city was walled and fortified early in the 1850s to protect it from the military threat of the neighbouring lamidate of Tibati. In less than a generation, the Fulbe managed to turn the Mbum groups who had occupied the area before the conquest into vassal allies. This was made possible by the incorporation of Mbum cultural elements, the prevalence of interethnic marriages, and the importance of the positions held by non-Fulbe title-holders in Ngaoundéré's court and army. Yet, ethnic and religious difference played a structural role in Ngaoundéré's political economy, as Fulbe domination was premised on the subjugation of the non-Muslim population to either servile or tributary status.[8]

---

[7] *Fulɓe* (singular: *Pullo*) is the word used in Fulfulde to designate the ethnic group that is conventionally referred to as Fulani (a word of Hausa origin) in English and *Peuls* in French. For the sake of convenience, in the following pages I render *Fulɓe* as Fulbe.

[8] On the relationship between Adamawa's political centre (Yola) and the sub-emirates, see Abubakar (1977: 110–16). On the differential incorporation of various groups in the lamidate's political system, see Burnham (1996a) and Sinderud (2008). On cultural bricolage in Ngaoundéré, see Burnham and Last (1994). The dating of the city's fortification in the 1850s comes from the oral tradition gathered by Mohammadou (1978: 287).

Hemmed in by other Fulbe states, Ngaoundéré looked towards its eastern and south-eastern margins, which were inhabited by 'pagan' Gbaya, Laka, and other groups. In the second half of the nineteenth century, the lamidate developed a raiding economy that targeted those eastern marches, which acquired a reputation as an 'Eldorado of the ivory merchants' (Flegel 1985: 7). Captives from periodic raiding campaigns, typically launched during the dry season, fed the slave trade with Sokoto and, to a much lesser extent, the lamidate's labour force. War parties could involve a sizeable portion of the city's population.[9] The opportunities created by the exploitation of the lamidate's distant periphery led to the emergence of a substantial trading apparatus, supported by large colonies of Muslim merchants and regular flows of caravans.[10]

Central to Ngaoundéré's consolidation and expansion in the nineteenth century were the *tokke* (plural of *tokkal*, a noun deriving from the verbal root *tokk-* or 'to follow'), which formed the basis of its administrative organisation. With 'their origins in the leadership patterns of mobile pastoral society', *tokke* were sets of followers, 'both Fulbe and members of vassal peoples, who were distributed in a scattering of different rural villages or residential quarters in town and who were allocated to individual office holders living at Ngaoundéré at the whim of the *laamido*' (Burnham 1980: 47). The implication of this conceptualisation of political space was that, unless they were affiliated to a *tokkal*, the groups resident in a specific territory were targets of tribute and slaving. The fact that members of the same *tokkal* lived in different villages and that families belonging to different *tokke* coexisted in a single village lessened the chances of secession by parts of the Ngaoundéré state, while allowing for the effective mobilisation of an army and the levying of taxes. These *tokke* continued to serve administrative purposes until the end of the colonial era.[11]

Ngaoundéré's political and economic landscape changed drastically with the brutal German conquest of what is today northern Cameroon.

---

[9] In a 1893 visit, Edmond Ponel (1896: 207), a French colonial envoy of de Brazza (Pietro Paolo Savorgnan di Brazzà), reported that 8,000 people remained in the city while 3,000 were absent while taking part in one such expedition.

[10] On the lamidate's raiding economy, see Flegel (1985), Ponel (1896), Charreau (1905), Burnham (1980), Burnham, Copet-Rougier, and Noss (1986), and Burnham (1996b). In population centres such as Kounde, an important base for Ngaoundéré's incursions into Gbaya-land, located on what is today the border between the Central African Republic and Cameroon, traders represented half of the 4,000–5,000 people living within the city walls during this period (Charreau 1905: 13).

[11] On *tokke*, see Froelich (1954b: 26–7), Burnham (1996a: 19), Burnham and Last (1994: 325), and Roitman (2005: 115–16). In the 1950s, the French authorities tried to dismantle these administrative units, which they had deemed expedient to preserve until then (Sinderud 1993).

The city was swiftly taken by the *Schutztruppe* (colonial infantry) on 20 August 1901. Lacking the means for a more ambitious approach, the Germans administered the northern part of their colony by employing *laamiɓe* as intermediaries. It was in Garoua that they established their main military garrison. In the lamidates of the Adamawa plateau, they followed events only at arm's length. The resident in Garoua thus became an *Oberlamido* of sorts. Until 1908, the German post in Ngaoundéré was occupied intermittently according to circumstances. It was only in 1913 that Ngaoundéré became the seat of a *Residentur* (administrative district).[12]

The colonial dispensation that had taken shape in the years preceding the fall of Ngaoundéré, and that had established borders between French, German, and British territories, made large-scale raiding increasingly difficult. The French–German agreement of 1894 complicated access to the sources of slaves and spoils. As far as the French were concerned, an initial pro-Muslim policy from 1892 to 1894 that had involved repeatedly helping Ngaoundéré combat its enemies mutated into a hostile stance that translated into attacks against the lamidate's agents in Gbaya-land in 1895. The British taking of Yola only a few weeks after the German capture of Ngaoundéré also meant that the slave trade directed to the west began to be policed at the new colonial border. Despite this, the Germans did nothing to curtail Fulbe power over other peoples and sporadic slave raiding in some parts of Adamawa continued unabated.[13]

World War One changed the colonial status quo. French and British troops arrived in Ngaoundéré in 1915 and went on to split the former German colony between them. In 1922, a League of Nations mandate acknowledged these facts on the ground. Like their predecessors, the French authorities made extensive use of *le commandement indigène* (native authorities) to administer the population. *Haaɓe* (people of servile descent, or simply 'pagans')[14] in Ngaoundéré's orbit were subject to constant abuses by the *laamido*'s agents in the first decades of French

---

[12] The visit of Governor Puttkamer in September 1902 provided an occasion for 68 chiefs and their retinues to travel to Garoua to greet the representative of the Kaiser. It established a custom of *laamiɓe* meeting in Garoua periodically to bring tribute to the resident (Temgoua 2014: 125–6). On the German arrangements for the administration of northern Cameroon, see Rudin (1938: 95–6, 186). On the German presence in Ngaoundéré, see Mohammadou (1983: 152–3) and Sinderud (2008: 45).

[13] On the relations between French agents led by de Brazza and Ngaoundéré in the 1890s, see Burnham (1996b). On Ngaoundéré's involvement in slave raiding and trade in the first decades of the twentieth century, see Burnham (1996a: 33) and Sinderud (2008: 43–4).

[14] Seignobos and Tourneux (2002: 132) highlight the non-Muslim dimension of the term; however, their dictionary deals mostly with linguistic usage in the far north. In Adamaoua, *haaɓe* (singular: *kaado*) signifies a servile condition (Burnham 1996a: 20; Sinderud 2008: 55–8).

rule. In some instances, the colonial authorities were forced to administer sections of the former lamidate without the mediation of the Fulbe. Thus, in 1928, a *canton* (district) was created to the south-east of Ngaoundéré in order to free Gbaya and Mbororo groups from the exactions of the *laamiɗo*.[15] The end of slave raiding had a profound effect on the city's economy. Having seen their main source of wealth dry up, *laamiɓe* in Adamaoua realised the commercial potential of cattle and relied on increased levies on cattle owners.[16] Jean Boutrais (1994: 179) has written of a process of 'repastoralisation' in the 1920s and 1930s, as the Fulbe of Ngaoundéré found refuge from these fiscal pressures in neighbouring rural areas. The cattle trade to the south, which had been actively encouraged by the Germans, grew in importance as stock expanded on the plateau. The colonial authorities responded by opening a veterinary station in Ngaoundéré in 1933 and progressively setting up a functional veterinary infrastructure.[17]

Ngaoundéré expanded gradually. To the south-west of the old city, the Germans constructed the first buildings of what became a large administrative camp as well as residential quarters for officials during the years of French rule. The city's weekly cattle market was organised in the early 1920s next to the western walls of the precolonial settlement; this was also the location chosen for the *Compagnie Pastorale*'s compound by the French *maquignons* (livestock dealers) who founded it. The year 1925 saw the settlement of the first Christian missionaries, Norwegian Lutherans, who set up shop to the south of the old city. The French built a 'native' Grand Marché in 1938 on what were purportedly the ruins of the palace that Arɗo Njobdi, the founder of the city, had erected in the 1830s. In 1952, the authorities developed a commercial district between the administrative camp and the old city that became the preserve of European and Lebanese merchants (Figure 1.1). Small waves of

---

[15] On the creation of the Gbaya canton and its links with the Karnu Rebellion in neighbouring Oubangi-Chari, see Burnham and Christensen (1983) and Burnham (1975; 1996a). In the plains, beyond the northern fringe of the plateau, the French also created a separate Dii district (Muller 2006: 144–5). There was also an attempt in the 1950s to create a Mbum canton under the authority of Nganha's *belaka* but it never came to anything (Sinderud 1993: 116–25).

[16] The archives offer sporadic evidence of the *laamiɗo*'s own cattle shipments to the south. On 19 May 1921, for example, he sold 171 head to the chief of Yaoundé's Hausa community. The transaction was documented on a handwritten scrap of paper with a French administrator bearing witness, a sign of its importance in ensuring a regular beef supply to the capital (ANY 2AC 8549, 'Evolution économique de la subdivision de Ngaoundéré'). The *laamiɗo* was also instrumental in allowing Europeans to enter the sector in the 1920s (Boutrais 1990: 76).

[17] Chapter 3 deals in more detail with the history of cattle trade in Ngaoundéré. Colonial livestock administration on the Adamaoua plateau divided the area into five *directions de secteurs d'élevage* (administrative units), with their respective outreach services, including 20 vaccination stations and 19 veterinary dispensaries (Boutrais 1999a: 608).

Figure 1.1 Shops in the commercial district undergoing reconstruction, Ngaoundéré, May 2004

migrants from Cameroon's south and west arrived in the years following World War Two. Their public consumption of pork and alcohol is said to have motivated the *laamido*'s decision in 1950 to ban them from residing within the old city walls. This marked the origins of a newcomers' *camp* that would later receive the official name of Baladji, after one of the streams surrounding the city. The French census of the city from that year counted 13,481 inhabitants, of whom 12,393 were subjects of the *laamido* and 1,088 were *étrangers* (strangers) living outside the walls. In the 1950s and 1960s, the new neighbourhoods of Joli Soir, Sabon Gari, and Madagascar were developed in the north following a distinctive grid pattern.[18]

The late 1940s and 1950s were years of intense administrative reform. In 1948, the colonial authorities made their first attempt to institute territorial forms of administration. The idea was to transform the system

[18] On the *Compagnie Pastorale*, see Boutrais (1990). On the Lebanese community of Ngaoundéré, see Roupsard (1991: 115–16) and Fimigue (1999). On the establishment of the Norwegian mission, see Dronen (2009: 53–64). The census data is analysed in Froelich's study of the city's economic life (Froelich 1954a: 9). On urban transformations in Ngaoundéré during the colonial era, see Vennetier (1991: 121–5), Hino (1993), Tchotsoua et al. (1998), Kemfang (1998), and DeLancey (2012).

based on sets of followers inherited from the precolonial era. Despite retaining 'a certain military efficiency', Froelich argued, over time the system had proven inappropriate for tasks such as tax collection and labour recruitment because 'the dignitaries [heading each *tokkal* unit] generally did not know the precise whereabouts of their [scattered] followers'. The aim was to make village and *tokkal* coincide, so that each village would constitute the *tokkal* of a village chief, the *laamido* presiding over 'this mosaic of *tokke*' (Froelich 1954b: 27). This complacent picture notwithstanding, archival sources show that this was not a smooth transition. The many ties between court dignitaries and their sets of followers did not disappear overnight and their administrative erasure took a heavy toll on efficiency, since it left the *laamido* dealing directly with village chiefs. In the following years, the French tried different alternative formulas, the results of which they judged unsatisfactory.[19]

In the context of rapid political and economic change in the late 1950s, the lamidate saw its authority under attack on several fronts. The French received constant complaints about abuses of authority from internal factions within the lamidate's affluent classes as well as from missionaries who claimed to speak on behalf of non-Muslim subjects. In 1957, the death of *laamido* Mohamadou Abbo, Bakary Bandjou's patron, was a turning point. In the preceding months, the *laamido* had seen his political credit compromised in the tightly contested ATCAM elections. A year later, the appointment of the city's first Cameroonian mayor established the trend for what lay ahead. In the early years after independence, the new government proved uncompromising in its suppression of the *laamibe*'s prerogatives. In 1963, Mohamadou Abbo's successor learned this first-hand when he was removed from office for administrative malfeasance. It marked the beginning of an era of decline for the chiefdom, from which it did not recover until the return of multiparty politics in the 1990s.[20]

---

[19] Ineffective experiments to improve the lamidate's administration included the creation in 1955 of a 'lamidate council' (an expanded version of the *laamido*'s *faada* or court, with a broader representation of the lamidate's social groups) and the appointment of 'sector chiefs' to mediate between the *laamido* and villages in 1956 (ANY 2AC 8559, 'Rapport sur les Reformes Politiques à Introduire dans la Subdivision de Ngaoundéré, Lataillade', 17 September 1958). See also Sinderud (1993).

[20] Partly due to the French concern for preserving the *laamibe*'s authority, northern Cameroon was one of the last parts of the territory to see the development of municipal institutions. On northern Cameroon's municipal institutions in the 1950s, see Tassou (2013: 103–6). On Ndoumbé Oumar, who was mayor of Ngaoundéré from 1958 to 1963, see Sojip and Nizesété (1998). On the independent government stance towards chiefs in Adamaoua and elsewhere in the north, see Azarya (1978: 182), Bayart (1985: 56), and Burnham (1996a: 68). In 1959, Ahidjo's warning to the *laamibe* during the second Union Camerounaise's congress in Ngaoundéré was unequivocal: 'What I am asking of them is that they act in such a way that [our country's] evolution comes about with them, for in the contrary case, they will be vanquished by it' (Johnson 1970:

Independence in 1960 made Ngaoundéré the seat of a *département* (district) within a large North Province, which had its administrative centre in President Ahidjo's home town of Garoua. This meant the expansion of its administrative services and an increase in the number of resident civil servants. Other migrants from Adamaoua and beyond, including Cameroon's neighbouring countries, also moved to the city during this period in search of economic opportunities, but the largest migratory flows resulted from the construction of the railway link between Yaoundé and Ngaoundéré and the paving of the Ngaoundéré–Garoua road in late 1974. However, the impact of the railway fell short of the economic revolution that had been anticipated. Hopes for the establishment of new industries, which the government fuelled by creating a 100-hectare Zone Industrielle de Ngaoundéré (ZIN) in 1973, were not fulfilled. Nonetheless, the magnitude of the transformation that the city experienced is hard to overstate. As Ngaoundéré became an important regional transport hub, it attracted significant numbers of Chadian and Central African immigrants. The arrival of the railway also meant the expansion of the city's electricity grid, which had been in place only since 1968. Many Cameroonian migrants attracted by the new commercial possibilities settled in Baladji and the adjacent Petit Marché, whose expansion contrasted with the relative decay of the Grand Marché and its Fulbe, Kanuri, and Hausa shop owners.[21]

In 1983, one of the first decisions taken by Paul Biya when he consolidated his position as head of state was to split the monolithic north into three provinces (Adamaoua, North, and Far North). Ngaoundéré thus became home to expanded government services and its civil service population grew accordingly. A year earlier, a National School of Agri-food Industries had opened its doors in the north of the city. This was the origin of the University of Ngaoundéré, which in its inaugural year, 1992,

---

161). The decision to close the *laamiɗo*'s prison in Ngaoundéré in July 1961 was a symbol of the decline of his powers. It was largely thanks to the balancing acts of Laamiɗo Issa Maïgari that the Ngaoundéré's chieftaincy recovered some of its former prestige in the 1990s. Laamiɗo Issa skilfully managed the crossfire between a fiercely anti-regime constituency and a government that made its financial support dependent on the chief's capacity to deliver votes (Burnham 1996a: 180 n.2; Hansen 2000; Mahmoudou Djingui 2000; Taguem 2003: 282–3). In the present decade, his successor has built up the lamidate's finances through a combination of unequivocal support for the ruling party and single-minded exploitation of available business opportunities, including public contracts.

[21] The ZIN was to be managed by the state agency Mission d'Aménagement et de Gestion des Zones Industrielles (Mission for the Planning and Management of Industrial Zones or MAGZI), which took 35 years to open a provincial office in Adamaoua. Estimates put the number of new arrivals between 1975 and 1976 at 1,890 people, 60 per cent of whom found a home in the Baladji neighbourhood (BCEOM 1984). On the economy of the city in the 1970s, see Gondolo (1978; 1986). On electricity, see Owona Ndounda (2009: 62, fn. 149). On the origins of the Petit Marché, see Kemfang (1998).

admitted over 1,000 students, most of whom did not come from Adamaoua. In the early 1990s, the depths of political and economic discontent in the city were laid bare in the massive support that the *villes mortes* campaign received. The electoral contests that ensued reflected the lack of popularity of the ruling Cameroon People's Democratic Movement (RDPC). In 1996, the first municipal elections of the multiparty era were won by an opposition candidate from the National Union for Democracy and Progress (UNDP). In the following years, however, the UNDP's appeal in Ngaoundéré and Adamaoua waned and the RDPC had a resounding victory in the 2002 legislative and municipal elections. Indeed, when I first arrived in the city in June 2003, I bumped into a political caravan of the ruling party as it travelled across the north of the country. Adamaoua had become the 'RDPC's uncontested fiefdom', or so post-election banners claimed. Although the official motive for the caravan was to thank voters for their massive support, most saw it as an attempt by government officials to counter the momentum generated by a memorandum authored by opposition politicians denouncing the neglect suffered by the three northern provinces.[22]

Such was the contentious political environment in which I first met the four people whom I introduce in this chapter. The portraits that follow are meant to offer a subject-centred perspective on the sectors of the economy on which later chapters focus.

The making of a public contractor

Ten minutes into the second half of a Sunday game at the Roumdé Adjia stadium in Garoua, the score left no doubt that the winner would be the home team Coton Sport. It was anything but surprising. Relying on generous sponsorship including that of the cotton parastatal Sodecoton, Coton Sport has dominated the national league since the mid-1990s. University of Ngaoundéré, their rivals that May 2011

---

[22] In the early 2000s, enrolment in the University of Ngaoundéré reached 10,000 students, 88 per cent of whom came from outside Adamaoua. For a detailed analysis of the 1996 municipal elections in the city, see Hansen (2000: 206–27). The poor performance of the UNDP in the early 2000s in Adamaoua resulted from serious internal divisions, the participation of its leaders in Biya's successive governments, and the weak support of non-Muslim populations. In the legislative and municipal elections of 2007, the UNDP recovered much of the lost ground. The central government response to this support for the opposition has been to fragment the two communes (urban and rural Ngaoundéré) that constituted the former *arrondissement* into five units (Ngaoundéré I, II, and III plus Nganha and Nyambaka). This process culminated with the creation in 2009 of a new overarching *communauté urbaine*, which is presided over by an unelected government delegate and has taken over numerous powers previously held by mayors.

Figure 1.2 The view from the VIP seats, Roumdé Adjia stadium, Garoua, May 2011

afternoon, had proved unable to stop them. Cotton Sport had just struck again, bringing the score to 4–0. Among the sombre-looking supporters of the visiting team sitting in the VIP box, Alhadji Djibrilla forced a defiant smile (Figure 1.2). 'You don't have this in Ngaoundéré, do you?' asked the Benoué District's prefect, pointing at Coton Sport's jeering crowd. Djibrilla was the only one left with the energy to heed the prefect's sarcasm: 'The stadium? You talk about it as if you had built it yourself!' The prefect retorted: 'Alhadji, have you changed cars again? You're always bringing new ones from Dubai. Tell me when the container arrives, so that I can go and see you then.' 'Maybe you'll find my door closed.' Djibrilla shrugged off the new provocation. It was less than a year since Djibrilla had joined a group of friends who had decided to take the reins of the University of Ngaoundéré's board of directors and attempt to rescue the struggling, debt-ridden club. They rose to the occasion, did the rounds of Adamaoua's politicians and business people, and raised sufficient funds to keep the team in the country's top league for another year. For some of Djibrilla's friends, the football club could be a convenient platform to take the leap into the world of politics. As one of them put it: 'With sports, the message gets across fast.' Partly because he had experienced the burden of political partisanship through several of his siblings who were civil servants, a political career was not an appealing prospect for Djibrilla. From the perspective of a public contractor like himself, football could be simply a good source of contacts with influential people. That afternoon, for example, the match had afforded him the opportunity to rub shoulders with the prefect of a wealthy district. As their teasing exchange signalled, Djibrilla and the prefect knew each other. The prefect's earlier posting had been in Ngaoundéré, as one of the senior managers at the governor's office. Public contractors thrived on this sort of connection, which could make the difference when the time came to bid for contracts. However, there were clear limits to the lengths to which Djibrilla was willing to go for his home-town football club. In fact, he hardly ever joined the team on their away fixtures, and he had travelled to Garoua for this game only because it had happened to coincide with a business trip to Maroua. As it turned out, his involvement with the club did not last. A couple of years later he decided to resign from the board. He had had enough of the headache of appeasing the coaches' and players' constant quarrels over money that characterise professional football in Cameroon (Pannenborg 2008).

I had first met Djibrilla in August 2003 through a friend of his from school. He was born into a large polygamous family. His father, who had arrived in Ngaoundéré after completing his studies, was a Pullo from Maroua. The father's status as a civil servant, his contacts in the cattle sector, and his strategic marriage choices (both for himself and for his older children) afforded him a reputable foothold in his adopted home town. By the time Djibrilla was born, his father had completed the pilgrimage to Mecca, owned several well-located houses in town, and had acquired a large farm east of Ngaoundéré, which boasted a sizeable herd of cattle.

Unable to obtain his baccalaureate, Djibrilla left school when he was 19 years old. He then pursued several occupations. At the outset, in what became his first experience of life in southern Cameroon, he worked for almost a year as a clerk in a textile store owned by a paternal uncle. He then moved to a small town in anglophone Cameroon, where one of his older brothers had been appointed sub-prefect. His brother got him an internship in the local municipality. There, he became familiar with the procedures and inner workings of Cameroonian public administration. That job was also the springboard for his first public contracts, which included supplying stationery and a couple of minor construction works. By 1996, better opportunities arose back in Ngaoundéré. Two of his brothers, who were only a few years older than him, had established themselves in the city as reliable contractors. His recent savings allowed him to pool money for use in some of his brothers' operations. Their father's death soon after Djibrilla's return also meant that he could turn his part of the inheritance, consisting mostly of cattle, into capital for his new business. Some of the managerial skills that I would see him deploy during my fieldwork – his affable and generous disposition towards officials, intense dedication to his business, meticulous planning and organisation, active searches for the most competitive suppliers, and close supervision of his workers on building sites – helped him get a good start.

When I first met him, he was in his early thirties. Seven years had passed since he had married and established his own household. Good-tempered and unassuming, he took pride in what he had achieved. In Maroua in March 2004, for instance, he declared with unconcealed satisfaction to an old friend who worked at the Ministry of Public Works, 'I don't have serious competitors in Ngaoundéré. They [the different state agencies] cannot do without me. There is no one in the city as reliable as me.' Self-confidence was his hallmark. His satisfaction also reflected how favourably, in his view, his work compared with that of other contractors in Adamaoua. For example, referring to the budget of his most ambitious project in 2004, a warehouse for a social marketing venture with international sponsors, he reminded me that a well-known contractor in Ngaoundéré had obtained four times as much from an international development programme for exactly the same sort of building – and, unlike Djibrilla, he had not offered a one-year guarantee. He often had disparaging words for contractors who based their businesses exclusively on privileged access to contracting opportunities and lacked the know-how and experience that fulfilling those contracts involved. In later years, when rural electrification became something of a speciality, he would boast that more than 30 villages across northern Cameroon owed their connection to the national power grid to his work.

In a short period of time, he attained a respectable position. The number of contracts he was able to take on increased over time, and from early on he had undertaken construction work outside Adamaoua, mostly in the North and Far North Provinces. He seemed well aware of the risks and challenges that the increased volume of business and this wider geographical scope entailed. Given his preference for a personalised management style and tight control over the fulfilment of each contract, he did not hesitate to decline invitations to bid for contracts that he viewed as beyond his financial, technical, or logistic means. Considering northern Cameroon's arduous road conditions, he was also careful not to embark on more than one or two contracts outside Adamaoua at a time.

During this period of expansion, Alhadji Djibrilla relied almost exclusively on his own financial capabilities. He used his bank accounts mostly for cheques and only occasionally for rather modest lines of credit. When appropriate, he supplemented self-financing with funds from family or other partners. This was not necessarily a response to a shortage of funds;

it could also be a way of keeping his business associates close – people on whom he would depend for obtaining contracts or carrying out and overseeing works for him. His relationship with one of his brothers, itself embedded within their very large and dense family network, was particularly important. They both benefited from access to contracts that two of their siblings – senior officials in different ministries – made possible. Beyond that, they would offer each other a share in many of the contracts they were awarded through other channels. They would also take advantage of each other's regular trips to the Middle East to import office equipment and furniture as well as luxury cars. During his brother's absences, Djibrilla looked after his business – processing paperwork, visiting building sites, or collecting payments for him as needed – and his brother reciprocated whenever Djibrilla travelled.

Djibrilla also pooled capital with a long list of partners. These included people who lacked the financial means or the technical expertise to fulfil contracts by themselves. More often than not, close collaborators were in an intermediate position between partnership and employment. Consider, for example, Bobbo, one of Djibrilla's three closest collaborators in the early years of his business career. Bobbo's initiation to public works had been rather serendipitous. Employed as a taxi driver in Ngaoundéré, one of his regular clients, a contractor from Douala, hired him as foreman on a large construction site. When his boss's business was completed in Ngaoundéré, Bobbo knew the time had come to branch out on his own. The year was 1999. Although he started with very small contracts, he managed to enlarge his capital slowly but surely. Almost inevitably, he approached Djibrilla, a former school friend who by then had attained a secure position among local contractors. Theirs was a multifarious collaboration. At first, Bobbo, who did not register a firm under his name until 2002, used Djibrilla's letterhead for his own contracts. In turn, Bobbo carried out assignments for Djibrilla and his brother. In 2003, when I first met them, they formed a team on almost every contract that either of them secured. Once a bid was successful, they decided how to share the profits according to their role in obtaining the contract and their individual contributions, in terms of money and labour, to its completion. Yet, their collaboration was not based on equality; the differences in their financial capacity, connections in government circles, and even ethnic identification (Bobbo considered himself Hausa) reinforced Djibrilla's higher standing. Interestingly, in the early years of their collaboration, people I knew in Ngaoundéré who were familiar with their respective ethnic and family backgrounds but not privy to the specifics of their business arrangements assumed that Bobbo was Djibrilla's driver.

The way in which Bobbo and Djibrilla divided their tasks reflected Bobbo's subordinate role. While Djibrilla prepared most of the legal paperwork, acted as their representative in important commercial transactions, and negotiated the 'cut' allocated to the officials responsible for awarding contracts and authorising payments, the routine chores fell on Bappa Bobbo, as children in Djibrilla's extended family would call him.[23] A road maintenance project they undertook in North Province in 2004, which I discuss in Chapter 2, offers an apt illustration. Djibrilla handled financially important transactions, such as renting a caterpillar, or delicate ones, like reaching an agreement with treasury officials on a fast-track payment. Yet, he only visited the work site once, and then only briefly, to see what needed to be done and to meet the prefect involved. In contrast, Bobbo stayed at the work site during most of the actual work to supervise workers and monitor progress. He also returned there for the formal reception of the payment. With time, as the number of contracts he secured by his own means increased, he became more and more autonomous. Bobbo's pilgrimage to Mecca in 2005 marked a moment of emancipation. To this day, however, he remains in almost daily contact in person or over the phone with Djibrilla and his brother. They still pool their financial resources regularly and even work together occasionally.

Although his financial capabilities and general skills certainly increased as the years went by, Djibrilla made a point of keeping his firm's operating costs low. With the exception of several medium-sized trucks, which he rented to other contractors whenever he did not need them, he had avoided purchasing any substantial construction equipment. For years, he conducted his business at home when not on the road, in public offices, or on construction sites. He began using an office in central Ngaoundéré only in 2007. It was a modest, discreet operation, without any identifying signs outside. As for labour, all his employees worked on a contract basis. In Ngaoundéré, there was a pool of site managers, masons, plumbers, electricians, and carpenters from which he drew as he saw fit. He considered this a flexible arrangement. If his first choice happened to be engaged elsewhere, he found others for particular jobs. For more sensitive tasks, particularly those involving handling money, he relied on a group of more trusted agents, many of whom were male relatives. Younger brothers or cousins, for instance, who had no better prospects or were in an intermediate stage between the end of their studies and a possible position in the civil service would oversee work sites, manage supplies of materials, and pay workers periodically. Others would specialise in driving trucks and running other errands. He also had trusted contacts at the Hôtel de Finances in Ngaoundéré, Garoua, and Maroua, who informed Djibrilla and his contractor brother of activities

---

[23] *Bappa* is the informal, apocopate form of *bappaño* ('paternal uncle' in Fulfulde).

and personalities there. None of these agents received a set salary, but they were given handsome rewards in return for specific jobs or information. Neighbours who visited on an almost daily basis managed side businesses for him, for example a small restaurant at the railway station or a fleet of old cars operating as taxis in the city.

In fact, Bobbo's transition to increased autonomy began a cycle whereby several of Djibrilla's most trusted assistants during his early years as a contractor graduated from their subordinate roles and established firms of their own. In this regard, 2008 and 2009 were challenging years for Djibrilla, as he had to find suitable replacements for some of his assistants and start training new people all over again. The transition also had financial implications, as Djibrilla felt compelled to bankroll his former employees in their first steps as independent contractors. However, not all of them were grateful or proved to be as successful as Bobbo. In July 2014, sharing his disappointment with regard to one of them, he told me:

Do you remember Yaya, *sukaa am* [my aide]?[24] He was in a rush [to make it big]. He married a second wife. [It was a matter of] pride! He sent ten people to Mecca; he built a very good house ... But it wasn't his money. It was other people's money he was handling. Well, he's bankrupt. If you see him now, he's a sorry sight. To think that I taught him much of what he knows!

Djibrilla thought he had managed his own new-found wealth much more wisely and gradually. In the couple of years after his return from anglophone Cameroon, his main priority had been to establish himself as a respectable *baaba saare* (father of the house). In that short period, he built a spacious house next to his brother-partner, with an adjoining mosque and, almost immediately afterwards, he celebrated his first marriage. In addition, he had been able to meet the expenses of his first pilgrimage to Mecca (and paid for his wife's hadj the following year). The couple, however, yearned to have children. For more than a decade, his wife had undergone numerous treatments prescribed by doctors and marabouts. Djibrilla had withstood mounting pressure to marry a second wife in order to have offspring. He had considered the idea seriously several times but never acted on it. In 2008, they had adopted a relative's baby daughter. Two years later, having put themselves in the hands of doctors in the Middle East, their persistence paid off and they finally had a son. By then, Djibrilla and his family were already living in a grandiose mansion, inspired by stunning foreign designs and filled with furniture and kitchen and bathroom appliances imported from Dubai.

---

[24] *Suuka* (plural: *suukabe*) designates a young adult and by association someone in a subordinate position more broadly. It can be used with pejorative connotations, sometimes hinting at a dissolute life (Boutrais 2002: 166).

Over the years, I heard numerous admiring comments from outsiders about how well Djibrilla's siblings had been able to preserve solidarity and unity among themselves even after their father's death. Their family was usually presented as an exceptional case among large, affluent polygamous families. Family represented a source of support and opportunities as much as a responsibility. Younger siblings depended on their older siblings when they needed support for their studies or access to civil service jobs or initiation into trade or other lines of business. Djibrilla had his fair share of dependent relatives, some of whom served him very well. Moreover, as the wealthiest of his mother's children, he assumed the maintenance of her large household while she was alive. The force of family bonds was most palpable in life-course events of religious significance, such as the return of family members from their first hadj, when those living in other parts of the country would congregate in Ngaoundéré to welcome the pilgrim home. Djibrilla's photograph albums bore testimony to the large receptions that marked his and his wife's trips to Mecca or annual festivals to commemorate the end of Ramadan or *Tabaski* (the feast of the sacrifice). The various ones in which I took part were understated by comparison with the sumptuous meals and prayers organised by important traders of the older generation in Ngaoundéré. Nonetheless, they revealed the range of people who made up Djibrilla's social world. Relatives and in-laws aside, I was always struck by the diverse class, religious, and ethnic backgrounds of the neighbours and civil servants who attended.

Real estate was a favourite investment for Djibrilla's extra funds. His contacts in the Fulbe-Muslim local circles and among officials from other parts of the country posted in Ngaoundéré meant that he was extremely well informed about available opportunities. He regularly purchased plots of land. He had become familiar with the intricacies of land-titling procedures and showed remarkable poise in his dealings with neighbourhood chiefs, prefects, and other relevant officials. His properties in the city included residential houses and apartment buildings as well as numerous *mini-cités* (dormitories with rooms to let for university students). By the late 2000s, he began also to target Maroua, a city where he had many business and family ties and which was anticipated to experience a construction boom with the opening of a university in 2009. In 2012, he built a house there to serve as his business base in the Far North. In his early years as a contractor, a modest investment of enormous affective value concerned his father's farm east of Ngaoundéré. It had remained undivided after his father's death and all the heirs had liquidated their share of the deceased's cattle holdings. From 2000 to 2005, Djibrilla undertook the rebuilding of the paternal herd. His view was that his older, better-off siblings' indifference with regard to continuing their father's cattle-herding activities was the result of an excessive immersion in city life in Yaoundé and Douala. By the late 2000s, Djibrilla regretfully gave up on cattle altogether. The farm, which he hardly ever found the time to visit, had proved to be a constant source of expenses that yielded disappointing results.

Among his side activities, Djibrilla's trade in second-hand cars perhaps merits special mention. It is little wonder that the Benoué prefect picked on it in his playful provocation during the football game in Garoua. Djibrilla's arrival in the stadium with a smart-looking Toyota RAV4 had not gone unnoticed. Djibrilla projected his business success and international connections through frequent changes of vehicle. He had made a name for himself because of his ability to import reasonably priced cars, mostly via Cotonou. This trade provided an outlet for excess liquidity and allowed him to build additional profits into his trips abroad. These transactions also enabled him to provide a gainful occupation to unemployed youth in his social circles who drove the vehicles to Ngaoundéré. Crucially, the clients were often civil servants and liberal professionals in whose good books it was useful for Djibrilla to be. This was consistent with his most distinctive business instinct, which was to invest money into building and consolidating relationships with powerful people, mostly in Adamaoua but also elsewhere in northern Cameroon and Yaoundé.

During a trip to Maroua in 2004, when I noted how efficiently he had secured prompt payment for a large contract, he told me: 'My connections [with state officials] are my wealth. That's why they pay me before others. [To forge them] takes charm and time ... but also money. They pay me because of what I put on the table.' Such expenses not only comprised payments tied to specific transactions, like the award of a contract or the speeding up of a payment, but also a striking catalogue of personal gifts. From small items such as imported garments or fabrics and assorted electronics brought back from his travels abroad to more substantial purchases such as the couple of prime head of cattle I witnessed him ship from Adamaoua to senior civil servants in Yaoundé, presents were meant to become memorable tokens of privileged relationships. As a cross-border trader, who grew up in the same neighbourhood as Djibrilla, once told me: 'He is someone who is extremely generous, and in the long run, that pays. People end up treating him well everywhere he goes.'

A cattle trader at a crossroads

It had been more than nine months since I was last in Ngaoundéré, and it was with great anticipation that I purchased my train ticket in Yaoundé on Sunday, 14 August 2005. I had spent a few days in Douala catching up with numerous acquaintances, after a week in Yaoundé working in the decaying records of the National Archives. Only five more weeks remained of my short research trip to Cameroon and I planned to spend at least three of them up north, mostly in Adamaoua. There were many things to look forward to, but I was particularly eager to reconnect with some of the cattle traders I had befriended during my previous stay. I did not have to wait long. That same evening on the train I bumped into Alhadji Badjo, whom I had first met in June 2004 in Ngaoundal (Djerem District, Adamaoua), the town where he lived. Now, by chance, we shared the same train compartment. It was not entirely surprising, for Yaoundé's cattle market takes place on Sundays and Adamaoua-based traders who do business there normally travel back to their homes on Sunday evening to start a new cycle of buying and selling.

The long hours spent going back and forth between Adamaoua and Yaoundé are an unavoidable element of many cattle traders' professional routine. Only a handful of traders can afford to travel by plane. But even then, scheduled internal flights have been so erratic in recent years that for long periods air travel has not been a reliable option.[25] The railway that links Adamaoua with Yaoundé and Douala has problems of its own. It has suffered from decades of underinvestment and lack of regular maintenance. Passenger trains still experience long delays because of derailments and other disruptions to the service. Privatised in 1999 through a 30-year concession agreement with a consortium led by the logistic multinational Bolloré, the railway company Camrail prioritised freight over passenger transport.[26] Even when trains run normally, it takes 15 hours to cover the 620 kilometres separating Yaoundé from Ngaoundéré.

Thus, cattle traders tend to spend many hours on the train every week. Those whose financial and commercial capabilities allow them to sell only a few head of cattle per trip must resign themselves to a second-class seat to minimise expenses. Better-established traders, such as Alhadji Badjo, can afford a sleeping berth. Either way, traders usually travel in groups. Train compartments then become spaces of intense sociability, where colleagues may rival each other in displays of wit or mockery, share

---

[25] The national airline company Camair, which had ten managing directors between 1993 and 2005, has been embroiled in countless financial difficulties. A botched privatisation process that started in 2005 was equally troubled and ended with the company's liquidation in 2008. A new state-owned airline operating under the commercial name of Camair-Co launched its first flights in 2011.

[26] The railway company was explicit in the rationale of cost-effectiveness for such priorities (Maunoir 2000: 20). The company's managing director did not mince his words on the subject: 'Passenger transport is 15 percent of our turnover and 80 percent of *des emmerdements* (hassle)' (Blanc and Gouirand 2007: 32). In December 2003, an additional agreement revised the subsidy regime for passenger transport. A new amendment to the 1999 agreement was signed in 2008.

market information, engage in religious or political discussion, gossip and joke, share provisions and (non-alcoholic) drinks, and pray together. Having purchased his ticket at the last minute, Badjo had been given a bed several cars away from most of the other traders travelling on the train. So we enjoyed a long tête-à-tête, interrupted occasionally by the comings and goings of four Arab-Choa traders from Mbaïmboum (North Province) who shared our compartment.[27]

Badjo complained bitterly about market conditions in Yaoundé. He felt that the difficult financial circumstances of butchers were crippling his activities, and he had not yet figured out a strategy for getting out of this vicious circle. This was a common plight among the traders I knew. Badjo's clients in Yaoundé bought cattle on credit. It took them one to four weeks to pay him back, if they did not default altogether. They could not repay him until they had slaughtered the animal and sold the meat. 'So if they run into problems, there is no way for them to pay or for you to recover the money. They have no capital. They are poor. I lose lots of money with them (*ɓe don ñaama ceede masin* [literally, they eat too much money]),' he explained. What he feared most, however, was dealing with intermediaries who sold cattle in other markets of the region, such as Gabon and Equatorial Guinea. With them, the chances of seeing his trust betrayed multiplied. They are transient figures, typically non-Cameroonians vaguely identified as Malian or Senegalese, whom the traders themselves barely know:

If I know who you are, I do not take the trouble of putting the sale in writing. I trust you. But when I deal with these people who go to [Equatorial] Guinea, I make them sign a voucher [*bon*]. Not that it helps much, though. I have been waiting five months already to get my money back from one of them without success.

I was already familiar with Badjo's story. At some point in the previous year, he had agreed to be interviewed. Although the interview had been in Fulfulde and only loosely structured, he made no secret of the fact that the format was too formal for his taste. Since then we had met on numerous occasions and our relationship had become much less awkward. Badjo had been born in the mid-1960s in the area surrounding Ngaoundéré. As he put it himself, 'We are rural folk (*himɓe ladde* [literally, people from the bush]).'[28] In 1974, his family was forced out of their

---

[27] Mbaïmboum (North Province), located on the Cameroonian border with Central African Republic and Chad, is a market that experienced a spectacular expansion in the 1990s (Bennafla 2002).

[28] This categorisation is often invoked with pejorative associations in Adamaoua's urban centres. Certain Fulbe business people in Ngaoundéré I encountered, who claim membership in some of the city's older families, viewed several recent cases of economic success as examples of such rural folk who had taken over 'their' city. Cf. Roitman's remarks (2005: 91) on *les venants* (newcomers and outsiders) from Maroua's

grazing lands by the tsetse fly invasion that hit the Adamaoua plateau hard from 1955 to the 1990s (Boutrais 1983: 103–16; 1999). A series of residential shifts ensued. Ngaoundal, which owed its foundation to the construction of the railway and soon boasted a sizeable population centre (Burnham 1996a: 41, 64), was their first destination. In 1978, his father decided to move to Meiganga, the main urban centre of south-eastern Adamaoua, in search of better opportunities. In the absence of promising results, they moved back in Ngaoundal in 1982.

While still in Meiganga, Badjo had begun to make modest inroads into the poultry trade. He consolidated his activities back in Ngaoundal and was able to devote his profits to the acquisition of cattle. In 1986, his life changed drastically. He married his first wife, his father died, and he made his first transaction in Yaoundé's cattle market. His father's estate consisted of little more than a house and what was by local standards a small herd of cattle of around 30 head, which was distributed among nine siblings. This allowed him to add four additional head to the seven that he had already accumulated by his own means. At Badjo's instigation, one of his new brothers-in-law, an experienced cattle trader, took him to Yaoundé to sell half of his stock. The operation was extremely profitable, so much so that he decided to embrace this trade as his main activity.

Such an auspicious start, however, was soon offset by a stroke of bad luck. A train hit and killed four of his adult cows. Regifercam, as the railway company was called before the 1999 privatisation, refused to compensate him for the loss. It took him considerable time and effort to restore his capital to its initial levels. However, the trend of Badjo's fortunes in those years was decidedly upward. In 1992 he paid for his first business licence, a sign that his activities had grown conspicuous enough not to pass unnoticed by the tax authorities. Over the following years, he added two more wives to his household, the third being the young daughter of one of the most influential cattle traders in the area. Soon afterwards, in 1998, he fulfilled his desire to make the pilgrimage to Mecca, which, by the time of our encounter on the train, he had visited on three more occasions.

In successive visits to Ngaoundal I developed a sense of what the foundations of his strong commercial position were. I learned that several farmers in the surrounding area regularly entrusted him their cattle, granting him months for repayment. Additionally, a couple of merchants who owned general stores in the town's market, channelled part of their cash flow through him. Badjo was an attractive business partner. His properties, large family, and reputation inspired confidence. One of the

surrounding area, whose influx is linked in popular discourse with changes in economic organisation and values.

merchants who invested funds to trade cattle through him reflected on the hazards of such an arrangement:

> You know how cattle markets are. When [traders] sell on credit and they are not paid back on time, your money is blocked there. If this happens, I am forced to take money from some other place [in addition to his main store, he had a smaller boutique in Ngaoundal and five teenagers driving motorcycle-taxis for him], until Alhadji Badjo is able to recover our money. There are times when the sum I give him does not yield profits, because selling cattle is not such a straightforward business as many think. In a way, it is as if what you are really doing is helping the trader with whom you work. It may happen that Badjo returns [from Yaoundé] having made far too little. He has spent almost a month struggling and he has only got a very small sum. Instead of asking him for your half, you let it go. Only when he has made enough money do we share it, otherwise [I only recover the money I have lent him and] I do not take my part.

To understand the reasons behind this and similar arrangements, consider this merchant's alternatives. At the time, there was only one microfinance institution and no banks operating in Ngaoundal. Created in 1997, the town's Mutuelle Communautaire de Croissance (Community Growth Savings Union, or MC2) did not live up to his expectations. Once he had to wait four days before he could withdraw a relatively modest sum from his account for a stock renewal trip to Ngaoundéré. He confided that this experience scared him away. He felt that his savings were not safe in a place with limited liquidity and thus closed his account after less than a year as a client. Since then, he had tried to circulate the surplus from his two stores and the moto-taxi business through agreements like the one he had with Badjo. He preferred this alternative to a bank account in a distant place with high operating fees. Circulating profits also helped him avoid keeping large sums of cash at home.

Badjo's success in the cattle trade was also based on access to railway transport. Making the most of lucrative business opportunities in southern markets for prime beef meant being able to ship cattle regularly, avoiding the losses and delays of transport on foot. Railway freight cars for cattle are scarce and, during peak times, space in them is fought over. In the late 1980s, tensions between Meiganga-based and Ngaoundal-based traders around their respective shares in freight cars departing from Ngaoundal station reached boiling point. Gendarmes had to be called several times to avoid violent outbursts, and the district and provincial authorities intervened to resolve the ongoing dispute, as the traders' leaders whom I interviewed recalled. The final outcome was very favourable to traders based in Ngaoundal, who, as a result, saw their allocated freight space more than double. Young, ambitious traders such as Badjo were able to capitalise on this opening in the early 1990s. Over the years, however, there had also been difficult moments when defaults by butchers or intermediaries who bought from him on credit made him unable to pay back the farmers whose cattle he was trading or the merchants who lent him money. Over time, Badjo claimed, experience had taught him to expect a setback after every bout of prosperity.

By the mid-2000s, Alhadji Badjo found that the improvements in lifestyle that accompanied his success became difficult to sustain. Over the years, he has built an imposing and centrally located house in Ngaoundal and has replaced every few years the four-wheel drive vehicle he uses for work. His wives have given birth to numerous children. He has also formed a sizeable herd in the grazing lands of Vina District, where he was born, which is now tsetse-free. 'What I see when I look at my present situation is all these mounting expenses! All my profits go to cover the expenses of my *saare* [household]. My business capital has stagnated,' he lamented that first time we met. More than a year later, on the occasion of our serendipitous shared train ride, his tone was markedly less negative. Even so, he still had many of the same misgivings.

It was almost midnight when the traders from Mbaïmboum sharing our train compartment decided to join in the conversation. We subtly moved away from the topic of the cattle trade. Badjo entertained us with a typical enough story of a marriage that had required formidable expenses. Last month, a friend of his had gone to Kousséri (Far North Province) to marry a young Arab woman, and, before the celebration was over, he had spent CFAF 3 million, including a bride price of 1 million. I could not help but think that the anecdote, ostensibly addressed to his Arab audience, provided a commentary on Badjo's own concerns: namely, his difficulties in keeping up with the expenses of his *saare*. In any case, despite its reinforcing of ethnic stereotypes, our travel companions found the story very amusing. On that note we prepared to get some sleep.

At the end of our train ride together, I had not made much of the fact that Badjo had not stopped in Ngaoundal but had instead travelled all the way to Ngaoundéré. Later that week, I was surprised to run into him on my rounds of the cattle markets in Vina District. I also met him during the weekly distribution of freight cars for cattle shipments to Yaoundé. A trader friend had introduced him into one of the two groups to which the railway company allocated freight cars in Ngaoundéré. He was happy to learn that he was likely to be assigned space for a few head the following week. In the coming weeks, it became apparent that Badjo was testing the waters with an eye to make the city his new base of operations. He listed several reasons for this move. Ngaoundéré was closer than Ngaoundal to the grazing land where he kept most of his own cattle. Vina District offered better trading opportunities than Djerem. Those among his children with an inclination to study were approaching the age to go to university, and the university in Ngaoundéré was the closest. Other reasons emerged later. For one thing, the death of his father-in-law and patron meant that he now depended on traders with whom he was on bad terms for access to railway transport for his cattle in Ngaoundal. Also, household dynamics and the deteriorating relationship between one of his wives and the other two made it advisable to split the household.

Badjo's plan proved feasible. Over the coming months, relying on his experience and on old professional relationships, he inserted himself into the city's cattle-trading circles rather smoothly. A year later, he built a house in one of Ngaoundéré's newer neighbourhoods, where his youngest wife moved. He has, however, kept his household in Ngaoundal, which he visits regularly. In many ways, his move to Ngaoundéré was about downsizing and ridding himself of the expectations that his wealth in the late 1990s had generated around him in Ngaoundal. In the early 2010s, after endless cases of butchers' debts becoming unrecoverable, he ceased selling cattle in Yaoundé's market and opted to focus exclusively on Gabon and Equatorial Guinea, where he has long-standing agents.

An undistinguished trucking career

When, in August 2005, I phoned Alhadji Yero, a former minibus driver turned trucker-cum-farmer whom I had met a year earlier, he insisted that we spend the following day together. He had a few errands to run, but, once they were taken care of, we would be able to visit his farm, 20 kilometres north of Ngaoundéré. After an early breakfast at his house, we drove to the Saga-SDV offices in the city's cargo terminal. Earlier that week, after a ten-day wait, he had been offered N'Djaména-bound freight from Saga at the truckers' union office. While I waited outside in the company of the usual group of intermediaries and other regulars hanging around, I listened to their litany of complaints about freight scarcity and low prices (Figure 1.3). Yero came out a few minutes later, visibly pleased, waving the cheque he had just received as advance payment. Our next move was to see the mechanic who was making the final adjustments to get his truck ready for the road. Since this involved, among other things, replacing a couple of tyres, Yero needed to cash the new cheque to pay for them. So, we stopped by Credit du Sahel, a microfinance establishment that had recently opened a branch in Ngaoundéré. A month before, Yero had received from them a small loan to cultivate maize and he was hoping to develop a close relationship with their branch manager. Much to Yero's disappointment, the manager told us that they couldn't cash the cheque directly. Instead, they needed Yero to first deposit the cheque in the account he had with Credit Lyonnais, one of the city's banks, and then write a cheque payable to the microfinance establishment. Like most other microfinance institutions in

Figure 1.3 Parking yard, Ngaoundéré cargo terminal, June 2011

Cameroon, Credit du Sahel lacked the capacity to negotiate cheques issued to their clients. This was the kind of complication Yero would rather avoid. Although we rushed to Credit Lyonnais, we found that it had closed for the day. Shrugging off this minor setback, my friend announced: 'It's about time we drove to the farm, don't you think?' And so we did.

The following morning, as he recounted later that week, Yero managed to have a word with his bank's branch manager:

I told him: 'I went to the butcher yesterday and called you to see if I should buy you some meat. You didn't reply and I didn't call again. Here you have a little something so that you can buy some.' And I gave him [CFAF] 20,000. 'Thank you very much, Alhadji. Thank you!' 'Here is the situation. I need to leave for Yaoundé later today. I would like to withdraw 600,000.' He said: 'Since you're travelling to Yaoundé, 600,000 is far too little. Take more! You have [deposited] two pending cheques for 1,400,000 and you recently withdrew 400,000. Take as much as you need.' 'Can I withdraw 800,000?' 'You can if you want to.' I wrote a cheque for 800,000, took the money, went to the cargo terminal, and took care of the final paperwork [with the freight bureau]. Before noon, I was able to get the truck on the road.

In the days when I accompanied Alhadji Yero while he conducted business, I had plenty of opportunities to admire the strength of his resolve. Born in 1958 in a polygamous household at the heart of Ngaoundéré's Maloumri neighbourhood, he grew up under the strict authority of his father, a Kanuri Qur'anic teacher. He left school at the earliest opportunity and, still a teenager, became a motor boy and then, in 1975, a taxi driver. His employer was Alhadji Daouda, a leading figure in SETRACAUCAM, the unitary union that controlled passenger transport in the city. Daouda was to become his father-in-law and a lifelong patron. Soon after Yero began to work for him, his mother died and he inherited from her a few head of cattle. In 1978, Yero decided to sell his cattle to purchase a second-hand taxi and have someone else drive it. This investment failed to bear the desired fruit, so a year later he sold the taxi and, through a friend of his deceased father, bought nine young bulls. In 1981, Daouda promoted him to driver of one of his cars (minibuses). At around the same time, his patron persuaded Yero to get rid of his bulls and buy cows instead. In the following few years, Yero's cattle suffered different misfortunes and were reduced to two cows and two calves. Since his patron felt bad about the losses that Yero had incurred following his advice, he decided to compensate him with a gift of 40 head. In 1986, on the condition that he did not drive it himself, Daouda sold him an old minibus on very favourable terms. This did not prove profitable and he eventually sold it. By then, the first small companies questioning the unitary union's monopoly had begun to emerge. In 1989, Daouda asked Yero to take up the management of his ranch, a job in which he lasted an entire decade. Yero was thus spared a front-line role in the conflicts between SETRACAUCAM and its rivals. The system that had been established in the early 1970s soon fell apart; in the old system, for each day of the week, the union designated the operators authorised to work on the Yaoundé–Maroua line. The fact that the young operators who flourished in this early period of liberalised passenger transport became known as *tasa ginnaaji* (a bus station run by jinns) will give an idea of the prevailing sense of chaos in the early 1990s.

The purchase of Yero's first truck came in 1999, when a well-placed relative helped him buy a 10-ton Mercedes that was being auctioned by a national parastatal. To pay for it, and for the repairs required, Yero tapped once more into his cattle herd. To drive the truck, he hired an acquaintance. After a few trips that generated unanticipated expenses, forcing Yero into further cattle sales, he decided to drive the truck himself. In this way he also ceased to be in Daouda's employment, achieving a long-held desire for greater independence. This formula worked so well that, in the space of a year, Yero was able to restore his herd to its former size and finance a second trip to Mecca – his first pilgrimage had taken place in 1985 and had been funded by Daouda as a reward for his loyalty. This was 'the story of the money I made when I sold that taxi back in 1979', he told me with a smile, concluding the exhaustive account of this long chain of transactions. As he liked to repeat, *na'i suddan asirri* (cattle would cover one's needs, or, more idiomatically, cattle would save the day).[29] In fact, his career, like that of many other truckers based in Adamaoua, could be seen as a succession of conversions between cattle and vehicles.

This brief period of buoyancy allowed Yero to purchase a semitrailer truck, the kind of vehicle with which he could obtain contracts with international freight forwarders such as Saga. He had bought it in 2000 from a close friend, with whom he had recently undertaken the pilgrimage to Mecca. His friend was a wealthy operator in the transport of goods and passengers and could afford to grant Yero a very flexible repayment schedule. Yero described it as a *coggu soobaajo* (sale between friends). His problems with diabetes, however, cut this prosperous streak short. In 2001, on account of his health, he had to give up driving and rely on others to drive his two trucks. This had a significant impact on profits. By June 2004, when we first met, he had not yet managed to pay for the semitrailer in full, something he had anticipated he would have done long before. Still, he counted himself lucky that if things did not work out as expected during a particular month, his friend was happy to wait until the following month. In fact, in the four years since he had bought it, the truck had experienced several accidents and a serious breakdown that led to the replacement of the engine, thus delaying the repayment process. By the end of 2004, his friend had finally agreed to waive the outstanding sum.

In spite of all the difficulties he had encountered in recent years, Yero was persuaded that, as he put it, he had 'everything required to become a successful transporter'. A recent experience in handling a minor crisis at Daouda's trucking business had supplied a powerful dose of self-assurance. His father-in-law was one of the few Cameroonian transporters who had benefited from a direct contract with the Chad–Cameroon pipeline consortium's subsidiary COTCO. His four semitrailers had serviced the pipeline project for about two years. However, in 2003, halfway through this period, neglect on the part of Daouda's foreman had led the consortium to threaten to terminate the contract. Daouda then asked Yero to take over. Once he did, things began to get back on track. After eight months of the trucks working to everyone's satisfaction, he was able to pass responsibility on to the foreman once more. Yero saw

---

[29] *Suddugo asirri* literally means to cover secrets. In the context of this phrase, those secrets refer to one's essential domestic needs, including nourishment, lodging, and clothing. Any public admission of concern or weakness in meeting those needs goes against established Fulbe ideals of proper behaviour. The rationale for covering such secrets is not to show any signs of want.

this as a triumphant test of his professional skills and his ability to handle all sorts of people.

When Yero said that he had everything required for success in the trucking business, the subtext was that something was missing. As the tension surrounding his visits to the local microfinance and banking establishments underscored, he lacked a strong financial base. Yero frequently found himself in tight spots, and his difficulties were not always resolved smoothly. Getting his trucks ready for a trip with the necessary visits to the mechanic and the requisite paperwork, or attending to road accidents, breakdowns, and all sorts of incidents often involved expenses that Yero could only cover by selling cattle. Nevertheless, in a conversation in August 2005, Yero remained upbeat enough to consider expanding his small fleet. He was exploring the purchase of a couple of semitrailers from an expatriate who had been doing the Douala–Bangui route and was planning to leave Cameroon. To finance the down payment, he was counting on obtaining a substantial loan from the bank manager, whose good graces he had been cultivating.

Five years later, when I visited his farm in July 2010, Alhadji Yero was eager to update me on all the improvements he had introduced since we had last seen each other. The changes in his agropastoral ventures were certainly impressive but I was most intrigued to find out how he had been able to make them compatible with the running of his trucking business. As it turned out, the need had not really arisen:

Don't get me started! [One of the trucks] had a serious accident three years ago. After the return from that trip, I decided to quit there and then. That was the end of it! The two trucks [I had] then are parked to this day. It was not even worth fixing them to try to find a buyer. [The business] wasn't working at all. I needed to take [CFAF] 1 million here, 2 million there, and sink them into the upkeep of the trucks, so that they continued working. Then, an accident or a mechanical problem would happen. I had to sell cattle to get the truck back here.

Yero's eight-year career in the trucking business highlights recurrent themes in my interviews with truck owners, drivers, and employees of freight forwarders. The linkages between the cattle and transport sectors, on the one hand, and the combination of investments in both passenger and goods transport, on the other, were two aspects that featured prominently in Yero's account and in those of many others. These trends reflect the widespread diversification strategies among Adamaoua's business owners. As in many other economic settings, commercial capital is perhaps the most common source of start-up investments in transport. Another thread running through my interviewees' narratives is the importance of patron–client relationships. Like Yero, many owners of small trucking companies, and a few of the large ones, had transitioned from driver to owner thanks partly to the support of their bosses. Often, this took the form of sales of vehicles from boss to driver. A truck owner could thus find a buyer for a vehicle he was ready to discard and strengthen the loyalty of a driver who now remained financially indebted. Sometimes, as when Daouda sold Yero an old minibus in 1986, such sales are made on the condition that the employee continues working as a driver for the employer. If the newly acquired vehicle works well and becomes a source of steady income, it is only a matter of time before drivers persuade their employer to let them go. This was frequently done on amicable terms. Another one of Daouda's former drivers, for example, who was 60 when I interviewed him in July 2004, still referred to his old boss as *mai gida am* (my patron, from the Hausa words for 'household head'). He had started independently in 1982 with a small truck that Daouda had sold him the year before. After investing heavily in passenger minibuses during the 1990s and experiencing heavy losses by the end of that decade, he had reverted to freight transport. For some three decades, he had benefited from Daouda's financial support and advice. Letting a driver go 'when the time had come', this transporter thought, had a bearing on the truck owner's reputation as a 'good boss', which in turn would secure the diligence and loyalty of future employees. In many other cases, however, the transition from driver to owner took place in spite of the employer's wishes.

Although Yero had ended up securing Daouda's blessing to cease working for him, he had had to overcome certain resistance. And, for Yero, it hardly seemed like a clean break, as he felt greatly indebted. Daouda's gifts over the years had been many and substantial, from 'giving me his child [as wife]' to paying for his first pilgrimage to Mecca, to reconstituting his decimated herd. In our conversations, Yero spoke of Daouda with admiration and gratitude. He also showed pride in having honoured his patron's trust and generosity through hard work and integrity. Although it was years since he had stopped working for Daouda, their relationship was still extremely close: 'We talk on the phone every day. *Min don hauri tan bana huunde gootel.* [We act in concert as if we were one thing.] Whatever I do, they know; whatever they do, I know. We constantly ask for each other's opinion.' For all of Yero's insistence on reciprocity and Daouda's benevolent paternalism, their relationship had had ups and downs. The deference that Yero showed by using the third person plural to refer to Daouda – common linguistic usage among Ngaoundéré's Fulfulde speakers – signalled their relationship as son-in-law and father-in law. But its correlate was considerable social distance, in wealth, age, and ethnicity – Daouda and Yero, although related through some distant matrilineal connections, defined themselves as Pullo and Kanuri respectively.

When Yero purchased his first truck in 1999, at first he had someone drive it while he remained in charge of managing his patron's cattle. It was only a few months later, after serious losses on the truck's first trips persuaded Daouda to let him give up the job at the farm, that he began to drive the truck himself. Ever since, Yero's increasing independence had put a strain on their relationship. Yero was happy to help Daouda out when needed, as he did in 2003 when he oversaw Daouda's semitrailers working for the pipeline project, but only as a temporary fix in exceptional circumstances. One morning in August 2005, on our way to the cargo terminal, Yero stopped by his patron's house for a few minutes. He came out shaking his head, laughing in disbelief. 'They wanted me to drive them around while they run a few errands. As if I didn't have enough things to do myself!' Sometimes, it took all Yero's tact to make Daouda understand that he had his own business to look after. A few weeks later, reflecting on how he had fared in the years since he had become his own boss, Yero told me: 'They protect me and help me in all domains. I also give them a hand. To this day, we're together. But doing their bidding has also hindered my progress. If it was up to them, I would still be working on their farm.'

In the following years, as his own farming business expanded, Yero became more and more frustrated with Daouda's dwindling fortunes, which he saw as a result of neglect, misguided decisions, and the refusal to listen to those who wished him well. As he put it in 2010: 'There is always a certain reserve in them. Their success came about in a different context. It was the way they did things during the dictatorship.' Such an approach to business was no longer viable, Yero thought. Daouda's pride and sense of honour were incompatible with the versatility required in present times. Using a recent glaring example of what he saw as Daouda's stubbornness, he asked me: 'If you have a problem with a driver, what do you do? Do you leave your truck parked for months on end? Or do you hire another driver?'

In Ngaoundéré, wealthy patrons with investments in transport often have dozens of clients, many of whom are former drivers. At the peak of his wealth, Daouda had a whole retinue of former and present drivers and other kinds of employees, as well as people he had helped purchase minibuses or trucks, whom he mobilised, among other things, to secure a position of strength in different professional associations and even, although only briefly, in party politics at the local level. Some, Yero among them, saw the maintenance of such a clientele as an ill-advised and old-fashioned business strategy. The majority, however, still regarded it as essential to weather the ups and downs of any career in transport. Most transporters, however, run very small enterprises and have little to offer to drivers other than employment. Yero's drivers, for example, could not expect him to sell them his old trucks on favourable terms or otherwise act as guarantor in their future purchases of vehicles. With little at his disposal to ensure his drivers' loyalty, Yero had to entrust his trucks and cargo to them as well as considerable sums of cash needed for the road. In a road environment marked by old trucks, poorly kept roads, checkpoints, and insecurity, the possibilities for drivers to betray their bosses' trust are endless. This is why Yero regretted having had his driving career cut short on account of his health in 2001. To begin with, expenses at checkpoints decreased considerably if the driver was also the owner of the truck. 'The owner has a value in the eyes of the gendarmes that the driver does not have,' Yero explained. Owners could overcome the abuse of the police and gendarmes by reporting them to their superiors or to bailiffs and prosecutors, something that Yero himself had done more than once. According to him, drivers lacked the intellectual resources and moral authority to do such a thing. Even more worrying for Yero were situations such as accidents, mechanical problems, and freight scarcity, which drivers could use to make money at their boss's expense. In his short trucking career, he had accumulated endless stories illustrating the dishonesty of drivers whose employment with him did not last long.

In a July 2010 conversation, as he looked back on his decision to quit freight transport for good, Yero showed no trace of regret: 'If I hadn't ever got into [transport], I would most likely have prospered greatly. Now that I've quit, I can breathe again. Instead of bringing in income, all it ever did was to make me lose money.'

'A matter of the heart'

By the end of September 2004, Bello, a young NGO consultant whom I had met only a few times, stopped by my office in the city centre. Presidential elections were around the corner and Bello was dressed in party garb. He had just attended an RDPC meeting. Although he was certainly not shy about proclaiming his political sympathies, Bello's visit had nothing to do with his campaigning. Instead, he wanted to chat about a symposium we had both attended at the University of Ngaoundéré two days earlier. A small group of academics, government officials, and private sector operators had met to discuss formality and informality in Adamaoua's economy. One of the presenters, a local community contact (LCC) of COTCO, the Cameroonian subsidiary of the Chad–Cameroon pipeline consortium, complained to the audience that there were no organisations in the province that deserved the name of NGO. He referred specifically to the group of organisations that had worked for the consortium within the framework of the pipeline project's regional compensation programme. In his view, these organisations were 'only a bunch of businesses in NGO disguise'. Even though the organisation where he was employed had not worked for the pipeline, Bello had found this criticism to be unfair. Many organisations had sprouted up in the last few years in Ngaoundéré, but, he thought, they should not all be lumped together. He was ready to grant that there were many people in the NGO world on the lookout for money – fast money, in fact – but there were also dedicated activists who were committed to transforming society and who deserved support and dignified working conditions. He had expected more understanding from someone like the LCC, whom he otherwise admired. The LCC knew full well that NGOs in Adamaoua were still in the process of acquiring experience, know-how, and a sound financial footing.

The point COTCO's employee had made about NGOs not deserving their name was true in a sense, Bello conceded. Indeed, no Adamaoua-based organisation had received the authorisation required by law to enjoy official status as an NGO. But who was to blame for this state of affairs if not the government itself? The NGO Act of 1999 had not specified the procedure to apply for authorisation. For a while, Bello explained, there had been jurisdictional battles between the Ministry of Territorial Administration and Decentralisation (MINTAD) and the Ministry of Foreign Affairs as to which of them would process such applications. The commission within MINTAD in charge of granting authorisations had only been set up in 2003. So far, the commission had authorised only a very small number of organisations whose promoters had connections in high places. In any case, from the perspective of most NGOs in Adamaoua, Bello complained, even the prospect of applying for authorisation was out of the question. One of the legal requirements was to have worked as an association for a minimum of ten years and this ruled out all but a handful of organisations in the province.

The uncertain legal position of most NGOs led to paradoxical situations. Bello invited me to consider the meeting that had taken place a month earlier, in August 2004, in Yaoundé's Palais des Congrès. MINTAD had invited representatives of civil society organisations across the country to a presentation of a series of new provisions aimed at improving the transparency and fairness of the upcoming presidential elections (and enhancing the government's frail democratic credentials). Bello, who had travelled from Ngaoundéré to attend the meeting, explained how they had been told that in the run-up to the elections a number of dissemination tasks were going to be entrusted to NGOs. 'When the minister stated that only officially authorised NGOs would be able to bid for such contracts, his announcement caused widespread outrage,' he recounted. He wondered why the same government that saw in them legitimate representatives of civil society would deem them unworthy of disseminating information on democratic principles and procedures to the electorate.

In his early twenties, Bello exuded youth and enthusiasm. He had grown up in a small town in Adamaoua and moved to Ngaoundéré in 2000 to pursue a university degree in law. This in itself was a considerable achievement, as the number of people born and bred in his home town who had finished their baccalaureate by then was very small. He was good looking and personable, and, in his last year of high school, he had grown close to several Peace Corps volunteers posted in his town. The volunteers involved him in several of the initiatives they tried to promote during their stay, which ranged from primary education to microfinance. Through these contacts, he had been able to familiarise himself with the development assistance circuit in Adamaoua and beyond. He soon built a reputation as a youth leader and received invitations to travel abroad, including one in 2003 to take part in the US State Department's international visitors programme. He possessed some valuable skills that enabled him to do well in such forums, including a knack for speaking in public, an impressive rhetorical flair, and excellent command of the English language. These skills he attributed to the political education he had received from an early age. His father had always been active both in the agropastoral cooperative movement and in local politics. In his teenage years, Bello had accompanied him to all kinds of meetings and rallies. Although his father had died when Bello was still in high school, he had since been able to rely on the mentorship and support of his father's circle of intimate friends, most of whom were in the local ranks of the ruling party. All these formative experiences perhaps explained why everything Bello did seemed informed by a political acumen that was striking in someone of his age.

For all their local influence and political connections, Bello's family was not well-off and he had had to find ways to get by. While in school, he had done all sorts of odd jobs; he had been particularly fond of a stint as advertiser for the cinema his town had had until the mid-1990s. As I learned some weeks after our conversation in my office, those jobs had also included work related to the Chad–Cameroon pipeline. This was not entirely surprising, as his home town had become one of the bases pipeline contractors had established during the construction phase. The pipeline construction was generally seen as a boon for the local economy. In a dire environment in terms of employment opportunities, the project offered lucrative openings. Bello, who was then in his second year of university studies in Ngaoundéré, did not want to miss out.

With a recommendation from a well-connected Cameroonian contractor, in January 2002 Bello began supplying foodstuffs to the pipeline's main catering companies. He used for this a dormant 'community initiative group' (GIC) his father had created before his death. The expected deliveries involved a frequency and quantity that Bello struggled to meet. He would source most of the produce from local gardens but had to travel regularly to Yaoundé for certain fruits and vegetables unavailable locally. The most serious challenge, however, was of a financial nature. 'When I had already got [my mentor's] recommendation and I was about to go and see the [catering company's] camp boss to discuss a contract, I had this moment of panic. How am I going to pull this off? I don't have the means!' he recounted. Producers would only sell if paid on the spot and Bello's clients paid once a month by cheque from a Yaoundé-based bank, and the only financial institution available in his home town, a savings union, could not cash the cheques for him. The savings union also refused to lend him the required funds, and, in the end, he had to resort to an old friend of his father who had made his fortune through trade in cattle and construction materials. Having overcome all these obstacles, Bello supplied fruits and vegetables to two pipeline camps for more than a year. Having a regular presence in the camps also led to other opportunities. Bello found builders' contractors delegating to him tasks they could not cope with themselves. All of this was lucrative for him but he acknowledged that it had been *'un travail de profanes'* (layman's work). It was also a line of activity that he abandoned as soon as the pipeline camps were dismantled. In fact, in the last months of pipeline construction he stopped doing the supplying himself. The job required staying in his home town more than he could or was willing to do, so he traded his status as supplier with a friend in exchange for a share of the earnings. Although the business kept his father's GIC's name, from that moment onwards it was his friend who raised the funds, purchased the produce, and made the deliveries. Unlike NGO work, which was 'a matter of the heart' for him, he told me, his role as foodstuffs' supplier for the pipeline consortium was 'simply about making money'.

In November 2003, at one of the workshops in Yaoundé to which he would regularly be invited as he became more and more integrated in networks of development professionals, he linked up with the former employee of an international NGO. An experienced aid worker in his fifties, Bello's new acquaintance had grown increasingly disenchanted with the saturated NGO scene in the capital and had identified the north of the country in general and Adamaoua in particular as a relatively open field. His plan was to establish a new organisation in Ngaoundéré that would capture some of the contracting opportunities that a series of development programmes and projects were going to generate in the coming years. Thus began Bello's entanglement with this new NGO. This was where he was working when we first met and where he would remain for almost three years. It was a period of hard work and learning as he went along. He became familiar with the bureaucratic devices of development work, from concept notes and proposals to logframes and monitoring and evaluation tools. He was introduced to the subtleties of courting decision makers in funding agencies and the authorities on whose blessing their unimpeded work depended. He did his share of *missions* (assignments) in rural zones where his organisation would conduct training sessions or run participatory workshops on areas ranging from HIV/AIDS prevention to entrepreneurship. These were absorbing tasks and they led Bello to neglect his university studies, which eventually he abandoned in 2005. It was also a period of financial insecurity. The NGO was perpetually underfunded, to the point of being unable to pay rent or utility bills for long periods. No one had a salary to speak of. They all relied on the highly irregular revenue the NGO derived from contract work. Once the NGO got paid, sums were distributed according to the staff's seniority, their role in securing contracts, and their part in the delivery of services. The expenses associated with bidding for project work or delivering services often had to be financed with the members' own funds.

In May 2006, Bello decided that it was time to go it alone. By then, he had realised that he was never going to have the same weight of other, more senior members in the NGO he had been working for. His two hats as NGO consultant and RDPC activist had allowed him to make contacts in Ngaoundéré and Yaoundé that he could put to use. New funding streams were going to become available for civil society organisations based in Adamaoua, and he thought he was well placed to receive support. Doing things on his own terms and not having to share the financial rewards with others were appealing prospects. In a matter of weeks, he had deposited the by-laws of a new association with the prefect and opened a small office on Ngaoundéré's main commercial street. The beginnings were not promising, as an important project bid to the French Programme Concerté Pluri-Acteurs (Consultative Multi-Actor Programme or PCPA) failed to bear fruit. This outcome was all the more disappointing because some of his former colleagues had been involved in the PCPA's decisions to award project money. He felt let down but persevered and went ahead with different projects, relying on his own savings and sporadic outside support. An important milestone for his new NGO was a contract he secured with the World Food Programme in 2008 for nearly CFAF 80 million in total, which ensured a modicum of activity and revenue for a couple of years.

As time went by, it became clear that the work his NGO was hired to carry out was just as likely to concern Adamaoua as the North, Far North and East Provinces. Bello began to perceive being based in Ngaoundéré as a limitation. In 2010, when he decided to settle down and marry the daughter of a wealthy businessman from his home town, a move to Yaoundé seemed to be a logical step. 'I came to the conclusion that in Ngaoundéré I was too isolated. Yaoundé works much better for me.' he told me. It was in the capital where most project opportunities arose. He made sure he kept his NGO's office in Ngaoundéré, which, after all, was what legitimated his distinctive position in Yaoundé's NGO scene. He visited Ngaoundéré occasionally to supervise his two young assistants, who enjoyed considerable latitude in everyday matters and were left to fend for themselves financially during long periods of downtime. He would schedule lengthier stays there when specific projects required his presence. In January 2011, Bello's admission into one of the country's elite training schools for the civil service demanded a readjustment. Although it proved challenging to stay on top of things at key moments in the academic year, he claimed to have managed by and large to make his studies compatible with his NGO work. In May 2015, for example, he spent several weeks in Ngaoundéré, where he played a lead role in organising a series of seminars on public–private partnerships within the framework of the European Union-sponsored Programme d'Appui à la Société Civil (Civil Society Support Programme or PASC).

What pushed Bello to the limit of his financial capabilities and personal endurance was not reconciling his training in the civil service and his NGO work but his decision to attempt an ill-fated foray into politics. Internecine battles over who would be designated RDPC candidate for parliament in his home town in the 2013 legislative elections made him think he could present himself as an alternative who would appeal to all warring factions. After months of constant travelling between Yaoundé and his home town, which involved taking part in endless internal party meetings, orchestrating many backdoor dealings, and running up debts to 'motivate' key decision makers, Bello saw his name vanish at the last minute from the definitive party list of candidates in his constituency. 'He was the only one of those who put themselves forward who had the baccalaureate. That's why people in the party didn't want him,' opined a sympathetic youngster who still could not fathom what had pushed Bello to attempt such a venture. To make matters worse, the ruling party ended up losing that parliamentary seat in the subsequent elections. The whole experience took a financial and personal toll on Bello. While he says he does not rule out giving local politics another try, an incipient career in a prestigious corps within the civil service would seem to offer sounder prospects. Whatever the case, his NGO seems to have become a far too irregular source of often short engagements and paltry income. Accordingly, Bello has increasingly tended to put it on the back burner. The chances of his NGO work expanding are slim, but it is a line of business likely to remain compatible with other pursuits.

★ ★ ★ ★ ★ ★

This chapter has offered readers an introduction to the past and present of economic life in Ngaoundéré. Given their generational distance and diverse specialisations, these four portraits of business people are meant to make apparent the multiple legacies of the 1990s, a decade marked by the socially pervasive tropes of crisis and reform whose aftermath this book explores. Yero and Badjo, the oldest of the four, are also the ones who did not make it past elementary school. Entrusted with the management of a ranch by Alhadji Daouda, his father-in-law and patron, Yero was spared the upheaval in passenger transport, his earlier line of activity. Rather, it was Daouda who experienced significant losses with the demise of the unitary union and the proliferation of new entrants. The opportunities created by the increase in freight of the early 2000s encouraged Yero to leave the ranch and try his luck in freight transport. Having established himself as a cattle trader in the late 1980s, Badjo took full advantage of the improved access to railway transport (and thereby to southern markets) Ngaoundal traders gained in the early 1990s. Drastic price fluctuations plus the recurrent bankruptcies of clients have since hindered his activities. In the early 1990s, Djibrilla quit school without having managed to get his baccalaureate and left Ngaoundéré. The first years away from his home town were tough but eventually served him well. Upon his return, he could supplement his family connections with the bureaucratic and financial wherewithal required to succeed as a public contractor. Bello, the youngest of the four, arrived in Ngaoundéré in the late 1990s to pursue university studies and thus became acquainted with the city's nascent NGO scene. This line of work has yet to become a dependable basis for his livelihood. Readers will come across Yero, Badjo, Djibrilla, and Bello again in the following chapters, which focus on the governance of specific economic sectors.

2   The ordering of public things

In February 2004, while having coffee with a Douala-based power broker from Adamaoua, our conversation meandered to the Association des Ressortissants de l'Adamaoua (ARA). ARA is a cross-ethnic association advocating for the development of the province that emerged during the early 1990s, when all sorts of civic associations flourished (Burnham 1996a: 135; Kemfang 2000: 67). It was not the first time I had listened to him reminiscing about what he saw as ARA's good old days, before partisan politics engulfed its activities. To give me an example of the kinds of low-key but valuable initiatives that originated within the association, he referred to his first-hand experience of a series of meetings that a select group of ARA members held with sympathetic government representatives in the mid-1990s. In response to ARA's accusations that the regime was punishing Adamaoua because of its support of opposition parties, the government representatives involved in this dialogue compiled a file detailing all the recent public investments in the province. ARA leaders were taken aback. 'The gap between those official papers and reality was grotesque!' my interlocutor noted with disgust. He went on to list a number of buildings in Ngaoundéré, specifying the amounts that were budgeted for their construction or renovation. He then invited me to consider the buildings' present state of abandonment and disrepair as evidence of how inflated those budgets had been.

I found myself picturing the locations in the city my acquaintance mentioned. I knew some of them well by then and, judging by their condition, I would never have imagined that they had been built or renovated so recently. Those budgeted figures offered an intriguing key to read the urban landscape. This conversation would resonate with numerous other negative characterisations of the public contracting system I was to come across later. Public officials and contractors were seen as making a readily apparent contribution to the erosion of public utility and the common good as mobilising metaphors (Mbembe 2001: 89–94). Inflated budgets and substandard works directly undermined the potential for improvement in public infrastructure and services. Public contracts had thus become a basic currency in assessments of political legitimacy, and the verdict was unambiguously damning. Talk about contracts relied on a number of established truths and had a stereotypical, taken-for-granted ring to it. In a travelogue piece on the Cameroonian crisis in the 1990s, for example, Achille Mbembe and Janet Roitman (1995: 334) sketch an 'extravagant and unproductive economy' thriving around public contracts. This chapter explores this field of economic activity ethnographically. It tries to make sense of the practices and processes through which public contracts were governed in a period when their reform became a prominent, albeit elusive, objective. It highlights a tension between, on the one hand, modes of operating premised on payments to officials, which place contractors in routine contravention of the law, and, on the other, the claims articulated by many of those contractors to ethical values such as professionalism.

More broadly, the chapter reflects on the significance of formality in economic governance. Bureaucratic forms and procedures have received insightful attention in recent anthropological studies. In his study of the Pakistani urban bureaucracy, for example, Matthew Hull (2012: 27) has proposed that clinics, classrooms, roads, and gutters that contractors build for the state be considered as bureaucratic things in their own right. Central to these assemblages of buildings, supplies, paperwork, and money are the links established between state bureaucrats and contractors. In pioneering research on public contracting in Senegal, Giorgio Blundo (2001: 80) conceived of these relationships as *surpersonalisés* (over-personalised). This chapter invites us to reconsider such a characterisation.

Public contracts as targets of reform

Cameroon's present-day public contracting system is the result of reform efforts that were launched in the mid-1990s and are still ongoing (Biakan 2011; Messengue Avom 2013; Nkou Songue 2014). In their own terms, these reforms have been designed to 'put in place a modern public contracting system, conforming to international standards in the field, and to good governance principles' (ARMP 2006: 3). The World Bank has commended the system's 'architecture' for 'generally corresponding to international best practices' (World Bank 2005: 13). These reforms must be understood in the broader context of depleted state coffers (and the resulting dependence on international financial assistance, which is conditional on the adoption of a shifting set of policies) and the emergence of corruption as a global policy challenge (and the accompanying anti-corruption apparatus). In such a context, the reforms' innovations in public contracting contain the promise of achieving enhanced versions of 'things public' (Latour and Weibel 2005).

This recent cycle of reform is part of a longer history of legal production. The transitional period during which French Cameroon prepared itself for independence saw the reassertion of the rules and procedures that had regulated contracts involving public authorities during the colonial era.[1] A string of decrees containing frequent modifications, which was largely aimed at filling gaps and updating existing rules, did not disrupt this pattern of continuity.[2] The World Bank's second *Country Procurement Assessment Report* (CPAR) for Cameroon in 2000 provided part of the impetus for intensifying the cycle of reform.[3] In 2004, the government approved a Public Contracts Code, which this time aimed to be fully comprehensive.[4] The Code proved enduring. Only in 2012 was the system modified again.[5] The numerous decrees have been supported by a long list of ordinances and circulars providing enhanced details for vague provisions, clarifying ambiguities, unifying divergent interpretations, and reminding officials of the importance of rigorous observance and enforcement.

However, legal texts governing public contracts are only one element in a broader policy effort. The authorities concerned have hosted workshops to better acquaint officials and contractors with the new rules, procedures, and penalties, often with contributions from international organisations and consultants, and they have launched media campaigns to popularise the changes. This is, after all, in accordance with the principle that information about public contracting should be made public, from the announcement of contracting opportunities and the conduct of contracting processes to the scrutiny of completed contracts. The authorities have embraced on an unprecedented level a pedagogic role aimed at disseminating information, raising awareness, and sensitising different publics.

Unsurprisingly, narratives of breaks with the past and of new beginnings have been prominent in the launching of reforms. Consider, for example, what, with distinctive flair, the government press (Dipanda 2004) had to say about the new Public Contracts Code:

The implementation of preexisting [legal] texts ... took place haphazardly [*au petit bonheur la chance*], with all the ensuing inconsistencies. Today, the rules of the game seem clearer to all contract bidders ... In the past, the responsibilities of different authorities looked rather confusing and files were endlessly carried around [*baladés*] in all directions. A strident pandemonium [*un embrouillamini*

---

[1] Decrees §59/144 of 14 August 1959 and §59/161 of 19 September 1959.
[2] The list includes: (1) decree §70/DF/1530 of 29 October 1970, later modified by decree §75/513 of 5 July 1975; (2) decree §79/035 of 2 February 1979, which was successively modified by decrees §80/272 of 18 July 1980, §82/12 of 8 January 1982, §83/440 of 26 September 1983 and §84/1488 of 21 November 1984; (3) decree §86/903 of 18 July 1986; and (4) decrees §95/101–2 of 9 June 1995.
[3] The relevant legal texts are decree §2000/156 of 30 June 2000; decree §2001/048 of 23 February 2001; and decree §2002/030 of 28 January 2002.
[4] Decree §2004/275 of 24 September 2004.   [5] Decrees §2012/074–6 of 8 March 2012.

criarde] and a needless waste of time that [the decree] signed last week promises to rectify.

Nonetheless, this promise of renewal and even rupture coexists with diagnoses that identify persistent problems. Variously referred to as *pesanteurs* (encumbrances), *dysfunctionnements* (malfunctions) and *dérives* (downward spirals), these problems are perceived to be deep-seated and even systemic (Nkou Songue 2014).

For over a decade, the institutional cornerstone of the reforms has been the Agence de Régulation des Marchés Publics (Public Contracts Regulatory Board or ARMP). The ARMP was established in 2001 in the aftermath of the World Bank's country assessment report. Its creation entailed the dismantling of the Direction Générale des Grands Travaux du Cameroun (Directorate General of Public Works of Cameroon or DGTC), which for years had been the centrepiece of a discredited system that rendered the state 'a social relation of domination founded essentially on coercive exchange, plunder and consumption' (Mbembe and Roitman 1995: 335). The extreme centralisation of public contracting over which the DGTC presided gave way to a decentralised system overseen by the ARMP. The ARMP exercises its control through independent observers present in contracting commissions at all territorial levels across the country, through its nationwide *antennes régionales* (provincial branches), and through external auditors responsible for drafting an annual report. Beyond this role as the gendarme of public contracting (Eloundou Bidjogo 2006), the ARMP's mission also includes managing a repository of public contract documentation, systematising and publishing data on public contracts, and raising awareness of (and promoting compliance with) the rules governing these contracts. A glossy newsletter (*ARMP News*), a functional website (www.armp.cm), and numerous outreach activities that have received extensive media coverage have helped raise the ARMP's profile.

Consider the ARMP team's first visit to Ngaoundéré on 20 March 2006, which was part of a nationwide campaign to disseminate a study commissioned to mark the first anniversary of the Public Contracts Code (Djarmaila 2006). The study was a response to the recognition that the Code's 'repressive apparatus' was 'not operational' and the enforcement of penalties was 'neither effective nor systematic', to use its own wording (ARMP 2006: 3). The study was also meant to exemplify the ARMP's didactic approach: '[The study] aims at inculcating everyone involved with a culture of respect of rules and of systematic punishment of every case of rule violation' (ibid.: 5). Contracting authorities, members of the contracting commissions overseeing the tendering process, and treasury officials from Adamaoua's five districts attended the seminar held at Ngaoundéré's Hotel Transcam. They received copies of the newly published collection of relevant regulations. The ARMP's experts instructed attendees on the 166 types of 'bad practices' observed over the course of the previous year and on the string of penalties that the regulations established for such practices. In a ceremony presided over by the governor of Adamaoua, the ARMP 's director warned everyone present that 'the time for penalties' had arrived. The following day, the ARMP held a second seminar with the province's magistrates to discuss effective strategies to enforce the new regulations. The ARMP was keen to get them interested 'in a sector that has long remained beyond the reach of criminal prosecution' (Eloundou Bidjogo 2006).

Although a detailed account of the public contracting reforms lies outside the scope of this chapter, it is important to note that, in time, the ARMP was seen to be ill equipped to go beyond what a critic called 'the logic of public declamation of its role' (Channon 2008). By 2011, when it had reached its tenth anniversary, its reputation had suffered severe blows. The dire state of affairs described in the independent auditors' reports year after year made it increasingly difficult for the ARMP to cultivate the narrative of improvement that underwrote its credibility as a reformer (Groupement 2AC-ACP 2008; 2011; Okalla Ahanda and Associates 2011). Confrontations with several contracting authorities, most publicly with Yaoundé's *délégué du gouvernement* (super-mayor[6]) in 2008 (Ntiga 2008), invariably ended with the ARMP on the losing side. Finally, in 2011, allegations of serious mismanagement within the organisation were substantiated by the national audit office CONSUPE (Atangana 2011). The government's response was to create a new Ministry of Public Contracts (MINMAP), which superseded the ARMP in many of its responsibilities. This new configuration entailed a return to centralised contracting procedures and an end to the involvement of governors and prefects in the contracting process. Capturing admirably the recursive logic of reformism, the government press assured its readers that this *coup d'accélérateur* (boost) to the reform of public contracting would lead to a 'renewed system' (Foute 2013).

From the perspective of the contractors, the succession of reforms has implied keeping up to date with changing administrative procedures, familiarising themselves with new actors, such as the heads of the ARMP provincial branches and the independent observers sitting on the local committees that assess bids, and paying new fees including those required to obtain the new certificate of non-exclusion from public procurement; the latter is one of the ARMP's sources of funding. As a rule, contractors did not place much faith in the transformative potential

---

[6] A *délégué du gouvernement* is an unelected government appointee who *leads a communauté urbaine* (metropolitan community) and rules over the elected mayors presiding over the different *communes* (municipalities) that constitute a large city.

of the new dispensations. Old actors who were newly empowered by the introduction of legal provisions to curb the practice of splitting contracts in order to avoid scrutiny, for example, became the object of mockery if not opprobrium. New actors who were willing to challenge 'business as usual' could be dealt with expediently, as was the head of the ARMP Ngaoundéré branch, who was suddenly removed from his job in February 2008 after having criticised Adamaoua's contracting authorities in public (Boyomo 2008b). Independent observers tended to be unadventurous. Being public contractors themselves (working for the ARMP), they have been subject to the same pattern of erratic payment as other contractors. This has made them amenable to the appeal of financial rewards in exchange for favouring particular contractors. Despite the ARMP's repeated announcements of an era of rigorous, systematic enforcement of regulations (Djarmaila 2006), this has largely failed to materialise. Violations are not always easy to establish, not least because few contracting authorities have been willing to meet the obligation to send copies of all contracting documentation to the ARMP. Even when it is established that violations have taken place, the ARMP lacks the power to impose penalties. As far as contractors are concerned, the reforms may have lengthened the chain of organisations, procedures, paperwork, and people involved in overseeing the public contract process, but the new figures and forms have been largely subsumed within long-standing repertoires of business practice.

A seat in Alhadji Djibrilla's station wagon

In March 2004, Alhadji Djibrilla invited me to join him for a short trip to Maroua (Far North Province), where his late father was born and most of his wife's family still lives. Over the course of four days, I witnessed how he combined scrupulous observance of family commitments with the efficient conduct of business. The ostensible reason for the trip was an *indeeri* (naming ceremony). His wife's *goggo* (paternal aunt) had just given birth to her first child. This event provided an opportunity for many other encounters with a broad assortment of relatives, friends, business associates, and acquaintances.

Before departing, we stopped at Djibrilla's mother's house in Ngaoundéré; this was part of his daily filial duties whenever he was in town. With his mother's blessing, we took National Route 1 from Ngaoundéré to Maroua. Our first stop was Garoua, the administrative centre of North Province. There we took the female members of our small party (Djibrilla's wife and his mother's cousin) to the house of a close relative so that they could get some respite from the extreme heat in the streets of Garoua. Then, Djibrilla, his business partner Bobbo, and I made the courtesy visits that are the bread and butter of public contractors.

Djibrilla and Bobbo wanted to congratulate someone who had just been appointed to an important job and to visit an official with whom they had a working relationship. They also were keen on finding out whether an earlier bid for a contract had been successful. To that effect, we made stops at the provincial offices of Fonds Spécial d'Équipement et d'Intervention Intercommunale (Special Council Support Fund for Mutual Assistance or FEICOM), the Ministry of Water and Energy, and the *sous-préfecture* (sub-district office). All these visits were unannounced and involved officials who were either from Ngaoundéré or had served there in the past.

A more targeted stop concerned payment for maintenance work on a rural road in a fairly remote part of North Province; this was one of their most recent jobs and had been completed only the previous month. The prefect of that district had encouraged them to bid for the contract. They lacked previous experience in road maintenance, but the modest size of the job encouraged them to pursue the opportunity. To make up for their inexperience, they had relied on the advice of an engineer who worked at the Garoua office of the parastatal company Matgénie, where they also rented a caterpillar for the job. Aside from the two-week rental of the caterpillar, expenses were well below a very inflated budget. Now Djibrilla was keen to receive his payment. We walked the short distance separating Garoua's *sous-préfecture* from the *Hôtel de Finances* and, after a half-hour meeting, Djibrilla reached an agreement with the relevant treasury official. Due to a shortage of liquidity, however, payments over CFAF 5 million had been temporarily put on hold. To circumvent this, Djibrilla and the treasury official arranged for him to receive the money in several simultaneous but formally separate payments. In exchange, the official got 10 per cent of the payment, which he would in turn share with the district's *receveur* (receiver general). The next step was to contact the latter to get his approval for the new scheme and to modify the paperwork accordingly. After a quick phone call, we went to see this young official at the luxurious house he had recently built in one of Garoua's new residential neighbourhoods. While Bobbo and I admired the immaculate finish of the house floors, walls, and ceilings (Bobbo with a touch of professional jealousy), Djibrilla and the *receveur* finalised the deal in an interior room.

From Garoua, we drove to Guider, the administrative centre of Mayo Louti District (North Province). After a short rest at the large *saare* of one of Djibrilla's aunts, we went to see a local official at his residence. Djibrilla had brought him a telephone from his latest trip to Saudi Arabia. Only after he offered us food and drinks did they go over the details of a previously negotiated contract. Djibrilla produced a folder with the relevant paperwork. To avoid complicated tender procedures and to facilitate payment after completion, he explained, they were going to divide the work into two smaller contracts, each one done by a different firm (only nominally, since Djibrilla owned both). The official deemed this an adequate arrangement, kept the documents, and promised that the award of the contracts would follow in a few months.

We arrived in Maroua late in the afternoon. The following morning, after brief visits to Djibrilla's in-laws and to a few of his father's nephews and nieces who still lived in the city, I accompanied him to the *Hôtel de Finances*. Our visit followed a familiar pattern. He first looked up the most recent lists of authorised payments, only to find that the contracts he had recently finished were not among those programmed for payment. He then went round knocking on the doors of several of his acquaintances. From those he found in their offices, he collected information on the current state of the provincial treasury's coffers.

Most agreed that, for the time being, there was not much to do but wait. One claimed to have heard from a reliable source that several hundred million francs had recently been transferred from Yaoundé. The provincial *trésorier-payeur général* (paymaster general; usually referred to as the TPG), who had final responsibility for programming payments, was out of the office. So Djibrilla had to settle for a phone conversation with him later in the day, in which he was told to wait for a week until the disbursement of civil service salaries was completed. Once the salaries were covered, the TPG would pay some completed contracts, although he could not promise that Djibrilla's would be among them.

Later that day, Djibrilla received a phone call from the *receveur* whom we had visited in Garoua. He had finalised arrangements for the contract for the road maintenance works to be paid and urged Djibrilla to return to Garoua as soon as possible. There, they would withdraw the money and travel with a military escort to the district administrative centre to comply with all the required formalities and receive the payment in the presence of the prefect. Djibrilla considered whether he should go himself or send Bobbo. He harboured doubts about Bobbo's ability to handle the operation successfully. As he reminded his wife, testing her reaction to an early departure immediately after her niece's *indeeri*, Bobbo had pocketed money that did not belong to him in the past. Djibrilla felt it would be better to take care of this operation in person. Moreover, since the amount involved in this particular payment was not very large, Djibrilla feared that Bobbo would be careless and might be robbed. Despite his misgivings, his wife's protests about the idea of leaving Maroua in a rush swayed his decision, so he ended up handing Bobbo the necessary documents to perform the transaction. As we drove him to one of the city's bus terminals, Djibrilla cautioned him to be especially kind to the prefect. The road maintenance work was carried out annually, and if they kept the prefect happy, they could count on future contracts. 'Give him a little something, CFAF 40,000, if you want,' he instructed Bobbo.

The following day I escorted Djibrilla on visits to a couple of acquaintances from Ngaoundéré. The first one was now working in the provincial offices of FEICOM. They had not seen each other in a few years, so there was much catching up to do on recent personal and professional changes. After a while, anticipating the public contractor's likely queries on the matter, he explained that Maroua's offices had no say in the award of contracts. 'There are contracts [to be had], yes, but it all happens in Yaoundé,' he told us.[7]

Our second visit was to the provincial offices of the Ministry of Public Works, where a much closer friend of Djibrilla worked. *Jum'aare* (Friday prayer) was approaching so we did not stay long. Before we left, though, he asked us to have dinner with him that evening. While Djibrilla left for the city's main mosque, I stayed at his wife's family house. Over dinner, Djibrilla told his friend about his recent jobs and I gave him a condensed account of my fieldwork activities. He in turn filled us in on the idiosyncrasies of Maroua's TPG: 'Unlike others we've had before, he makes no attempt whatsoever to ask Yaoundé for funds. All his concern is to make sure that whatever money arrives is distributed according to his interests.' Djibrilla mentioned the rumours he had heard the day before at the *Hôtel de Finances* about a recent transfer of funds to the provincial treasury. His friend told him not to raise his hopes. 'That money has been sent because Minister X put pressure to have one of his people here paid. Most of that sum will go to him, and the rest is already committed to other people,' he explained. He advised Djibrilla to contact the TPG without fail the day after the provincial civil servants got paid. If not, his chances of receiving the money anytime soon would be very slim.

As we drove back to our hotel, we received a phone call from Bobbo. During the bus trip to Garoua, he had misplaced some *bons timbrés* (stamped vouchers) that were essential to process the payment. This meant delaying the whole operation until the following Monday. Djibrilla could not hide his disappointment: 'He's not wise. He is always in an excessive hurry. He wants to get things done too fast ... I should have gone myself.'

The next day we got an early start. Immediately after *subaha* (sunrise prayer), while the imam of the nearby mosque was still delivering his sermon, we left for the *indeeri*. It was a very special occasion for the new mother, who at 40 had given birth for the first time. When we arrived, we joined a group of some 60 men, including the child's father, who sat on

---

[7] This centralisation of decisions relating to contract bids, which was intended to make them more transparent, was not very successful in preventing corruption. Doubts surrounding FEICOM management, expressed by its board of directors as early as July 2005, ultimately led to the sentencing of 14 of the fund's top officials, including the managing director, to long prison terms in June 2007.

mats arranged on the street. In whispers, picking up on the fact that the father was Kotoko, some guests contrasted the Fulbe ideal of sobriety with what they considered to be the Kotoko tendency to overdo family ceremonies. After ten minutes of waiting, the name of the girl was announced and the customary prayers performed. Drinks and foodstuffs, which the women of the family had prepared during the previous days, were passed around. After half an hour, people started to leave, their enjoyment cut short by the praise-singers' mounting exhortations. We went inside the house to congratulate the mother, greet other female family members, and take a few photographs. Djibrilla's wife stayed with her aunts and cousins while we went to the city centre to run a few errands. The next morning, we drove back the 374 kilometres separating Maroua and Ngaoundéré, stopping only at Pitoa (North Province) for a glance at its weekly market. Back in Ngaoundéré, Djibrilla's mother welcomed us warmly and immediately began to distribute her son's purchases among the different members of the household.

Procedures, papers, stamps, and signatures

Public contracts are closely regulated and markedly technical. A minimal familiarity with countless offices, terms, document formats, and procedures is something no public contractor can do without. The folder of documentation that contractors such as Alhadji Djibrilla take to the *Hôtel de Finances* in order to get paid is sizeable. Typically, it includes photocopies of the official contract summary issued by the contracting authority and of the *procès-verbal de réception* (authenticated account of satisfactory delivery), which signal that the contractor is entitled to receive full payment. To these two key documents contractors need to add the *plan de localisation* that establishes the whereabouts of their business premises and four other tax-related documents: an outstanding tax payments clearance certificate, a tax status form, a certificate of tax payment, and a certificate of non-bankruptcy. Each of these photocopies needs to be certified by the authorities that issued the originals; most also require a revenue stamp. Missing documents mean experiencing blockages and delays, like those suffered by Djibrilla on account of Bobbo's lack of diligence when trying to get paid for their road maintenance work.

Payment, however, is only the final stage of an often protracted contracting cycle. Once they receive their budgetary allocations, authorities at the municipal, sub-district, district, and provincial levels announce upcoming contracts. It is supposedly at this stage that contractors first learn about available opportunities. Information acquired before and after such announcements has considerable tactical value. In some cases, as illustrated in Djibrilla's visit to a local official in Guider, contract programming results from previous agreements with contractors.

Bons de commande (contracts concluded by direct agreement between the authority concerned and the contractor, which, on account of their low financial value, avoid competition and independent review procedures) are by far the most common contractual category. The practice of dividing up a larger contract into smaller segments, known as *fractionnement*, is common and has been documented ethnographically in other contexts (Blundo 2001: 92; 2006). Not only does it allow contractors to avoid the uncertainties of a bidding process, it might also make payment for completed contracts smoother, as in the case of Djibrilla's road maintenance work in North Province. Officials wanting to capitalise on their job tend to favour this form of contract. Since *bons de commande* do not require a committee to select contractors, officials who decide them and who are keen on getting a cut do not have to share it with anyone else.

In the case of *lettres-commande* (contracts preceded by a request from the authority concerned to specific contractors for an estimated budget and subject to review by a committee) and *marchés publics* (contracts subject to a publicised call for bids and awarded by committee through a competitive process), leaks about ceiling prices and the bids of competitors could be as important as anticipating which contracts are going to be offered. In these categories, members of the relevant *commission des marchés publics* (committee for public contracts) tend to actively favour their contractors of choice. Committee members trying to privilege individual contractors might clash between themselves. To avoid this, they try to reach agreements before the committee's official sessions take place.[8]

Once the contracts have been awarded, the awardees are required to register their contracts with the tax authorities. This procedure of *enregistrement* involves the advance payment of a *droit d'enregistrement* (registration duty) amounting to 2 per cent of the budgeted total. The contract is

---

[8] Contract totals determine the appropriate contractual category. The upper limit for *bons de commande* in recent decades has remained at CFAF 5 million. *Lettres-commande* were indicated for totals between CFAF 5 million and 30 million until 2012, when a presidential circular justified lifting the threshold to CFAF 50 million on the grounds of managerial efficiency. Contracts upwards of CFAF 30 million (50 million after 2012) are considered *marchés publics*. It should be noted that the regulations also leave room for large contracts to avoid the requirement for a call for bids under exceptional circumstances, including very broadly understood situations of urgency. Until 2012, these contracts, known as *marchés de gré à gré* (contracts by mutual agreement) required special authorisation from the prime minister. Since 2012, the Ministry of Public Contracts has been entrusted with issuing these authorisations, a change that has reduced their prevalence (Nkou Songue 2014: 42).

then assigned a registration number that the contractor will have to supply at further stages along the contracting process.

Contractors engaged in construction work may request an advance before completion. Otherwise, the payment process is initiated once the works are completed to the required specifications and are officially delivered to the satisfaction of the contracting authority. The prospects of getting paid sooner or later hinge on a variety of factors, but recurrent shortages of funds and the amount of red tape often turn the process into an exercise in endurance. Treasury cash flows have an obvious impact. Many contractors pointed out that peak periods of tax revenue (quarterly and, most noticeably, annual payments of income and value-added taxes) coincided with a smoother payment process. Also, some years are better than others. For example, in 2003 and 2004, depleted state coffers meant that contractors had to wait for many months and sometimes more than a year to receive payment for completed works. Payment arrears eroded the financial resources of all but the best established contractors. A number of contractors were forced to suspend their activities and others went out of business for good. The scarcity of available public funds had the additional effect of increasing contractors' readiness to offer a cut in their fee in exchange for payment – and of increasing treasury officials' demands for such cuts.

Consider the plight of Jeanne, a MINEFI junior official who moonlighted as a contractor. In November 2004, she found herself in a tight spot. She had outstanding invoices for several classrooms she had built in the Djerem and Mbéré districts, dating back 11 months, totalling CFAF 36 million. Of that sum, she would keep only 28 million. The rest belonged to other contractors who had pooled money to finance the works and to the treasury official who was taking a cut for processing the payment. She explained that, until the money arrived, she could not continue her business:

Ten days ago, I've had to stop working at my current site. And, once the bricklayers return to town, it is difficult to take them back to the bush [for work]. I have used up my savings and I have taken money from *la réunion* [the meeting].[9] The due date has come and I cannot pay back, when normally I need to use the money [from a loan] twice within a year to make something out of it. Otherwise, what you get only covers the interests you have to pay.

Sometimes, she admitted, she felt tempted to give up. She recounted all the things she had gone through since she had obtained the contracts to

---

[9] The 'meeting' here signifies the *tontine* in which she takes part. It is common today in Adamaoua to refer to such mutual assistance groups metonymically as *la réunion*, a word used so often in this context that Fulfulde speakers have borrowed it. In the case at hand, the people from Jeanne's home village in West Province have formed a *tontine* in Ngaoundéré.

build the classrooms: registering the contracts and taking care of the paperwork in September 2003; overseeing the construction in December 2003; having the completion verified by the relevant officials in January 2004; and waiting for the elusive payment ever since. As she put it: 'It is truly *un parcours du combattant* [an obstacle course].'

In 2005, the public finance cycle improved significantly. A new head of MINEFI replaced Meva'a m'Eboutou, who had been minister from April 2001 to November 2004 and had become something of a contractors' *bête noire* (Ngogang 2004). International pressures that made reaching the Highly Indebted Poor Countries (HIPC) initiative's completion point dependent on efforts to balance the country's internal debt also played a decisive part in the improvement. On average, payment delays became much shorter. Similar ups and downs have taken place in recent years, although – so far – delays have never reached the levels of 2004.

My trip with Alhadji Djibrilla to Maroua first made me aware of how much a contractor's chances of getting paid could vary across the country. At a time when payments were blocked completely in Adamaoua and to a lesser extent in Far North Province, it took him only a few hours to sort out pending payments in North Province. This is not an unusual state of affairs and it underscores the importance of factors such as the degree of influence of the province's treasury at the national level and the modus operandi of the top treasury officials. Those days with Djibrilla also highlighted how the standing of specific contractors and their 'generosity' towards officials influenced the processing of payments.

Few difficulties in obtaining payment were as intractable as the ones described by Alim Pierre, a contractor based in Ngaoundéré, in a September 2004 interview. The situation was all the more 'puzzling', he said, because 'in public contracts everything to the last detail is put in writing'. The problems concerned two contracts that Alim had undertaken in 2001. After he completed the construction and submitted all the appropriate paperwork for payment, he was told to wait. Numerous months and visits to the *Hôtel de Finances* later, Alim concluded that the TPG had in fact transferred the money to his own bank account. It was then, before the end of 2002, that Alim took the bold step of suing this senior treasury official. The law was on his side: the contracts in his name, the copious related paperwork, and, crucially, the records of the Bank of Central African States (BEAC) that proved that the money had been transferred to the TPG's account. Yet this meant upsetting the interlocking agreements that keep the wheels of public contracting turning.

Alim's lawsuit was delayed by protracted procedural disputes over the correct judicial venue. Finally, on 22 July 2004, the judge determined that the TPG had misappropriated the funds and sentenced him to one year in prison, ordering him to pay Alim his money plus interest. Eight months later, on 17 March 2005, the Ngaoundéré court of appeal dismissed the defendant's appeal and confirmed the previous judgment. The dispute became a front-page headline in the main newspaper in the north of the country (Guivande 2005). Although the matter reached the Supreme Court, Alim was never able to seize any of the ex-TPG's properties in order to get paid. Airing this dispute in court had also come at a cost. Alim was subsequently ostracised from many of the professional circles he had previously inhabited.

A contract's paperwork creates a series of obligations and entitlements for the contracting parties. These effects are perhaps most striking in the case of completely fictitious contracts, which largely concern consumables, although they are not unheard of in construction work. More frequent are cases of contractors who, in order to avoid expense, carry out the commissioned job only in part or with substandard work and then have it approved by complicit officials. One of my interviewees, who had been a prominent contractor for the Chad–Cameroon pipeline regional compensation programme, was exposed as having been involved in one such scheme. The contract concerned electrification works in Ngangassaou and Ngan'ha, two villages in the vicinity of Ngaoundéré. Broadcast by CRTV Adamaoua (the provincial branch of the national public television channel), the opening ceremony brought together a group of government and ruling-party officials. A month later, repeated complaints from the villagers revealed the project's deficiencies to the public. Much to the embarrassment of the officials who had certified the works as satisfactory, a third of the planned electricity poles had never been erected and the cables installed did not meet minimum safety standards (Dahirou 2004). Meanwhile, to buy time, the contractor in charge disappeared from Ngaoundéré for six months.

Such extreme cases aside, appropriate paperwork tends to successfully obfuscate the gap between the documented procedures and actions and actual events. Only by relying on official documentation could someone like Alim Pierre envisage the extraordinary feat of deploying the force of the law against a top provincial official. Such is the power of bureaucratic devices that when a prefect decided to retaliate against an uncooperative *receveur* (treasurer) in July 2005, the most effective course of action was to lock him out of the office containing the tools of his trade, and to prevent him from processing any payments for close to a month.[10] Procedures, documents, signatures, and stamps constitute public contracts. And yet, as the next section shows, they do not exempt officials and contractors from the sociability that also shapes these contracts.

---

[10] The *receveur*, working for the Ministry of Finance in Meiganga (Adamaoua Region), found himself in this embarrassing situation as a result of a conflict with the Mbéré District prefect. The *receveur* had refused to sign the district's book of *bons de commande* due to suspicions of irregularities (Takoua 2005).

The sway of *le suivisme*

Contractors commonly talk about the constant task of reminding officials of their existence in the terms *se faire voir* (making oneself seen), *faire un saut* (popping round), or *passer dire bonjour* (dropping by to say hello). During a casual conversation with one of my informants whom I shall call Alhadji Sehou, he vividly referred to these practices as *le suivisme*. This French word, which comes from the verb *suivre* (to follow), is generally translated as 'herd instinct', 'blind conformity', or simply 'inertia'. In Sehou's usage, however, the term acquires a slightly different meaning. It derives from the notion of *suivre le dossier*: that is, all the efforts deployed by contractors to track the progress of their case from the moment they first entertain the idea of bidding to the time when the contract is completed and they receive full payment. *Le suivisme* offers an apt entry point to explore the nature of the relationships between contractors and state officials.

For Sehou, who was the founder of a well-established NGO but had also dabbled in construction work for several ministries, *le suivisme* encompassed the undignified subservience of contractors to the whims of venal officials. Many contractors, however, wholeheartedly embraced the investment of effort, time, and money that is required in keeping active relationships with as many officials as possible. For Alhadji Djibrilla and many of his colleagues, the courtesy visits, tentative approaches, and negotiating sessions with officials were if anything a test of charm and skill, as well as an often enjoyable exercise in what might be called 'civility' (Herzfeld 2009: 79–84). For many in Adamaoua, such standards of civil behaviour appeal to religious or ethnic frames of reference. During the Ahidjo era (1960–82), Muslim notions of propriety and Fulbe ideals of self-worth remained hegemonic in the northern part of the country, which at the time constituted an immense single province (Azarya 1978: 156; Bayart 1986: 10). This was particularly the case in the civil service, where, as Philip Burnham notes, the unremovable governor Ousmane Mey 'operated virtually a mono-ethnic policy in favour of appointees drawn from the Fulbe or the "Fulbeising" category' (1996a: 39). Thus, with the exception of major infrastructure projects that were carried out by foreign companies (such as the Italian firm Cogefar, which undertook the construction of the Yaoundé–Ngaoundéré railway link in the early 1970s), Fulbe with good connections to the regime, preferably from Ahidjo's power base Garoua, captured most public contracts in Adamaoua.

In 2003, I met a couple of elderly Ngaoundéré businessmen who had made their fortune through the supply of consumables and construction works for government departments in the 1960s and 1970s. To many of my informants, they were icons of a bygone era, out of touch with the transformations their home town had experienced in the last decades. As a close acquaintance of one of them put it, for contractors of that generation 'the slightest contact with anything remotely Christian or Western' was a source of irritation. They were 'practically illiterate [in French]' and as a rule refused to use 'the little French they knew'. Trivial occurrences such as spending a night in a hotel represented 'moral quandaries' for them. The contrast with contractors such as Alhadji Djibrilla is illuminating. Unlike his predecessors, Djibrilla had been schooled in the multi-ethnic classrooms of the national education system, he had spent long periods in the south of the country, and he worked on a regular basis with Cameroonians of diverse ethnic and religious backgrounds. Northern senior officials in Adamaoua's territorial administration and ministerial services were now the exception rather than the norm. The small, homogeneous public contracting sector of the 1960s and 1970s had also given way to a much larger and more diverse group of Ngaoundéré-based contractors. Someone like Djibrilla took pride in the broadmindedness, conviviality, sense of humour, and generosity that he was capable of showing time and again in all sorts of contexts in order to keep his business running. Whereas the older generation might have seen an obliging attitude and dependence on others as the opposite of *pulaaku* (Fulbe-ness, or Fulbe ideals of propriety and virtue), even those in the younger generation who saw themselves as Fulbe tended to see no insurmountable obstacles in reconciling *pulaaku* with the niceties of *le suivisme*.[11]

When the monetary stakes are high and all efforts to successfully complete a contract fail to bear fruit, the resolve of even the most hardened *suivistes* will be put to the test. Consider Alim Pierre's account of what happened when, five months after the official delivery of the completed works, he tried to find out what was delaying the payment:

[The TPG] tells me the money has not arrived yet. When leaving the office, I run into an official I know who asks me: 'How come you get paid and I don't get a little something?' 'But I have just seen the TPG [and he tells me the payments are still pending],' 'No way! You've been paid. He went over all pending bills and paid them.' I rush into my bank and ask them to check whether I have received a transfer recently. They say I haven't. I begin to make my own inquiries. I go to the BEAC in Garoua and they confirm that there's been a recent cheque [for the amount involved] but they are not authorised to give me [any details]. I go and see the TPG once more, and he tells me the money has not arrived yet ... He keeps me at bay with more lies for quite some time until one day, in Yaoundé, I receive confirmation that the money has been disbursed but the transfer has been made to a Credit Lyonnais bank account. My account is at BICEC! Once

---

[11] *Pulaaku* has attracted considerable academic attention in different West African settings. For two Cameroon-focused contributions, see Schultz (1979) and Burnham (1996a). For a continent-wide review of studies on *pulaaku*, see Leblon (2006).

back [in Ngaoundéré], I confront [the TPG] without success. I then bring a lawsuit against him.

Although its factual accuracy cannot be taken at face value, this account is significant in that it is structured around a series of visits to the province's treasury.[12] The purported realisation that these encounters with the official in charge were dead ends provides the closing knot in the narrative thread. It is also noteworthy that in this account Alim finds out that the TPG has authorised payment for the contracts from a junior treasury official. This illustrates the importance of following one's case closely. To learn about contract opportunities or to assess the status of their invoices, contractors need constantly updated information. Such information may help contractors get ahead in preparing competitive bids or uncover pretexts used by officials in order to justify late payments. Much misinformation circulates. Contractors often hear about these matters from officials not directly concerned with the contracts at stake or from their own colleagues, whom they regularly encounter on their rounds to the *Hôtel de Finances* or other offices. Contractors try to check their facts with as many insiders as possible. Thus, for example, when Djibrilla learned of a substantial transfer of money to Maroua's treasury, he asked his friend at the Ministry of Public Works to confirm the rumour.

Let me now turn to a July 2004 exchange between a small-time Muslim contractor and a young treasury official, which further highlights the dynamics of *le suivisme*. I had joined them for lunch in a restaurant near the *Hôtel de Finances* in Ngaoundéré. I knew Saïdou, the contractor, well. Born in Ngaoundéré, his main source of income did not come from his own contracts, which usually concerned the provision of IT support and office supplies, but from the myriad little jobs he performed for Aliou and Abbo, two prosperous businessmen who were partners in numerous construction contracts. Sandra, the treasury employee, came from West Province and had worked in Ngaoundéré for about a year. 'José, this is Sandra. She is Abbo's wife,' Saïdou introduced us. 'How come you give your brother [Abbo] a wife and you don't even tell him?' retorted Sandra, establishing the light tone of the long conversation that ensued. What

---

[12] Alim's version of events stood in stark contrast to accounts that circulated among other contractors and to the version that the TPG himself adopted at the appeal stage, once his initial outright denial that he had transferred the funds to his own account was dismissed by the judge. According to these rival versions, the TPG had used his influence to steer in his favour the bidding process for the two contracts at issue. In exchange of a fifth of the total sum involved, Alim had agreed to act as a nominal bidder and oversee the completion of the works, which the TPG himself was funding. When confronted with Alim's demands for a larger share of the profits than the one initially agreed, and hoping that he would force Alim to abandon such aspirations, the TPG had opted to make the payment to his account rather than to Alim's.

The sway of *le suivisme* 81

follows is my rendering of part of that conversation concerning contract payments.

SAÏDOU: *Le Papa* [Daddy, their nickname for the incumbent provincial TPG] is too strong!

SANDRA: He wants to have control over everything that's going on, to the very last detail ... Last week, he went through all recent payments because he suspected his instructions had not been respected ...

SAÏDOU: I always have the same conversation when I go to see him: 'What are you [Saïdou] doing here again? You only bring me nasty things.' 'It's bills for you [the TPG] to okay.' '[You bring me] a [CFAF] 60,000 telephone [bill]!' 'Come on. That's nothing. Aliou spends 100,000 a month in telephone.' 'But Aliou is a businessman ...' 'And you [the TPG]? You are ten times more of a businessman!'

SANDRA: Of course, [the TPG] is a businessman. Only he's conscientious about what he does.

SAÏDOU: Things are increasingly difficult. It's been seven years now I have spent trying to make money in this, and it's not any easier than it was when I started. Last week I came close to crying in order to get my bills paid. After trying first one for [CFAF] 800,000, and then another for 240,000 unsuccessfully, I had to resign myself to one for 38,000.

SANDRA: He says he wants to end paying all bills from 2003 first.

SAÏDOU: No way! I know he has been paying a lot of stuff from 2004.

SANDRA: Maybe it's because you and your bosses are too tough, always in a rush to get your money.

SAÏDOU: With Aliou, you may be right ... But not with Abbo. He has a tender heart.

SANDRA: Perhaps I'll toughen him up. [Giggling]

SAÏDOU: José, did you hear what she just said?

SANDRA: What have I said that's so funny? [Still laughing]

SAÏDOU: Oh, nothing! Anyway, there's not much you can do against Abbo. You don't even know which bills are his. [In order to make the control of their activities more difficult, he and his two bosses used different firms to operate.]

SANDRA: Well, in fact I do. He's told me that all the ones coming from the Ministry of Agriculture are his.

SAÏDOU: Yes, that's true. He loves those people too much!

The excerpt reveals the intimacy that officials and contractors can cultivate. Joking eases the crossing and negotiation of the boundaries that separate not only Saïdou and Sandra but also Saïdou and the TPG (who, like Sandra, happens to be a 'southerner' and a Christian). Notice the language of kinship: the TPG being called *Le Papa* and the assertions that Saïdou and Abbo are brothers and that Sandra and Abbo are married. Joking in this way creates the closeness sought by both officials and contractors. Equally significant are the references to affection as opposed to pure instrumentality and the associated single-minded quest for money. In their exchange, Abbo's feelings towards the local employees of the Ministry of Agriculture are portrayed as being so strong that they might end up betraying the importance of his business activities to the tax authorities.

Power in contracts

Le suivisme is also markedly hierarchical. As is apparent to any frequent visitor to Cameroonian state offices, the playful pleading for special attention and the teasing entreaties not to neglect one's acquaintances are in many ways a sign of deference towards the addressee. In Alim Pierre's account, such was the case of the official who requested 'a little something', thus unwittingly warning Alim that the payment order for his contracts had been issued. Even so, the possibility of subverting these hierarchies is frequently brought up. Thus, Saïdou, a small-time contractor, has no qualms about reminding the TPG of the inconvenient truth of this official's considerable involvement in the contracting business; in turn, Sandra, recently admitted to the lower rungs of the civil service, might decide to 'toughen up' Abbo, one of Ngaoundéré's largest contractors.

These hierarchies are gendered. Female officials and contractors are not only a minority but often have to learn to cope with an insidious undercurrent of gossip. Muslim women who have made a career in public contracting, for example, show a clear preference for using their young male employees to handle the groundwork (submitting paperwork, directing workers on an everyday basis, and sorting out basic logistical needs). Still, relatives and acquaintances, male and female alike, frequently censure the behaviour of many female contractors. The remarks of a distant cousin of one woman, for example, capture well the ambivalence of some of these criticisms: 'She never stays at home. She's a woman who's always trying to find her place in life. *Elle met son corps en jeu* [she uses her body] ... In the end, she's become very rich. She has even paid for her younger brothers to go to Mecca.' Female contractors tend to strike a fine balance in order to handle officials (mostly men) adeptly while keeping them at arm's length and conforming to norms of propriety. Christian contractors such as Jeanne, whose financial difficulties I discussed above, can also feel discriminated against on gender grounds. Once she recounted the problems she had experienced while looking for a new spot in the city centre for the general store she owned as a side business. Several landlords refused to rent their properties to her because she was a single businesswoman. 'There are no entrepreneurial women here. Me, I wanted to be the exception. I wanted to succeed, but in Ngaoundéré people don't accept those who come from elsewhere,' she explained.

Jeanne's case (she was born in West Province and considers herself Bamileke) also illustrates the impact of ethnic identity on the sociability that emerges around public contracts. Ethnic stereotypes are very visible in discourses on the workings of public contracting, emanating both from participants in the sector and from outsiders. The changes that occurred between the 1960s, when most state officials and national contractors in the north were either Fulbe or assimilated Muslims, and the mid-1980s, when a majority of southerners were appointed to decision-making posts, have not passed unremarked. These changes opened up possibilities for southerners and non-Muslim northerners to participate as contractors. Some Fulbe contractors have not fully accepted such changes and are quick to blame ethnic favouritism for their business difficulties. The manager of a farming cooperative who doubled as a small-time contractor, for example, vented his anger to me about the 'nightmare' he had to go through in order to get paid for a series of completed contracts: 'It's the Garafi governor who's to blame.[13] It's not taken him long to hook up with the TPG and form a Bamileke clan. They have set up ghost companies, headed by relatives or members of their *réunions*, to which they channel most of the available public money. It's there [at the *réunions*] that everything is decided.'

Conflicts framed in ethno-regional terms do not necessarily presuppose opposition between northerners and southerners. Consider, for example, the July 2005 conflict between a prefect and a *receveur* that I mentioned earlier. The Mbéré District prefect had submitted a contract voucher book for the *receveur* to sign. Having identified some irregularities, out of professional zeal and because of the large sums involved, the *receveur* decided to travel to Ngaoundéré to consult his superiors before signing. Once he became aware of the *receveur*'s departure, the prefect retaliated by sealing off the treasury office, which remained closed for almost a month until the TPG persuaded the governor to intervene. For my purposes here, it is interesting that a *L'Oeil du Sahel* article covering the incident mentions in passing the ethnic undertones that otherwise tend to remain implicit. The newspaper account explains how 'the prefect threw a memorable fit [when he noticed the *receveur*'s absence], uttering vague threats and letting it be known that he is Bulu and they are still in command' (Takoua 2005).[14] Ethnic stereotyping of contractors is as common as that of officials. A contractor who criticised Alim Pierre's

---

[13] Garafi is the most common term in the northern vernacular to refer to Bamileke. It is often used with pejorative connotations. It derives from 'Grassfields', which is how West Cameroon has long been known, given its typical landscape of humid savannah. Stereotypical opinions about the Bamileke monopolising economic opportunities through networks of ethnic solidarity are common in northern Cameroon and elsewhere in the country (Dongmo 1981; Warnier 1993; Socpa 2006). On 'the myth of the Anglo-Bamileke threat', see Sindjoun (1996a: 63).

[14] The Bulu are taken to be President Biya's ethnic group, although often the label of choice is the broader ethnic category of Beti.

handling of his conflict with the TPG, for example, concluded his invective with a mention of Alim's ethnic identity ('These Gbaya are dangerous people!'). It is significant that neither the journalist reporting on the prefect's abuse of power nor the contractor censuring Alim's conduct deem it worth mentioning the ethnicity of those who are portrayed as victims in their accounts (the Bamileke *receveur* and the Beti TPG respectively).

Negative perceptions of public contracts premised on ethno-regional readings of prevailing relationships and practices are indeed common. Thus, for the Douala-based power broker who had been involved in ARA in the 1990s, what made the dire standards of numerous public works in Ngaoundéré particularly tragic was the fact that many of the contractors involved were the city's own 'children'. As he put it, these contractors from Ngaoundéré 'think that they are smart, that they have outdone others in obtaining those contracts'. Instead, they were being 'turned into accessories to corrupt officials who could not care less about Adamaoua'. They did not seem to fully realise that 'they harm themselves, their home region, and their people'. In this account, contractors are portrayed as blinded not only by a desire for self-enrichment but also by a sense of accomplishment derived from having prevailed over other competitors. From such a standpoint, the contractors' rewards, financial and otherwise, are obtained at the expense of local aspirations for improved public services and infrastructure. For many high-minded critics, the practices that Alhadji Sehou designated as *le suivisme* were especially contemptible because they play into the hands of officials whose loyalties lie elsewhere and who have no hesitation about jeopardising local futures.

In spite of the conventions, constraints, and stereotypes that imbue the sociability around public contracts, the negotiations and agreements that underlie these contracts tend to be fluid. This fluidity stands in marked contrast to the rigid formalities that govern public contracting procedures and explains the prevalence and scope of the various ways to circumvent and subvert such formalities. Agreements like the one that purportedly existed between Alim and the TPG before they fell out, which make public contracting what it is in practice, offer no guarantee other than the personal commitment of both parties to respect them. Failure to honour agreements can certainly put individuals' future participation in the system at risk, as both Alim and the TPG learned firsthand. The knowledge of what is at stake may thus encourage officials and contractors to compromise when necessary. It does not, however, dissuade them from attempting to redefine the sometimes implicit or loose terms agreed. These are agreements subject to constant renegotiation: nothing is final until the last payment is made. The most banal of dialogues will help illustrate this point. I witnessed this in April 2004 when eating grilled meat in a street restaurant with a young contractor. He was supplying the Ngaoundéré branch of a parastatal with a substantial amount of imported office furniture. The pro-forma invoice was now ready and pending approval. While we were having lunch, the contractor phoned and summoned the official in charge, who did not take long to show up. After taking a look at the invoice with the listed items and prices and being reprimanded by the contractor for getting it dirty with grease, the official started the following exchange:

OFFICIAL: You won't forget that there is still a small matter pending, will you?
CONTRACTOR: A small matter? What do you mean?
OFFICIAL: Something we have to sort out at the time of payment ...
CONTRACTOR: I thought we already had an agreement. I suppose we will stick to it.
OFFICIAL: Well, you know we need to talk.
CONTRACTOR: Oh, don't worry! We will talk and see.

This fluidity of working agreements is related to the fact that, in this economic domain, contractors and authorities relate to each other as parties to business transactions. Giorgio Blundo, in his early work on everyday corruption in public contracting in Senegal, emphasised this aspect: 'These are rather negotiations between equals (and, sometimes, it is the private sector actors who are in a situation of social and economic superiority)' (Blundo 2001: 80). In light of this, accounts that put the full force of *le suivisme* squarely on the shoulders of contractors fail to do justice to the interactions between officials and public contractors. In fact, in exceptional circumstances, public officials' need to generate interest among contractors may acquire particular urgency. I witnessed such a situation in September 2004, when the Vina District prefect was compelled to organise a meeting with Ngaoundéré's contractors. There were over CFAF 160 million earmarked for planned works in the district that risked going back to Yaoundé unused, the prefect informed us. He declared his sympathy for contractors suffering from systematic payment arrears and promised to do his best to help solve the problem. In return, he urged contractors to make an effort to ensure that these contracts without bidders did not remain 'orphaned'.

The taxation of public contracting

In a conversation we had ten months after I first met Alhadji Djibrilla, I asked him why he did not have an office from which to conduct business. Was it because he did not need one? His answer was a small revelation:

I do have an office. It is because of the tax people. The first time I had an audit, the inspectors refused to go to my house. They have their own procedures and

I try to do what I am asked. So I rented a small office at Carrefour X [a central spot in Ngaoundéré]. I take all my papers there and, in a matter of days, they are done. It only happens rarely, once a year at most ... Yes, I just keep [the office] for the audits; otherwise it remains empty.

I had never suspected the existence of that empty room and I found it intriguing. It was a glaring example of 'the occlusion of intimate knowledge' between bureaucrats and their clients (Herzfeld 2005). It also revealed the gap between the routine management of Djibrilla's activities and the conditions tax authorities required in order to exert their control.

This refusal to perform their task at taxpayers' homes and the denial of any intimacy between officials and taxpayers were all the more remarkable given Djibrilla's line of business. He, like all public contractors I knew, thrived on establishing close relationships with officials in Adamaoua and beyond. As we have seen, he also relished the opportunities that his involvement in Ngaoundéré's football team afforded him for rubbing shoulders with government officials. Not only were civil servants frequent guests at his house, but he was also a regular visitor to their offices and an occasional guest in their homes. The officials in charge of awarding contracts or authorising payments were certainly not the same as those who carried out tax verifications. Yet, they shared working space at the Ministry of Finance's local offices (in the case of treasury officials), or were next-door neighbours in the relevant *quartier administratif* (in the case of prefects, sub-prefects, and delegates of the different ministries). Both public contracts decision makers and tax officials benefited from Djibrilla's generous attention. The neutral technical labour, unencumbered by personal relationships, that tax auditors conducted in an unused office, in accordance with recent Tax Directorate guidelines, was a striking simulacrum.

Public contracts in Cameroon historically involved tax exemption. Numerous calls, including – most pressingly – those of the International Monetary Fund, to improve the transparency of public accounts, to differentiate expenditure and revenue-raising roles and functions, and to simplify tax systems by eliminating exemptions were heeded by the government in 2003. In that year, the prime minister proclaimed that from then on public contracts would be subject to all taxes.[15] On the face of it, the taxation of public contracts should be a rather unproblematic task. Regulations make it a requirement for any public contract bidder to submit copies of a long series of tax-related documents: a valid business licence, official verification of their place of business, taxpayer card, and a recently issued certificate of tax payment. Even *bons de commande* and *lettres-commande*, which avoid bidding procedures, have to be registered

---

[15] Decree 2003/651/PM of 16 April 2003.

with the treasury before the work is started. In practice, what these documents represent and how they reflect compliance is not always straightforward.

Consider the requirement to register contracts and pay the fee that registration entails. Once this formality is taken care of, the treasury issues a registration number, which will subsequently appear on all official documentation pertaining to a contract until the relevant works and services are delivered and remunerated. However, the potential for exploiting the effects produced by the mere invocation of a number is not lost on many contractors across the country, who are well aware of the bureaucratic challenges that the Cameroonian revenue authorities face. This became apparent in March 2003, when the Ministry of Finance announced the discovery of a *réseau de faussaires* (fraud network) surrounding registration duties. In a period when the tax administration was being revamped through a quantitative assessment of its performance, its long-term decline in revenue prompted an inquiry, which resulted in the detection of widespread fraud. Some 50 firms were caught routinely reusing old registration numbers referring to entirely different contracts. The culprits were given a chance to avoid being fined or prosecuted if they paid the sums they had evaded (Amayena 2003).

Often, the enterprises recorded in official documents may reveal little about the identity of those financing and fulfilling the contract. Contractors frequently submit bids under somebody else's name. This is common in the case of civil servants, including chiefs and elected authorities, who resort to *prête-noms* (fronts) to make it less obvious that they have brought their influence to bear in order to succeed in tendering processes. Established contractors may have other reasons to multiply the number of firms registered under their name or that of their relatives. For example, Abbo and Aliou, the contractors for whom Saïdou did multiple jobs, utilise different firms in order to lessen the impression that they are systematically favoured by several contracting authorities. Those taking their first steps as independent contractors may also ask to borrow their mentors' or colleagues' letterheads when submitting bids. Thus, for about three years Djibrilla's partner Bobbo carried out his own contracts under the umbrella of one of Djibrilla's firms. Jeanne also did her first jobs as a contractor using the name of a contractor with whom she had become acquainted in her work at the treasury. Arrangements vary depending on the importance of the contract. For small contracts, *le carburant* (money for petrol) might be sufficient compensation. For larger contracts, a share for the person providing the letterhead would typically be agreed beforehand.

A requirement that became particularly salient at the time when I began my research is the aforementioned *plan de localisation* (business location map), an instrument of tax administration that was introduced in 2000 with the explicit aim of consolidating the taxpayer base.[16] The *plan de localisation* was conceived as a preliminary step in creating a *dossier fiscal unique* (taxpayer's single file), which was meant to put an end to fragmented and dispersed information on taxpayers and tax payments. Now, these files would offer a comprehensive view of the records of every taxpayer, who would then be assigned a *numéro identifiant unique* (single identifying number). Knowing the whereabouts of taxpayers constituted the most basic step towards increased compliance. Despite this requirement, the mobility of public contractors continued to have an impact on the state's ability to tax them. Those contractors operating in different parts of the country pose specific challenges. In 2004, a young tax official from Ngaoundéré explained to me that public contractors were only too aware of how onerous it was for the tax authorities to handle the *découpages territoriales* (territorial demarcations): 'They take advantage of the weakness of our administrative organisation'. Those like Djibrilla, who carried out a substantial part of his work outside his base of Adamaoua, could benefit from the incomplete picture that the provincial tax office had of their activities. As the new director of the ARMP lamented in his speech during an event hosted by the national business association in September 2014, 'a shared, interoperable, and integrated computer system for the management of public contracts is still lacking'. Although they are part of the same ministerial structure, tax and treasury offices suffer serious blockages in data sharing. Properly handled, contract registration data would almost effortlessly provide the tax authorities with an image of contractors' expected annual turnover. However, information on the beneficiaries of registered public contracts was not adequately processed or centralised. Treasury payments to contractors suffered from the same problems. Records of such payments were not consolidated or made available for tax control purposes. The end result is that the information tax authorities are able to obtain through independent sources on public contractors' activities is full of gaps. The conditions are thus in place for an open-ended, annual give and take between contractors and the staff of the relevant tax centre.

When a tax return was submitted, it was not uncommon for officials to refuse to accept it. If they judged the income declared to be low, they told contractors to think twice about it and report a higher, more plausible income. In the same spirit, some contractors liked to sound out officials about what they could expect if they declared a given level of income before proceeding to file a return. Hence, the income declared was often

---

[16] The taxpayer's obligation to provide a *plan de localisation* is contained in Article L.1, Fiscal Procedure Handbook, Tax Code. The administrative procedures for the verification of location were first set out in Instruction no. 362/MINEFI/DI of 15 June 2000.

the outcome of previous negotiation. The belief that completely doing without such preliminary approaches would expose them to unfairly harsh treatment was broadly shared among small and medium-sized contractors.

Nevertheless, these preliminary agreements between taxpayers and officials and the payments under the counter they might entail do not offer full protection against audits or *redressements* (rectifications; from *redresser*, literally to straighten up) of their tax forms. Consider Bobbo's experience in early 2004. It was only in 2002 that he decided to stop operating under the mantle of Djibrilla's enterprise and create one of his own. He initially paid the *impôt libératoire* (the flat-rate tax for an annual turnover of less than CFAF 15 million) but his businesses had expanded noticeably. In discussing his tax return for 2003, tax officials had advised him to report an income slightly above 15 million, which involved moving from the *impôt libératoire* to a business licence in the *régime de base* (less than CFAF 50 million). About a month later, he was taken aback to find out that his return had been subject to a rectification that added CFAF 6 million to his annual turnover.

As far as audits are concerned, none of the parties involved have any illusions about what they might yield. Inspectors know that whatever documents they are allowed to examine are carefully selected, and perhaps even concocted, to minimise tax liabilities. Contractors, for their part, know that tax officials have leeway to determine the final tax burden, even though their means to assess actual income are extremely limited. If we return again to Djibrilla's case, for all his conspicuous prosperity and his frequent presence in the Ministry of Finance, the precise details of his business activities remained strikingly diffuse for the tax authorities. What officials chose to conclude about these activities in the mid-2000s was not exclusively a function of observing a series of scrupulously impersonal document-based procedures in his 'ghost office'. Audits were only one element – and a far from common one, for that matter – in a longer process dominated by personalised backstage bargaining between Djibrilla and the tax officials involved. What preceded and followed auditing procedures rarely bore any resemblance to the administrative purity that inspired the staging of the audit itself.

Pronouncements on tax evasion in Cameroon often make much of the lower tax liability that results from this more or less negotiated reporting of income by public contractors and other business people. It is important to remember, however, that even those public contractors who grossly underreport their income in tax returns still pay substantial sums in taxes. Readers are already familiar with contract registration duties (5 per cent for *bons de commande*, 2 per cent for other types of contracts). Payments for contractors' work are further subject to withholding tax. As in the 'pay as you earn' system, the contracting authority deducts an advance payment of income tax of 1 per cent of every invoice it pays to the contractors. VAT withholding, a less intuitive but financially more consequential procedure, means that contractors also have 19.25 per cent deducted from every payment they receive. Although VAT withholding is premised on the notion that contractors can then ask for a refund of the VAT credits that they have been unable to offset (VAT they have themselves paid to their suppliers), in practice many of those credits are as good as lost. To begin with, only companies with a turnover of CFAF 50 million and over can apply for a VAT refund. Then, applying for a refund entails an audit that most contractors would rather do without. Finally, the processing of VAT refunds can take years. Consider again the case of Bobbo. Since 2002, he has seen the authorities who hire his enterprise withhold VAT from every payment. Until 2007, when he finally moved from the *régime de base* to the *régime simplifié*, he was not entitled to recover any VAT he paid to his suppliers. In 2011, after four years under this new taxpaying category, he had yet to file his first VAT refund request. Taking such a step, he told me, would equate to *s'en prendre aux Impôts* (taking on the tax authorities), a risky journey that he was not ready to set out on. So, despite the limitations of the authorities' knowledge of taxpayers and the irregularities that characterise tax administration procedures, considerable public revenue is raised from public contracting.

On top of all these tax payments and duties, of course, there are many other payments that no discussion of the taxation of public contracts can avoid. Such disbursements are wide ranging. They include commissions paid by contractors to those in a position to direct tendering processes in their favour, facilitation money paid to treasury officials to expedite outstanding bills, and side payments to tax officials ready to sign off on the contractors' underreporting of income. Attitudes among contractors towards these payments also vary. Many satisfy themselves with the self-serving but hard-to-dispute contention that their choice is one between engaging in illegal payments or giving up public contracting altogether. Alhadji Djibrilla, for instance, had no qualms about discussing how much he paid and to whom. Everyone did it, he pointed out, only some more graciously and skilfully than others. It was a transaction like any other, an additional item in the list of running costs of his business. Some contractors even depart from this tone of inevitability and present themselves as willing participants in a game of reciprocal exchanges. Thus, when in November 2004 a contractor took me to see a recent job he had undertaken, the refurbishment of one of Meiganga's *lycées*, he insisted on making a point of whose decision it had been to reward treasury officials for speeding up the final payment: 'I gave the people at [the *Hôtel de Finances*] their part and they made sure I got paid. But I did it of my own accord. Nobody asked me to pay.'

Therefore, overall, public contractors are subject to considerable levels of official and unofficial taxation. Given that their business is premised on dealing with state institutions, this is not particularly surprising. However, it is worth underscoring the fact that the ways in which these taxes and exactions are collected are far from inconsequential. Firstly, they account only very partially for all the income that public contracts generate and they fail to assign this income to individual taxpayers. Secondly, they entail breaches of the law, often shared by officials and taxpayers. The result is that, despite all those payments, public contractors' credibility as dutiful taxpayers is extremely low.

* * * * * *

Public contracts are a tightly regulated and highly formalised field of economic activity. Contractors not only need to carry out the construction works or deliver the supplies their contracts refer to but also have to abide by a long list of administrative procedures designed to ensure that state organisations and agencies get good value for money. This chapter has shown that these contracts assemble people as well as buildings, supplies, documents, and money. Public contracts thus rely on assiduous cultivation of personal relationships and draw on recognisable but dynamic repertoires of civility, such as *pulaaku*. Although earlier work on public contracting in Africa (Blundo 2001: 80) has described these relationships as *surpersonalisés* (over-personalised), there is a sense in which such a personalisation makes a lot of sense and appears excessive only in relation to an ideal type of bureaucracy that has limited purchase even in contexts where states pride themselves on avoiding intimacy between public officials and citizens (Riles 2004: 396). These relationships are not an extraneous addition to public contracts but instead are the substance of which these contracts are made.

Because of the collective interests at stake during a period when the state has confronted serious financial shortfalls and when the fight against corruption has become a global concern, public contracts in Cameroon have been subject to intense official scrutiny and social commentary. In recent decades, Cameroonians have been very cognisant of the architectural text of unfinished, crumbling buildings and the political subtext of illegal modes of appropriation of public wealth outlined by Mbembe and Roitman (1995: 355). Public contracting and the practices that one of my interviewees glossed as *le suivisme* constitute a domain under suspicion, in which illegal dealings are perceived to jeopardise the promises of collective betterment that public investments contain. This was the view of the ARA-affiliated Douala-based civil servant who invited me to consider the budgets of a series of decaying buildings in Ngaoundéré. Similarly, how could the residents of Ngangassaou and Ngan'ha not feel let down in April 2004 when the long-awaited electrification of their villages turned out to be a fiasco? Yet, for all the extravagance and wastefulness of such egregious cases, this chapter proposes a more balanced portrayal of public contracting. There are certainly many authorities who have 'their' contractors and even more officials who systematically capitalise on their position to extract payments from contractors – or to turn their position into money, as the French word used by my interlocutors, *monnayer*, vividly conveys. Such phenomena are the bread and butter of long-standing repertoires of business practices. In this regard, the reforms' new tools of control have been largely circumvented and the new actors incorporated in those repertoires. Less eye-catching, however, is the fact that the routine work of dozens of public contractors based in Ngaoundéré can be described as sound and even conscientious. Their budgets are more often than not considerably inflated to accommodate generous profit margins as well as commissions and other payments made to public officials, but they are proud of their work and ready to answer for its quality and standards. For contractors such as Djibrilla, cultivating relationships with those officials and giving them their established share are not incompatible with an aspiration to become respected professionals known for doing a *kuugal laaɓdum* (clean job).

3 'Cattle saves the day'

On 18 August 2005, a *moto-taxi* took me to the Ngaoundéré railway station. The station building's tall, pointed concrete structure jutting above the entrance, which its architects had conceived as a symbol of the young republic's desire to modernise the north of the country and make it less isolated, was in serious need of repair at the time. Facing it in the distance, some cattle traders sat on the benches of the wooden stalls with corrugated roofs that serve as cafés and shops. Others stood in the unpaved esplanade used as a parking lot, around the pickup trucks and cars of the more established traders. It was a Thursday, the day when, unless there has been a derailment or any other disruption to traffic, the railway company Camrail announces how many freight cars will be available for cattle shipments to Yaoundé. Thursday morning is not a random choice for allocating freight cars. The system is designed to fit within the established rhythm of weekly markets. Knowing with certainty the number of cattle they can ship allows traders to manage their stocks accordingly. Thursday is also the designated day for Ngaoundéré's market, the largest in Adamaoua. Immediately after they find out their weekly allocation, traders can attend the market to make any necessary purchases. The day of shipment is also set to allow sufficient time for livestock to arrive at Yaoundé, whose main market day is Sunday, and Douala, where peak activity occurs on Mondays.

Since the mid-1990s, the railway company has granted the right to ship cattle from Ngaoundéré to two groups: Éleveurs et Commerçants à Bétail de Cameroun (Cameroon Cattle Farmers and Traders, or ELCOBCAM) and the Comité (the local chapter of the National Association of Cattle Traders, or ANCBC). The available freight capacity is distributed equally between them. Camrail restricts the presence of cattle traders in the station manager's office: only one delegate of each group is allowed. In this way, the company avoids being entangled in the conflicts involved in determining individual traders' share of the space made available to the two groups. When I arrived that day, ELCOBCAM's representative was already there. Everyone was waiting for the Comité delegate – a recurring situation that seems to express his seniority relative to his ELCOBCAM counterpart. The time spent waiting for his arrival tends to be one of contained anxiety. Traders have made their requests to their respective group leader in advance and want to see if the allocated number of cattle will match their expectations.

On that particular Thursday, the delegate arrived at around 9.15 a.m. After greeting all the senior traders, he went into Camrail's offices accompanied by ELCOBCAM's representative. Fifteen minutes later, they came out to the parking lot holding the green vouchers that list the freight cars they have been given. While ELCOBCAM sorts out the distribution of freight cars at the house of their leading figure, the Comité makes its decision in a highly charged performance at the railway station immediately after Camrail's announcement. When they saw their delegate coming out, the 20 or so Comité traders and their agents rushed to meet him. Oblivious to their many solicitations, he curtly announced that each group had been given seven freight cars and locked himself into his parked car. On days such as this, when the allotted space is not enough to satisfy the traders' requests, it may take him a while to make calculations and think through the adjustments that will lead to the final distribution.

Some ten minutes later, the delegate got out of his car and began scribbling on scraps of paper meticulously torn from his notebook. Each corresponded to a freight car and contained the names of the traders who would share the space as well as the number of cattle they would be able to ship. Visibly impatient, most traders surrounded the delegate at very close quarters. He called out the name of one of the lucky traders, handed him the piece of paper with his decision scribbled on it, and proceeded to write down the next one. The *chargeurs* (cattle loaders), who until then had shown their subordination by standing at a distance, approached the traders they worked for in order to receive precise instructions about the animals they needed to attend to. With each announcement, the uncertainties surrounding the weekly distribution of space dissolved – with varying degrees of satisfaction. The delegate finally handed out the seventh, and last, scrap of paper, marking the end of the distribution process. Outstanding requests, he informed them, would be postponed to the following week.

The delegate's announcement hardly came as a surprise. The requests that Comité members had made that week amounted to more than 11 freight cars. One of the disappointed traders, who had asked for a full freight car (30 head of cattle) and had got nothing, grabbed the delegate by the arm and cornered him against the car to vent his anger. It took a few minutes for him to cool down and he was assured that next week his request would be fulfilled. Another important trader who had been denied space that week was not present. His agent approached the delegate but, given his junior status, avoided body contact and was careful not to lose his composure when expressing his disappointment. At around 10 a.m., traders and *chargeurs* gradually began to leave in order to get ready for the cattle market. Still surrounded by several other people intent on reminding him of their pending or upcoming requests, the Comité delegate stayed at the station for another 20 minutes.

Economic activities around cattle production for meat in Cameroon are extremely fragmented. From the grazing grounds to the butcher's shop, individual, family, or small-scale businesses populate this field of activity. Ranches, including state ones, are rare, and by and large they achieve disappointing commercial results. There are no wholesalers to speak of and the largest butchers are supermarket chains in the main cities and catering firms supplying oil platforms and other large corporations. Cattle merchants themselves fit into this broad picture. Big trading concerns have been historical exceptions. The largest traders in Ngaoundéré are those who specialise in 'exports', the local convention to refer to any sales of cattle outside Adamaoua; these will be the main focus of this chapter.[1] Every week the railway station becomes a point on which most of these traders and the cattle they trade converge. Key regulatory dynamics that shape the volume, monetary rewards, piecemeal documentation, and professional identities of the trade manifest themselves on these weekly occasions. This chapter tries to makes sense of those dynamics. A thread running through the text concerns the widespread portrayal of cattle merchants as refractory regulatory targets. Such a representation has deep historical roots but gained more currency in the 1990s, as a contested, under-resourced, and disaffected civil service showed itself to be unequal to its tasks in an unevenly liberalised cattle economy. The chapter points to the need to look beyond an obvious opposition between slippery traders and helpless authorities.

Vying for a share of the southern markets

Since the mid-1990s there have been no set limits on cattle shipments to Yaoundé. However, the scant number of freight cars the railway company makes available on a regular basis represents a substantial constraint. After the 1999 privatisation, cattle freight was relegated to a marginal place in the railway company's commercial strategy on the grounds that it is not a profitable part of its business (PRASAC 2003: 100). Freight cars have long been in a state of disrepair and they are clearly insufficient to cover periods of high supply and demand of cattle. In the regular arguments concerning the reduced availability of freight cars that I witnessed when accompanying the cattle traders'

---

[1] This terminology is congruent with the existing cleavage between north and south Cameroon (Froelich 1954a: 24; Douffissa 1993: 207). For many traders, south of Adamaoua constitutes *yaasi lesdi* (foreign land).

representatives, Camrail's managers invariably stuck to their new guidelines. Unlike its parastatal predecessor, they insisted, their company's main objective was the maximisation of profit. Camrail's top manager in Ngaoundéré and the *chef de gare* (station chief), his immediate subordinate, would remind traders that their ability to 'foster the loyalty of [*fideliser*] long-standing clients' like them was very limited. Cattle, Camrail's managers liked to point out, were Yaoundé-bound cargo (even cattle being sent to Douala normally travel the Yaoundé–Douala stretch by truck, which on that part of the journey is more time- and cost-effective than the railway). The company's profit-based orientation meant that it prioritised clients with Douala-bound shipments over those who needed transport only to Yaoundé.

Traders' dissatisfaction with Camrail related not only to its low transport capacity at peak periods. One of their main grievances concerned the unreliability of the scheduled services. The unloading operations (fruit, mostly plantains, being transferred from freight cars coming from the south to trucks going north) that normally precede the loading of cattle often take longer than the time scheduled for them. Additionally, when crossing freight coming in the opposite direction, cattle is considered low priority and put on hold (between Yaoundé and Ngaoundéré, the Transcamerounais is a single-track railway). More substantial delays would result from derailments or other technical problems. Such interruptions of railway traffic create uncertainty about whether the animals will reach Yaoundé and Douala in time for the main market days. If delays in providing freight cars or arranging loading reach a certain point, the shipment is suspended until the following week. Even more worryingly, when serious problems emerge along the line, cattle are trapped in freight cars for several days, making the prospect of losses very likely.

Despite all its shortcomings, railway transport offers the best option for high-end cattle, whose price per head in southern markets can justify the cost of shipping them. Transport on foot takes much longer, causes animals to lose weight, and increases the chances of accidental casualties. And road transport is substantially more expensive, although road paving completed in 2012 (from Ayos to Bonis) and 2013 (Garoua Boulai–Ngaoundéré) has made it much more attractive. For all intents and purposes, at the time of my fieldwork, regular access to important markets such as Yaoundé, Douala, Libreville, Bata, and Malabo depended on doing well in the weekly allocations of freight car space. Nigerian markets aside, these are by far the most lucrative outlets for cattle in the region. It is hardly surprising that competition over Camrail's cars was so fierce.

In Ngaoundéré, requests for freight car space need to be made in advance to the respective group representatives (ELCOBCAM or Comité). In times of particularly intense trading, these demands are made well beforehand, up to three weeks in advance, and subsequently ratified or revised. When the number of cars available in a given week is close to the number requested by traders, the leaders of the two groups generally reduce them pro rata. When the mismatch between requested and available space is more substantial, they grant some traders' requests (with a smaller or larger reduction) and postpone those of other traders to subsequent shipments. This is what happened on the morning of August 2005 described earlier. The generally accepted criterion for privileging some traders over others is their requests' precedence in time, but other factors such as the traders' commercial weight, regularity, and reputation also come into play.

This system is subject to considerable distortions. The groups of traders operating in each railway station distribute freight space only to their members (although such status is not formalised but rather established by consensus and practice). In Ngaoundéré, this means that cattle owners or traders who want to try their luck in southern markets on a one-off or sporadic basis have to convince a member of the Comité or ELCOBCAM to include them in their weekly requests for space. Depending on the existing relationship, they may agree to do this for free or in exchange for a commission. In any case, in weeks when the capacity of railway transport is clearly insufficient, traders tend to inflate their requests as a matter of course, aware of the likelihood of a downward revision. In the unlikely event that they get more freight car space than they can fill with their own cattle, they can always discreetly pass it on to other people who are ready to pay for it. Although group leaders and more established traders frown upon this reselling of car space and publicly condemn it, this does not deter some traders from such practices. In these relatively closed commercial circuits, where everyone knows everyone else, traders find it impossible to make exorbitant requests that are obviously beyond their financial means. However, moderately inflated demands are a common occurrence during peak periods. Group leaders are certainly aware that they need to take traders' stated requests with a pinch of salt in these busy periods. By simply keeping track of the proportion of unfulfilled requests that vanishes from one week to the next, they get a sense of which traders have a proclivity for overstating their transport needs.

In times of market bonanza in Yaoundé and Douala, the group leaders who allocate freight car space are subject to overwhelming pressures. This was very apparent in my earlier description of the Comité delegate's typical handling of the situation and his resort to lengthy, laborious written calculations before he announced his decision. I am tempted to see in those scribbled notes the administration of a *pharmakon* (Derrida 1981) that would mediate between the many imponderable merits of each of the traders' requests and his final decision – if there were such a

Figure 3.1 Weekly distribution of freight car space among cattle traders, Ngaoundéré railway station, October 2004

thing. But much backstage intimation precedes these performances on Thursday mornings. Over the week, the group leaders, as a matter of course, deal with phone calls or visits by cattle farmers and traders checking on the status of their requests and the prospects of having them fulfilled. They must deploy considerable poise and tact in balancing the demands of numerous interested parties. In the nervous moments that immediately precede and follow their weekly decisions, the moral authority they inspire and even their ability to impose their physical presence are put to test (Figure 3.1).

The *kabbol* (loading of cattle; from the root *habb-*, 'to tie up') can also be a time filled with tension. Although, in principle, freight space has already been distributed earlier, nothing is set in stone until the cars are finally loaded. This is often a protracted process that requires coordination among railway employees, cattle traders, herders, and *chargeurs*. Freight cars are not always available when expected and the communication between railway employees and those handling the animals is anything but fluid. A variety of incidents can take place, many of which derive from the fact that only rarely does a single trader get a freight car for himself. More often than not, several traders share a car, which, depending on the kind of wagon, accommodates either 30 or 40 head of cattle. Some traders may not manage to put together enough cattle to match their allocated car space. They may also fail to find someone interested in taking it – a payment on the side is normally expected for surrendering car space, although it may be done for free if no bidder is forthcoming. Unless they are only a few head of cattle short, such traders will not be able to cover the expenses involved in travelling to Yaoundé and may renege altogether on sending any cattle that week. Such a decision will necessarily affect the traders with whom they happen to share the freight car in question. Since Camrail charges a lump sum per freight car, partial payment of freight is not a possibility. As a result, one of the cars that had been allotted might suddenly be up for grabs, or even, in very rare cases, remain unused.

Other problems may arise. Many traders oversee the loading process personally but others entrust its supervision to herders, *chargeurs,* or even a fellow trader. Everyone is on guard against possible intrigues. Since loading often takes place in the middle of the night, someone can try to sneak in a few additional animals, leaving out those of an inattentive trader. The arguments that follow such incidents can be long and heated. Stranger things can happen too. On 2 October 2003, for example, I witnessed an episode reminiscent of the impromptu transport arrangements of the late 1980s. A derailment had meant that there had been no shipment the week before. This represented a serious hindrance to most traders' plans, so that week everyone expected a fiery atmosphere. In the morning, Camrail had announced that each group would get seven freight cars, which in normal circumstances would have been considered a fairly decent number, but, after the derailment, was far from enough to meet the traders' requests. The loading of cattle had started in the early afternoon, much earlier than usual. The few traders watching, with whom I was waiting, seemed in good spirits. The mood changed suddenly when one of them received a phone call with disturbing news. It turned out that seven additional freight cars, in addition to those Camrail had distributed in the morning, had appeared in Ngaoundéré. The station manager had decided to send four to Ngaoundal the day before. As for the remaining three cars, a young, impetuous trader in the Comité group had managed to get first claim on them on account of his good connections with the station manager. The trader was now trying to fill them with his own cattle and with those of other traders to whom he was allegedly trying to sell the space. When they found out, the traders whose shipments had had to be postponed were furious. The ensuing dispute proved all the more intractable because that particular week the Comité delegate was in Yaoundé at a meeting. The person who had replaced him was an important trader but he lacked the authority to assert the group's right to dispose of the extra cars according to the list of outstanding requests. After much wrangling, first on the phone and then in person, the young trader got his way and loaded the three cars as he saw fit, albeit while making some minor accommodation for a couple of the disgruntled traders.

The loading process is also a time when cash exchanges hands. The most substantial payment concerns the rail transport itself. Traders also need to pay *chargeurs* for their labour and for the straw that covers the wooden floors of the freight cars and ensures safe travel for the cattle. But this is not all. Loading operations also trigger the payment of an income tax advance and for a compulsory veterinary inspection authorising the animals' transfer. Since the colonial era, the movement of cattle crossing administrative boundaries has been subject to veterinary authorisation. Ever since the possibility of sending cattle by train first materialised in 1976, these shipments have required the payment of a fee for a *laissez-passer* (let-pass) to be issued by the Ministry of Livestock, Fisheries, and Animal Industries (MINEPIA). The tax advances, which are notionally set at 1 per cent of commercial turnover, have a much more recent history. The governor of Adamaoua introduced these advances in 1999 through an ordinance.[2] The measure was justified by the critical state of the provincial treasury that year. However, it provoked such an outcry that the governor was forced to revise downward the taxable value of a head of cattle (from CFAF 200,000 to 150,000) on the basis of which the advance was calculated. According to a leader of the national traders' association, the authorities at the time had told them: 'Bear the brunt of this measure, pay what we ask you to pay [the tax advances], and like that you get it over with [i.e. you pay no further taxes].' Such words did little to appease the massive opposition to the advances, but traders who wanted to keep transporting cattle by train were left with little choice but to pay.

The collection of veterinary fees and income tax advances merits further explanation. While the tax authorities entrust Camrail with collecting and remitting these taxes, MINEPIA sends a veterinary agent. This is reasonable, since MINEPIA's fees are justified by the veterinary inspection. More often than not, this is either a summary or a virtual inspection; however, the veterinary agent needs to be present to issue the *laissez-passer* and collect the fees. The expectation from both MINEPIA and Camrail agents is that the traders sort out these payments among themselves. Typically, once the loading is well under way and the final composition of each freight car has been decided, money from all the traders involved is laboriously gathered together and counted, first at the level of each freight car, then at the level of each of the two groups of traders. A representative of each group then takes the cash to the office

---

[2] Provincial ordinance no. 45 of 17 September 1999.

where Camrail's cashier is located. The cashier counts the money again to make sure that the sums due are being paid in full (freight, VAT, tax advance), records the name of one trader per freight car as payer, then stamps a copy of each of the car vouchers as paid, and gives them to the traders. The veterinary agent tends to appear at some point during the loading process to take care of the relevant paperwork and receive the fees collected by the group representatives. Often, if the wait has been long, the veterinary agent finds refuge in Camrail's cashier's office, and it is there that all payments are sorted out. Whatever the case, it is important to note that this collection system does not allow MINEPIA or the tax authorities to know exactly who is paying the fees and taxes.

Remembrance of cattle past

Throughout my research, participants from all sectors were keen to impress on me what a distinctive activity cattle husbandry in Adamaoua is. It has long been an economic specialisation on the plateau, whose humid savannahs and natron-rich springs make it attractive for grazing. In the lamidate of Ngaoundéré's expanding sphere of influence during the second half of the nineteenth century, with the impetus of barter, trade, raids, tribute, taxation, marriage payments, and other gifts, cattle moved around a constellation of *dumɗe* (slave farming villages) and pasture areas following seasonal rhythms. However, it was the gradual decline of the periodic raiding of the lamidate's periphery as a source of captives, ivory, and numerous other spoils under German and French rule that gave cattle an unprecedented importance. Cattle became a more significant element of the finances of Adamaoua's *laamiɓe*. As noted in Chapter 1, the resulting fiscal pressures pushed many Fulbe to seek refuge in the bush in a process of 're-pastoralisation' in the 1920s and 1930s (Boutrais 1994: 179).[3]

The need to feed growing urban centres in the south and to supply armies became the two driving forces behind the colonial authorities' involvement in the cattle economy. In Ngaoundéré, the creation in 1920 of what later became the Compagnie Pastorale et Commerciale Africaine (or La Pastorale, as it is still commonly known in Adamaoua) marked an important watershed. The group of French World War One veterans who founded the company established an initial herd through a cash loan to the *laamiɗo* and entrusted it to a group of Fulbe cattle owners (Boutrais 1990). With the active support of the authorities, La

---

[3] Cattle was already a significant element in the operation of Ngaoundéré's raiding and trading apparatus in the late nineteenth century (Charreau 1905: 12–13). On cattle trade during the German period, see Temgoua (2014: 159).

102   'Cattle saves the day'

Pastorale's venture entailed a restructuring of an already substantial trade. Adjacent to the old city walls and contiguous to La Pastorale's compound, a large weekly cattle market was established in Ngaoundéré. During the 1920s, a dynamic trading network was consolidated around the market, a network in which La Pastorale and other expatriate traders rubbed shoulders with myriad *indigène* ('native') merchants, whom the authorities viewed with suspicion if not with overt hostility.[4] The bulk of the supplies came directly from Ngaoundéré cattle owners or from other newly established weekly markets in the surrounding areas. Herders would transport animals on the hoof to southern urban centres, first and foremost Yaoundé and Douala.

Because it made meat supplies for the troops critical and it had a lasting effect in expanding food demand in the main urban centres in the south (Guyer 1987), World War Two offered a favourable context for increased state interventionism in the cattle trade. During the war, the French administration became involved in purchasing cattle, sometimes directly from merchants and sometimes through Adamaoua's Société de Prévoyance (SP), the colonial 'provident society'.[5] Beyond these actions, which were aimed at solving periodic scarcity, the authorities imposed significant wartime regulatory measures. These included controlling the volume of cattle being sent from Adamaoua to the south and a system of commercialisation in Yaoundé whereby the administration enforced a single price and advanced payments to traders in cash. Given the difficulties that the administration encountered in recovering from the butchers the money it had advanced, the system of advance payments was short-lived.

Although the single price mechanism proved more lasting, its rigidity became increasingly untenable as the volume of cattle traded doubled in the second half of the 1940s. The *chef de région* voiced the dissatisfaction of Adamaoua's cattle farmers and traders in a letter to the High Commissioner in Yaoundé, dated 5 April 1950, in which he expressed his opposition to '*dirigistes* [interventionist] solutions, [which] we do not have the means to organise or impose'.[6] In 1951, when the authorities finally decided to 'liberalise cattle trade' (i.e. dissolve the single price

---

[4] Ngaoundéré's administrator, for example, wrote in 1924: 'The fact that our commercial centres are exclusively exploited by one single category of native traders, whom we are led to think have partnered in a *mise en coupe reglée* [ordered plundering] of the region, unavoidably contributes to a rise in [cattle] prices that disrupts [*desaxe*] markets, a rise so sharp as to be immoral' (ANY 11898/II, 'Rapport 4ème trimestre de 1924').

[5] ANY 2AC 6095, 'Ravitaillement en viande de Yaoundé'; ANY 2AC 9143, 'Société de Prévoyance de l'Adamaoua (1950)'. Adamaoua's SP, which was founded in 1937 and included *laamibe* and other office holders in its managing committee, intervened in cattle supplies to the south until 1949.

[6] ANY 1AC 551 (23), 'Région de l'Adamaoua, Ravitaillement en viande du Sud-Cameroun'.

system), they did it in the name of their reliance on 'the butchers' ability to organise' and on 'the collective spirit of Adamaoua's cattle farmers' (Lacrouts and Sarniguet 1965: vol. 1, 207) – a pronouncement that, in its omission of the role of traders, is indicative of the authorities' disposition towards them. The most enduring legacy of World War Two interventionism was the control of southbound cattle convoys. To ensure a constant and regular supply that would match demand, the authorities instituted in 1939 a system that controlled and modulated commercial flows along the main routes to Yaoundé at three strategic points: the veterinary posts of Banyo, Tibati, and Meiganga.[7] As the sector grew, such controls became increasingly problematic.

Underlying the controversy surrounding the single price system was the authorities' concern for consumers in Yaoundé and Douala. This reflected the broader policy goal of keeping the price of foodstuffs down during the post-war period (Guyer 1987: 126–30). In Ngaoundéré, this concern with rising prices translated into a sustained effort to control access to the cattle-trading profession and rid the sector of intermediaries. The *chef de région*'s political report of March 1946 is worth quoting at length in this regard:

[In order to bypass regulations], licensed [cattle] traders get additional licences for their buyers. These buyers go to the bush to find the Pullo herder who is on his way to Ngaoundéré and take all his cattle without even discussing the price. Then, once in Ngaoundéré, these animals are sold at a price that includes the intermediary's commission. We have tried to take measures to put an end to these practices by making licences more difficult to obtain, and forcing cattle farmers to come to Ngaoundéré in person. We have also established fixed trading hours for the cattle market, in an attempt to stop the ploys that would take place early in the morning or late in the afternoon: cattle purchased, taken away, brought back and sold a second time. But it remains legally difficult to prevent a native from obtaining a licence.[8]

Jean-Claude Froelich's detailed study of Ngaoundéré's 'economic life' circa 1950 offers a vivid picture of the challenges involved in enforcing the maintenance of 'arbitrarily very low [beef] prices' (1954a: 24). By then, Froelich notes, cattle trade had become the most dynamic and lucrative activity in the city. The cattle traders' delegate was an influential figure who sat on the Council of Dignitaries and represented the province in Douala's Chamber of Commerce. In relation to Yaoundé's supplies, the delegate managed to impose 'a certain discipline', but, given the circumstances, the traders' 'repugnance' (as Froelich puts it)

---

[7] Ordinance (*arrêté*) of 30 January 1939; later replaced by an ordinance of 8 November 1945.
[8] ANY 2AC 8566, 'Rapports Politiques, Région de l'Adamaoua, Subdivision de Ngaoundéré, Mars 1946', p. 10.

to send cattle to the capital is hardly surprising. The French administration could do little to stop trade to other Cameroonian destinations or exports to Nigeria (the latter continued unabated despite their formal prohibition, imposed by a 1946 ordinance).

During this period, other means of transporting cattle became available. In 1950, with the active support of the French administration, La Pastorale started using air transport for slaughtered cattle. Another foreign operator, the Compagnie d'Élevage et de Cultures de Cameroun (CECC), known locally by its owner's name, Calmette, followed suit soon afterwards. These shipments targeted the colonial civil service and military communities in Yaoundé, Douala, and other cities in the region such as Brazzaville, Pointe-Noire, and Libreville (Froelich 1954a: 27; Lacrouts and Sarniguet 1965: vol. 1, 181; Gondolo 1978: 139–40). Around the same time, some traders began to ship cattle to the south by truck. Far from replacing foot transport, as some had predicted, the use of road transport for the most part was restricted to select, heavyweight animals.[9]

Independence did not bring any drastic changes to cattle commercialisation. The 1960s was a period of increasing pressure on the state's role in shaping the market. The veterinary posts in Meiganga, Tibati, and Banyo faced difficulties in modulating commercial flows to the south. On the one hand, the authorities had proven incapable of anticipating the variations in demand in southern cities. Since the control posts were at least a month away from Yaoundé on foot, this meant that decisions on supply adjustments were almost always too slow to take effect. In theory, MINEPIA assigned a quota of cattle per week to each post for the year. In practice, however, these quotas were exceeded as a matter of course. Moreover, traders based at a distance from the control posts, such as those in Ngaoundéré relative to Meiganga and Tibati, and those in Tignere relative to Banyo, did not receive updated information on the numbers of cattle waiting to go through. On the other hand, the increased turnover – which, according to official figures, had almost doubled between 1951 and 1961 – accompanied by constant price rises had translated into much higher economic stakes. Certain groups of traders had more leverage than others on the officials in charge in particular posts. Obtaining favourable treatment could prove particularly valuable when the market was saturated, as in the situation Lacrouts and Sarniguet (1965: vol. 1, 177) reported in Tibati in 1964, when they found a waiting list of over 2,000 animals.

---

[9] During the 1950s, truck shipments accounted for only a modest proportion of the total, at around 10 per cent of all cattle shipped outside Adamaoua (Lacrouts and Sarniguet 1965: vol. 1, 154).

The 1970s saw the disappearance of foreign participants in the sector. La Pastorale's dominant position in cattle trade became less viable in an environment in which measures contributing to the 'indigenisation' of national economies were popular.[10] Early in that decade, small traders, who were being priced out of the market by La Pastorale's increased local purchases (more than 4,000 head per year at the time), made numerous complaints to the authorities (Boutrais 1990: 80). These resonated with government policymakers who envisaged state involvement in raising and marketing cattle. In 1975, a presidential decree declared that foreign operators should restrict themselves to raising livestock and were no longer authorised to buy livestock in markets. Its rationale was the protection of national operators from La Pastorale and Calmette's *concurrence déloyale* (unfair competition). This fatal blow coincided with the creation of state ranches and the promotion of private ones.[11] La Pastorale closed its slaughterhouse in Ngaoundéré and interrupted its air shipments. Its herds gradually decreased in size and the company was finally sold to a local businessman in the 1980s (Ngayap 1983: 261).

The completion of the Transcamerounais railway in 1974, which linked Ngaoundéré and Yaoundé, opened up the possibility of shipping cattle to the south by train. The railway practically eliminated road transport as a viable alternative for cattle. By the late 1970s, it had absorbed two-thirds of the shipments from Ngaoundéré (Gondolo 1978: 137). Road and railway transport also rendered obsolete the control system of cattle supplies. In principle, these means of transport were not subject to administrative quotas, and this provoked highly irregular supplies. The cost of railway transport coupled with rising cattle prices translated into higher capital requirements for traders.[12] The result,

---

[10] La Pastorale had based its success not only on the colonial authorities' protection but also on its integration in local socio-political structures. Thus, for example, although the titled land in Goumdjel, its main ranch in Adamaoua, was a mere 3,000 hectares, La Pastorale enjoyed use rights over more than 100,000 hectares of prime grazing land. These rights, for which it had secured approval from Fulbe chiefs, were not exclusive. Pasture was shared with other local cattle farmers (Boutrais 1990: 76). The downside of this strategy was its precarious legal footing. In the context of independent Cameroon, this situation became a source of vulnerability and subjected the company to increasing conflicts with neighbouring farmers.

[11] This was funded under the mantle of a World Bank-sponsored National Project for the Development of Livestock Farming, launched in 1974. The state ranches had very limited impact on the cattle sector beyond the inflationary episodes that their initial cattle purchases induced in Adamaoua markets (Boutrais 1990: 84). As for family ranches, well-connected urbanites, ranging from civil servants to merchants and truckers, were the main beneficiaries of the property and loans devoted to their promotion (Boutrais 1983: 127–42; 1990: 87–91; Douffisa 1993: 143–8).

[12] Transport by train was more expensive than transport on foot: 3,191 CFA francs compared with 1,150 francs per head (Gondolo 1978: 137). As far as cattle prices were concerned, a strong inflationary trend had been noticeable since the 1950s. In the decade from 1953 to 1963, for example, average prices increased 55 per cent

judging by official figures on licensed traders, was a smaller number of traders with a higher average turnover.[13] Because of the tsetse invasion in the north-eastern reaches of the Adamaoua plateau (Boutrais 1983; 1999b), these were also difficult years for cattle farming in Ngaoundéré's surrounding area.

The economic downturn of the mid-1980s affected cattle trade as greatly as other activities. In 1983, an outbreak of rinderpest had already seriously disrupted commercial flows. The drop in demand and the steep fall in average prices in 1986 were to have lasting effects.[14] Government authorisation of massive imports of foreign beef also depressed the internal market (FAO 2003: 100). Moreover, although it created some extremely profitable (and unauthorised) export opportunities in Nigeria, the 1994 CFA franc devaluation resulted in substantial capital losses and even bankruptcy for many cattle traders. As we saw in our earlier account of Badjo's career in Ngaoundal, the initial years of the crisis were also chaotic as far as the organisation of transport was concerned. Railway company officials had free rein to decide whose cattle received priority and used this discretionary power to obtain an additional income in bribes from traders. Ngaoundéré and Ngaoundal stations became the foci of intense conflicts between different groups of traders.

The most significant attempt to find a way out of the turbulence of those years was a 1990 meeting of delegates representing the main cattle-trading groups in the country – a structure of representation that, as we have seen, had its origins in the colonial period. The leading figures of what later, in 1993, became Cameroon's National Association of Cattle Traders (ANCBC) seized this opportunity to put in place a self-regulating mechanism that would stop excess supplies from reaching southern markets and therefore prevent a decline in prices. Each group of traders would be allocated a number of freight cars per week in accordance with their estimated market share, and train shipments would take place only twice a week from the main stations. Moreover, the railway company would only deal with each group's elected delegate. The system worked reasonably well for a few years and led to a significant recovery in cattle prices. However, its opponents grew in number and strength. On the one hand, some important farmers who had recently

---

(Lacrouts and Sarniguet 1965: vol. 1, 208). In the late 1960s, prices rose even more sharply, amounting to another 50 per cent increase in the 1968–73 period (Boutrais 1990: 80).

[13] Although they must be used with caution, figures on licensed traders show a clear downward trend: 92 in 1964, 80 in 1971, 61 in 1974, 54 in 1976, and 42 in 1977 (Deen and Johnson 1972: 23; Gondolo 1978: 133).

[14] In Meiganga, for example, the value of a castrated bull went from 117,000 CFA francs in 1985 to 79,000 francs in 1987. Albert Douffissa, who was a veterinarian in Mbéré District at the time, offers a vivid description of this period (Douffissa 1993: 193, 204).

decided to involve themselves in the trade and butchery sides of the business were dissatisfied with the limitations the quota system imposed on their operations. On the other hand, numerous small traders complained that the delegates systematically favoured big traders over small ones (PRASAC 2003: 73). At a time when the government needed to prove its commitment to liberalisation, the opponents of the quota system succeeded in getting the support of the authorities. The mechanism whereby supplies were regulated collectively came to an end in 1995. In Ngaoundéré, a second group operating alongside the ANCBC's Comité was formed in 1994 under the acronym of ELCOBCAM. As we have seen, the railway company has since distributed freight cars evenly between the two existing groups.

Cattle trade as an economic niche

The market infrastructure that has emerged out of the history I have summarised above imposes serious obstacles on entering the cattle-trading profession. Take a rather typical market day for Alhadji Badjo, whose acquaintance readers made in Chapter 1. I accompanied him to Tello's *tikke* (cattle market) on a Tuesday morning in late August 2005.[15] Tello is a village whose growth dates back to the migration of cattle-less herders from Far North Cameroon in the 1920s and 1930s (Boutrais 1991: 103). Because of its strategic position between the pastoral plateau and the agricultural plain, Tello is now one of the main commercial hubs of the eastern part of Vina District. The pickup truck that Badjo shared with other traders was parked not far from the small mosque, at a short distance from the market precinct. As he approached the market, the varied coats of the cattle and the colourful attire of customers contrasted with the bright green grass and blue sky. It was almost noon and the trading was well underway (Figure 3.2). In a matter of seconds, Badjo embarked on the customary round of exchanging greetings with numerous colleagues, friends, and acquaintances. Given the need to make the most of the few hours that markets last, courtesies are cut short. Traders and intermediaries circulate among the clusters of herders and cattle. The larger their purchasing needs, the more incessant the movement. *Jangugo luumo* (to read the market) is how traders refer to their preliminary survey of the market grounds, when they get a sense of

---

[15] Weekly cattle markets are known throughout Adamaoua as *tikke*, in reference to the ticket or receipt market participants receive after paying transaction fees (Boutrais 2001: 55). The term apparently dates back to the 1920s. In the recollection of some informants, drawing on stories they had heard from pioneers in the trade, the establishment of the *tikke* system was associated with the increase in the cattle trade to meet the needs of the colonial civil service and army.

Figure 3.2 Cattle market, Tello, August 2005

the kind of animals available and the starting prices. To equate cultural artefacts (a cattle market, in this case) with texts is a trope that is familiar to anthropologists. Seeing traders in action, however, gives us an idea of the performative work involved in reading such a text.

Badjo first needed to assess which animals were for sale and which were not – many animals are taken to the market simply to accompany the rest and to keep them as calm as possible. Moreover, many animals are not for sale individually, as owners prefer to sell in lots. Approaching any cattle cluster entails greetings and pleasantries, whose intensity and length vary depending on the existing relationship with those involved. At times, particularly in the early stages of the market, Badjo might ask for quotes for animals he did not intend to buy in order to get a sense of the market mood and price levels. Quotes may not be forthcoming, often because the actual seller is engaged in another transaction elsewhere and the herder in charge may have only a vague notion, if any, of starting prices for the animals. Withholding a quote temporarily can also be a way of testing the buyer's interest, although it may discourage buyers who are short of patience or time. While inquiring about prices, Badjo silently calculated how much he could get for a specific animal in Yaoundé, given that animal's health and butchery potential. Bearing this in mind, he could possibly make an offer that set in motion the haggling process. All this he tried to do subtly and swiftly. Every now and then, he had to put his buying targets on hold, since courtesy demanded that he did not interfere when another trader was negotiating.

First approaches are almost always inconclusive; buyers generally try to show as little interest as possible to avoid weakening their bargaining position. Expressing too much eagerness goes against notions of composure and self-mastery that govern market etiquette. Playfulness constitutes a basic resource to keep people talking while diverting attention from the commercial issue at hand. It can bring a touch of lightness and assuage tensions. This is where other traders, intermediaries, herders, and farmers' aides become useful props to create an amiable atmosphere conducive to reaching a deal. When approaching people they do not know or know only vaguely, a sense of humour can help traders create a narrative thread for future meetings and thus lead to a fruitful relationship.

Before concluding any transaction, Badjo typically engaged in a preliminary negotiation on the merits of the animals and their price. There was also room for less open bargaining. Traders often ask for private asides with sellers, intermediaries, or other traders. Unless they are convinced they have found a definite bargain, traders return to the same animals several times before reaching an acceptable price or finally deciding against purchasing them. On the one hand, they need time to assess how such a purchase might compare with other available options as well as how it might fit with their budget and commercial needs. On the other, expressing doubts is a way of putting pressure on sellers, who could find themselves with unsold animals at the end of the market day. Buyers know only too well, however, that delaying the closing of a deal can backfire. There is always the possibility of some other trader getting the upper hand.

Badjo was looking for cattle with butchery potential that would sell well in Yaoundé and cover his transport expenses. Not all traders are in Badjo's position. Many traders in Tello are *baranda* (small-scale traders) who have not yet raised enough capital to try their luck in markets outside Adamaoua. They specialise in buying in two or three markets in Vina District to then sell in Ngaoundéré on Thursdays, where prices are significantly higher. Quick operations of *sooda–sorrita* (buying and reselling) characterise their brand of trade. They look out for exceptionally cheap animals and often buy cattle when the market is in its closing stages and sellers are desperate to sell their animals. At other times, they try courting farmers at the market, who may let them have one or two unsold head on credit. There are also numerous *sakaina* (intermediaries) who do not plan on buying any cattle themselves but rather try to facilitate other people's transactions. They do this by getting a seller to commit to sell to them at a particular price, then finding a buyer ready to pay a higher price and pocketing the difference. The services of intermediaries can be especially useful when a trader needs to buy numerous cattle in the relatively short span of a market day. This particular afternoon, Badjo had bought only three animals and had not dealt with intermediaries.

Once the animal is purchased, the buyer's mark is painted on it; the colour indicates its destination. In each market there are organised convoys to take cattle to the next stage in the local trade circuit so that traders do not need to make separate arrangements for transport. Although the burden is shared, generally it is the seller who is responsible for making the payments involved in the transaction, including the communal tax, the veterinary fee, and the compulsory contribution to the local cattle farmers' union. After more than an hour of energetic business, Badjo noticed that it was time for the *zuura* prayer. As we walked towards the market mosque, he told me that he did not have ambitious plans that particular week. Before he could venture into more substantial purchases, he needed to recover the money butchers in Yaoundé owed him from the previous month. This week, if he got the freight car space that he had requested, he intended to ship six head of cattle south. This was still early in his move from Ngaoundal to Ngaoundéré.

Badjo's day at Tello's market gives an indication of the exclusionary dynamics that derive from the sociolegal framework in which transactions take place. This was one of the key elements of Abner Cohen's celebrated analysis of the landlord system that structured cattle trade in Ibadan (Nigeria) after independence (Cohen 1969). Although much more fluid than the situation described by Cohen, in part because there is no equivalent to the important role membership in Sufi brotherhoods played in traders' professional identity in Nigeria in the early 1960s, cattle trade in Cameroon today also involves operating in a market where price levels are not publicised and reliable information about prices depends on intense and active socialisation with participants in the cattle economy. Fluctuations in cattle supply and demand, resulting both from the seasonal character of the sector and from a volatile economic environment, also make it advisable for traders to diversify into cattle raising and fattening. To do so, they must secure access to affordable grazing land, which in Adamaoua's rural landscape depends as much on formal legal entitlement as on harmonious relations with chiefs and villagers. Furthermore, cattle from weekly markets such as the one in Tello and from the traders' own livestock holdings comprise only part of their supplies. Traders obtain some of those supplies directly from cattle farmers, outside official markets. Those farmers would not agree to such unauthorised transactions if the buyer were a stranger.[16]

---

[16] Concerns related both to animal health and to taxation and price controls led to the outlawing of cattle transactions outside official markets in the colonial era. This prohibition has been maintained ever since (Article 19, Decree no. 76/420,

Lack of market security also makes the cattle trade unattractive to newcomers. This is not only linked to cattle theft and assaults on market-goers on the road perpetrated by *jargina* (armed robbers), known also as *coupeurs de route* due to their roadblock tactics, which, in northern Cameroon, is a chronic problem (Burnham 1996a; Saïbou Issa 2004; 2010; Roitman 2005). The lack of standardised systems for the identification of animals, such as ear tags, the verbal character of almost all transactions, the absence of market scales or rigorous veterinary controls, and the prevalence of payments in cash all contribute to heightened risks. When confronted with breaches of contract on the part of butchers, for example, only traders who are well integrated within existing commercial networks can benefit from the collective pressure of their peers. This is a key sanction mechanism in a context where the court system and other formal legal remedies are not realistic options. Similarly, the non-professionalisation of some of the auxiliary services required from the moment cattle are purchased until they are sold – market brokerage, marking cattle with paint or branding irons, transport, herding of convoys from supply to destination markets, and loading cattle in freight cars or trucks – makes access to those services difficult for outsiders.

This socio-legal infrastructure accounts for the significance of what Cohen (1969: 19) called 'essentially non-economic factors' that determine who acquires knowledge and experience, builds relationships, and raises the financial capital required to succeed in the cattle trade. In Adamaoua, such factors have turned this trade into a niche that, with almost no exceptions, only men who are Muslim and speak Fulfulde can access. 'There is not a single scale in Cameroon cattle markets,' a well-known trader lamented in March 2004 in one of the meetings the ANCBC regularly organised in Ngaoundéré during my fieldwork. His calls for the 'modernisation' of the sector – and those of other traders – often highlighted the need for more 'transparency' in the markets. It was not only a matter of accurate weighing but also of tighter veterinary controls and safeguards against cattle of dubious origin. Veterinary controls of cattle entering the market grounds and the veterinary fee paid for every transaction are meant to ensure that only healthy animals are traded. Yet this guarantee is tenuous at best. Similarly, the *sarkin sanu* (chief of cattle) and other representatives of the respective *laamido* or village chief, who, as auxiliaries of the veterinary services, are entrusted with watching over the safety of transactions and preventing stolen cattle

---

14 September 1976). In spite of this, transactions outside markets have been a structural constant in the sector until the present day. In the 1960s, Lacrouts and Sarniguet (1965: vol. 1, 161) estimated that established markets accounted for only 20 per cent of cattle purchases made by Adamaoua traders. Douffissa's work (1993: 208) shows that this phenomenon reached enormous proportions in the Meiganga area in the early 1980s.

from entering markets, have no real means of fulfilling their role other than their moral authority. Cases in which these 'traditional' authorities purportedly engage in transactions involving stolen cattle surface every now and then.

In private, many traders admit that they like the present functioning of markets, because, in spite of the risks, it rewards their skills. They must have a good eye to make reliable estimates of basic information such as the animals' weight and legitimate ownership, or the absence of disease. They must also possess a keen sense of how well certain animals are going to sell at specific destination points. If traders' prospects largely hinge upon this mixture of observation skills and market exposure and know-how, how are these acquired and transmitted? Although there are remarkable exceptions, the vast majority of traders, even when they grow up in urban environments, have absorbed pastoral knowledge since childhood. This knowledge, however, needs to be supplemented with specific commercial skills that are acquired at a later stage through different channels. It is possible to develop familiarity with the workings of the market and its participants by working as errand boy, branding cattle, loading them into trucks and trains, or taking herds from their grazing areas to the market for sale. Young people may also work as herders in charge of taking cattle convoys to the south, as agents of farmers or traders in southern markets, or as assistants to intermediaries, traders, and butchers.

The learning curve of potential traders depends on how important their assigned tasks in these subordinate occupations are. Farmers, traders, and butchers may be more inclined to trust sons, nephews, or brothers – a preference that can lead to faster induction into the trade. Similarly, patrons who marry their daughters to a client may be more invested in creating opportunities for their sons-in-law. More experienced traders accompany novice traders on their first forays into the trade. As Boutrais (2001: 60) noted, this 'following' somebody, as it is expressed in Fulfulde (from the same verbal root of the *tokke* units discussed in Chapter 1), does not necessarily involve any financial arrangement. Consider, for example, how Badjo's brother-in-law first took him to Yaoundé's market. At other times, the transmission of professional know-how is mediated by employment and partnership.

The cattle trade presupposes insertion into multiple networks. Relationships with fellow traders are of critical importance, and competition can be fierce. Those specialising in certain markets frown upon the encroachment of traders who normally work in other areas, which is why Badjo had to tread carefully after he shifted his main source of supplies from Ngaoundal to Ngaoundéré. Small-scale traders are often undercut by more established traders if they are perceived as interfering in their transactions. However, despite competition and marked hierarchical differences, there is also a considerable degree of cooperation and mutual assistance. In markets, colleagues seek each other's advice on the health, weight, origin, and price of animals. While sharing a ride to a market, waiting for the weekly distribution of freight cars, or spending long hours in a sleeping berth on the way to Yaoundé, traders share information about market trends, existing opportunities, and the financial situation of particular butchers. Advice may be offered and news shared, but these are also spaces in which misguidance, exaggeration, and deliberate misinformation proliferate (Douffissa 1993: 204). Furthermore, cooperation may involve joint purchasing of animals, sharing vehicles, lending money for a few days, passing on assigned freight car space, and possibly sharing clients' orders. It also means that, when faced with difficulties in contractual relations with farmers and butchers, traders can count on the support of their peers.

As Jean Boutrais (2001: 58) has pointed out: '[Cattle transactions] are inscribed on a social formation that goes beyond cattle traders and encompasses a whole series of other participants linked by ethnicity and kinship, and by relations of dependency and clientelism.' This quote aptly underscores the fact that these relationships, as much as those between traders themselves, are power relationships. The 'other participants' in the cattle sector include farmers and butchers, herders and market authorities, *sakaina* and vendors of veterinary products, truck owners and railway company employees, *chargeurs* and *convoyeurs*, gendarmes, veterinarians, village chiefs, and tax officials. Long-term association with a farmer gives traders precious access to cattle on credit. Good contacts with railway managers may mean extra freight car space. Close monitoring of a butcher can anticipate and pre-empt a default. The creation and consolidation of these ties are major challenges every neophyte faces.

In a context where sellers generally demand instant payment and butchers invariably buy on credit, capital can represent a significant obstacle for people interested in entering the profession. Cattle loans or gifts from one's parents or other relatives – and, even more commonly, inheritances – feature prominently in the life histories of traders. However cattle are accumulated, they constitute only the starting point for establishment as a trader, if an individual is already on the way to becoming one. When Badjo's father died, for example, he was able to make the most of a very modest inheritance because he had worked in the markets surrounding Ngaoundal for almost five years and had devoted his savings to buying a few head of cattle. The idealised *cursus* (mode of advancement) from herding tasks to cattle trading described in earlier studies (Boutrais 2001) is more and more distant from the present range of possibilities. Those who take convoys to the south may be the exception. Traders who have mainly relied on savings from employment in the cattle sector to finance their first steps are in the minority.

Traders also tap into other sources of finance outside personal or family savings. Aspiring traders turn to cattle owners who are willing to entrust their animals on credit. Only tested and experienced traders, however, normally benefit from such opportunities; it is hardly ever an option for those getting started in the trade. Although these situations remain exceptional, they play a central role in traders' financial strategies, particularly since a single transaction often involves much larger numbers of cattle than marketplace transactions. Several farmers in Djerem and Vina Districts, for example, would entrust their livestock to Badjo, often giving him up to three months for repayment.

Although most traders have opened accounts with them, banks and microfinance institutions have largely ignored cattle traders as potential loan recipients. Managers in these financial institutions often stereotype cattle traders as unsophisticated, semi-literate money hoarders. Instead, most traders take part in one or several *tontines* (rotating savings and credit associations), generally known in Adamaoua by the Hausa word *adashi*, but these represent only a marginal part of cattle-trade financing. More important for traders' capitalisation is the establishment of symbiotic relationships with people who are active in other economic domains. Badjo, for example, for years received injections of funds from two merchants based in Ngaoundal whenever they had excess cash flow. In a small town where there was only one poorly managed microfinance institution and no banks, circulating profits through agreements with cattle traders was an attractive alternative for them.

The circulation of cattle as a regulatory target

Controlling the circulation of cattle and the people around them has historically been a persistent if intractable governmental concern. A major incentive for tighter controls has been the need to contain the spread of diseases. One of the most enduring measures in this regard was the establishment of a *barrière sanitaire* (health barrier) in the village of Mbé, which the colonial veterinary services set up to avoid cattle coming into Adamaoua from the north of the plateau. This was formally lifted only in 2001. The controversy that always surrounded Mbé's barrier shows that animal health objectives have not always been easily separable from other goals. For decades, the supply of veterinary services has been premised on the payment of an annual tax per head of cattle and numerous other fees. After independence, the strong veterinary corps created by Ahidjo's government became ubiquitous.[17] As Jean Boutrais (1999b:

---

[17] Colonial livestock administration on Adamaoua plateau divided the area into five *directions de secteurs d'élevage* (administrative units), with their respective services,

622) wrote: 'Besides health controls, the Ministry of Animal Husbandry intervened in all stages of animal production, including rangeland management, composition of herds and legal norms for cattle markets and shipments.' These multifarious tasks and goals have been reflected in the legal texts that have regulated the circulation of cattle since the colonial era. In them, circulation outside the designated *pistes à bétail* (cattle trails), commercial transactions outside established markets, and slaughtering outside the official slaughterhouses are all outlawed. However, there are serious obstacles to the enforcement of these prohibitions, which are currently contained in a couple of old decrees.[18] These obstacles only increased after the 1990s, when veterinary officials saw their numbers dwindle and their powers decline.[19]

The inventory, demarcation, and upkeep of cattle trails have attracted considerable energy since the 1930s (Fréchou 1966: 79). The map of official trails in place during my fieldwork had been established by two ministerial ordinances in the 1980s.[20] Yet, despite such efforts, 'the systematic failure to restrict cattle circulation to designated trails' (PRASAC 2003: 77) was widely acknowledged. In an interview in November 2004, the MINEPIA provincial delegate did not evade the issue: 'We lack the means to prevent [the unauthorised circulation of cattle]. There is much talk about cattle trails ... Well, frankly, once animals leave Ngaoundéré and go back into the bush, there is little we can do.' This admission of impotence coexists with an often-voiced concern with exports to Nigeria. This cross-border trade, which is subject to elusive and expensive export licences, poses the paradox of an economic activity that continues unabated despite routinely violating official rules. Its vitality relies on enduring but flexible arrangements between traders and a constellation of local authorities at border-crossing points who draw unofficial revenue from the trade.[21]

---

including 20 vaccination stations and 19 veterinary dispensaries. This infrastructure was further expanded in the 1960s with support from the European Development Fund (Boutrais 1999b: 608).

[18] Decree no. 76/420 of 14 September 1976; modified by decree no. 86/755 of 24 June 1986.

[19] Readers will remember the reference in the Introduction to efforts to reduce the Ministry's payroll through programmes encouraging voluntary departure and early retirement and the decision to liberalise veterinary services and products (Boutrais 1999b; Gros 1993).

[20] Ordinance no. 105/MINEPIA of 9 June 1984; ordinance no. 02/MINEPIA of 20 July 1988.

[21] On cattle exports from Adamaoua to Nigeria, see Muñoz (2014: 318–22). This cross-border trade is subject to drastic seasonal fluctuations because of the impracticability of trails during the rainy season, among other reasons. Commercial flows are also closely tied to currency exchange rates. The trade is attractive for its low capital requirements (cattle are transported on foot as opposed to other, more expensive means of transport) and quick turnover (sales are paid immediately, as opposed to other markets where sales

Restricting transactions to established markets is not any more workable than curbing the use of unofficial trails. As mentioned earlier, nothing prevents traders from sourcing a substantial number of their animals directly from farmers with large herds. Nonetheless, substantial trade flows go through the network of markets that have Ngaoundéré as their centre. These weekly markets constitute an essential site in the apparatus of governmental control. Markets presuppose a designated time and place for commercial transactions conducted in public. As happens in Tello, no matter how small or inaccessible, any *tikke* features the presence of, at the very least, a veterinary agent from MINEPIA, a *sarkin sanu*, and a municipal official. In large markets such as Ngaoundéré, numerous other staff control the entry of animals and keep count of them.[22] As their vernacular name (*tikke*) indicates, markets are also places where transactions are registered in writing. Whenever a purchase takes place, sellers have the responsibility of declaring it on the spot and making the required payments per head of cattle. It is rare for buyers and sellers not to make these payments. Officials keep a handwritten record of the parties to every transaction and the number of cattle involved, although the issuing of receipts has long ceased to be established practice.

On the other hand, cattle markets (and slaughterhouses) in Adamaoua have long been known to provide an opportunity for the diversion of public revenue. An article from the state-owned *Cameroon Tribune* gives a sense of the prevalence of this phenomenon (Beya 2003). The reporter draws attention to the discrepancy between the taxes collected and the number of cattle traded and slaughtered in Mbéré District. According to the tax authorities, in Meiganga, where estimated levels of activity in the cattle sector should have generated CFAF 6 million in veterinary taxes per year, the municipality had never collected more than 600,000. In Dir, another municipality in Mbéré District, where 'cattle is the unrivalled backbone of the economy', things were 'even more serious':

On the occasion of a recent sub-prefect's visit, voices rose crying out against the harm that this situation is causing to the *commune* [municipality]. Of five cattle markets in Dir, the tax-collecting officer noted that apart from the revenue coming from Dir-Centre, he has never received any money from the other veterinary centres. Who specifically profits from veterinary taxes? It is difficult,

on credit are more common). The Nigerian government's devaluation of the naira in June 2016, together with the insecurity resulting from the Boko Haram insurgency, reduced this trade to almost nothing in that year's dry season. Earlier studies of cattle trade across other sections of the Cameroon–Nigeria border include Boutrais, Herrera, and Bopda (2002) and Engola-Oyep and Herrera (1997).

[22] The problems involved in interpreting the numbers generated, which are used in official statistics, are discussed at length in Hubert Fréchou's study of the 1960s (Fréchou 1966: 68). Counting practices have not changed much since then.

very difficult to tell with any certainty, since accusations are coming from all sides. Mayors accuse veterinary agents. These, in turn, retort that it is municipal officials in charge of collecting taxes, acting on mayors' behalf, who are to blame. In short, there is some sort of neglect on the part of the authorities and a set of collusive practices [between them and traders and butchers]. (Beya 2003)

Such practices had motivated the launch of a nationwide Programme de Sécurisation des Recettes de l'Élevage et la Pêche (Programme for Enhanced Revenue Reliability in Animal Husbandry and Fisheries or PSREP) in 2000 (Muñoz 2014). Indeed, it was because the PSREP insisted on the involvement of the tax authorities in the process of collecting these funds that news items like this one appeared.

Before the PSREP, the management of veterinary fees had been the sole prerogative of MINEPIA. As the ministry's provincial delegate explained to me, 'The programme's aim was to steer funds that sometimes got lost [in the collection process], because there were many collectors involved. It was a matter of the state being able to reclaim its own revenue.' By the end of 2003, after overcoming a period of silent resistance from veterinary officials and pragmatically choosing to focus on Adamaoua's largest markets and slaughterhouses, the programme managed to curb the most glaring instances of misappropriation. As a senior official in Adamaoua's tax administration summed up with palpable satisfaction:

Since the *chefs de secteur* [heads of cattle-grazing zones] work in rural areas for the most part, they behaved *en electron libre* [as loose cannons]. They undertook the collection of these duties, only to put the money in their pockets. The state has decided to protect these funds [against such practices] and we have succeeded.

The routine irregularities that the PSREP sought to address go to show how, in spite of their highly public nature, even markets can prove elusive regulatory targets. The fleeting crowds of traders and herds gathering in the market grounds every week leave no trace other than the handwritten records established by officials whose integrity is questioned as a matter of course.

If the circulation of cattle from grazing lands through a network of markets to slaughterhouses offers opportunities for government control that are unevenly utilised, what about the circulation of people concerned with the trade? Controlling access to cattle markets has been a long held but difficult to realise ambition. As the *chef de région*'s report of 1946 quoted earlier acknowledged, attempts to bar intermediaries from Ngaoundéré's market were rather futile. The crusade against what Froelich (1954a: 24), in an eloquent choice of words, called *le pullulement* (swarming) of intermediaries appears again and again in the reports and correspondence of colonial officials. Froelich recounts how, in the course of a few years, the Ngaoundéré authorities managed to cut the number of the city's cattle traders from 190 to 60. This success must have been largely illusory.[23] It was not enough to limit the number of licences without offering any further support to authorised traders. Little got in the way of those officially excluded from operating.

After independence, the Ministry of Animal Husbandry introduced a requisite *agrément* (administrative authorisation) for all cattle traders. Compliance with this, however, ceased to be enforced with rigour in the early 1990s, a sign of the depth of the economic crisis and the political unrest of those years. Notionally, traders should have to apply for annual authorisation and pay the accompanying fees every January. But, in the last decades, prefects have not been able to issue the list of authorised cattle traders until much later in the year.[24] In the early months of the year, veterinary officials periodically remind market-goers of the need to submit their applications. Their calls are ignored for months until a combination of persuasion and mild threats of sanctions compel some traders to comply. Only by the year's end does MINEPIA put together a minimally satisfactory number of applications from Ngaoundéré-based traders and sends the list to the Vina District prefect for publication. 'To trade cattle without an authorisation, that is *le maquis*,' I heard the provincial head of MINEPIA remind traders in a fit of exasperation in a September 2004 meeting. The traders present, who happened to be among those who reluctantly applied for an authorisation every year, also knew that, if such an equivalence existed, it would mean that life in the *maquis* was something banal and inconsequential. The traders' failure to comply is intimately linked to the redundancy of this particular formality. Quite simply, although, according to regulations, authorisations are required to purchase livestock in markets,[25] the lack of such authorisations does not bar anyone from trading.

Ensuring that all traders obtain the requisite *patente* is also besieged by difficulties. These annual licences, which fall within the remit of the tax authorities, should be applied for by new entrants to the trade within two months of their start date. Already established traders have up to two months to renew their licence every year. The cost of the licence is determined by the previous year's turnover (or, in the case of new entrants, an estimate of their projected turnover). Traders with a low

---

[23] In 1956, the authorities reported 97 cattle traders in Ngaoundéré, who were said to form 'an increasingly numerous, rich and powerful corporation' (ANY 2AC 8570, 'Rapport Annuel 1956', p. 53). A 1957 report on veterinary services observed that across Adamaoua '[cattle traders'] numbers have never been as high' (ANY 1AC 3406, 'Région de l'Adamaoua, Centre d'Élevage, 1957', p. 42).

[24] Although authorisations are MINEPIA's responsibility, prefects are in charge of publishing the official lists. In 2003, for example, this was not done until 11 October. In the following two years, the list came out in early November in 2004 and mid-October in 2005.

[25] Article 22, decree no. 76/420, of 14 September 1976.

turnover (less than CFAF 15 million at the time of my fieldwork) are exempt from the licence as well as from income and value-added taxes; they are required to pay the *impôt libératoire* instead. Unlike the authorisation, these obligations involve a portable document that is liable to be checked. As far as access to markets is concerned, these documents are not checked when entering market grounds. However, on my visits to cattle markets in Ngaoundéré's surrounding area, I witnessed how sometimes police and gendarmes at checkpoints would ask self-declared traders to show their licence or *impôt libératoire*. While this can become a source of annoyance that many traders would rather do without, it is nothing that cannot be settled with some small payment to inquisitive 'bureaucrats in uniform' (Blundo and Glassman 2013). As a result, at the start of my fieldwork, it did not take me long to realise that many intermediaries and traders operated without paying either a licence or the *impôt libératoire*. Others opted to pay the *impôt libératoire*, although sometimes at a lower rate than the one indicated for the type of activity and turnover involved.[26] Other common tactics included small-scale traders pairing up to get a licence or operating under the cover provided by the licence of a more senior trader whom they regarded as their patron. Traders who chose to apply for a licence tended to be among those whose business took them to markets outside Adamaoua.

Taxing the cattle trade

In 2002, as the Ministry of Finance launched its *direction par objectifs* (management by objectives) programme, Adamaoua's tax authorities became subject to periodic revenue targets. From that point of view, 2004 was a challenging year. The creation of the Direction des Grandes Entreprises (Large Taxpayers Office or DGE) the year before had meant that the files of the seven largest businesses based in the province had been transferred to Yaoundé. Also in 2003, the completion of the Chad–Cameroon pipeline had caused a drastic drop in the Exxon-led consortium's expenditure in Adamaoua. These changes translated into severely

---

[26] The *impôt libératoire* includes four different rates (categories A to D), depending on the kind of activity and annual turnover. According to their testimonies, traders were taxed at a more favourable rate in exchange for paying CFAF 2,000–5,000 to municipal officials 'off the books'. At the time, in Vina District, the *impôt libératoire* category B amounted to CFAF 21,000. The *patente de base* for cattle traders was normally set at CFAF 56,000. It is worth noting that if traders had been paying the *impôt libératoire* at the applicable rate (category D), this would have amounted to CFAF 75,000–100,000, which would have made it more expensive than the *patente*. The reason for this is that the *impôt libératoire* is a global tax that exempts one from other taxes, such as VAT or commercial income tax. The paradox is that, as regards cattle trade, such exonerations are not respected in practice. Under present arrangements, the 1999 ordinance imposes a tax advance on the commercial income tax of anyone who transports cattle by train.

diminished collection figures and put pressure on the provincial tax services to find alternative sources of revenue. Targeting cattle trade made sense within this effort of *élargissement de l'assiette fiscale* (broadening of the taxpayer base).

The railway shipments to southern markets were perhaps an obvious place to start, but collecting taxes from cattle trade can prove both difficult and expensive. The small size of business units, the instability and seasonality of trade flows, the dearth of records of transactions, and the limited use of banking are some of the factors that explain this. There are few available 'handles' (as tax professionals call them) to tax such an activity. Yet, once a week, traders in Ngaoundéré use Camrail's freight cars to send anything between 300 and 500 cattle to Yaoundé. The authorities' decision to use this particular tax handle was not particularly striking.[27] Nor was it a novelty. As we have seen, an income tax advance based on the value of these shipments had already been established in 1999. It was now a matter of taking that previous step to its logical conclusion and ensuring that the traders paying those advances also applied for licences and filed tax returns. A seminar on 'the modernisation of the cattle trading profession' organised by the ANCBC in February 2004 offered a warning of things to come. A provincial senior tax official, one of the seminar guest speakers, followed a review of the tax rules and regulations to which traders were subject with the admonition to 'start paying taxes before things get serious'.

The 'operation', as the tax authorities called it, was launched through a letter dated 10 August 2004. Signed by the Ministry of Finance's *Directeur Général des Impôts* (General Manager of Taxes or DGI), the letter was addressed to Camrail's chief executive officer. Drawing on the established vocabulary of the ongoing nationwide tax reform, the letter lamented the fact that cattle traders had chosen to ignore 'their duty to contribute to the funding of public spending' and announced his intention to '*sécuriser les recettes* [enhance revenue reliability] in this domain'. He requested that Camrail's station managers require traders wishing to ship cattle by train to produce a *plan de localisation* (business location map), a valid business licence, and a certificate of tax payment issued in the last three months. In addition, he wanted station managers to report every month to the local tax centres on the numbers of cattle shipped on their trains per trader.

Having been sent to Camrail's headquarters in Douala, the letter became public knowledge in Ngaoundéré only in late August. Its effects

---

[27] A historical example of the revenue potential of such nodes of circulation is the influx of cattle to the most renowned of Adamaoua's *lahore* (natron-rich natural springs), which used to take place during the dry season in the colonial era and provided an opportunity for the imposition of levies by *laamiɓe* and chiefs (Boutrais 1974; Delcroix 1937).

began to be felt soon afterwards. In early September, I witnessed a couple of instances in which traders who had been allocated the freight car space they had requested decided at the last minute to withdraw. In one case, the trader had not reported any commercial activity to the authorities; in the other case, a trader who operated under the *impôt libératoire* had declared a level of activity well below his actual turnover. Others, in similarly irregular situations, overcame their misgivings and carried on with their weekly transactions.

Individual tactics aside, traders also mobilised collectively. In anticipation of foreseeable events, Ngaoundéré's traders held an internal meeting on 2 September 2004. The ANCBC president set the meeting's agenda and led the discussion. He made a few introductory comments on the DGI's letter. In his view, the letter was a reaction to the decline in recent years of cattle shipments by train to the south, on which the collection of tax advances depended. He then went over the different tax regulations. Some disagreement followed on specific issues such as official deadlines for obtaining licences and for filing quarterly tax forms. These were expediently settled by one of the wealthier traders, who phoned his accountant on the spot and provided precise answers to their questions. Once this summary of existing regulations was completed, the president described the inconsistencies in existing arrangements for the collection of tax advances and speculated about the potential implications of the new measures announced by the DGI. Under the present system, there was a mismatch between nominal freight car users (a single name per car) and the actual owners of the animals in each car. This discrepancy, he concluded, left the tax authorities without the means to assess individual traders' turnover.

The later part of the meeting was devoted to a discussion of proposed courses of action and, specifically, of the traders' collective position in future meetings with state representatives. A variety of opinions was expressed. One trader declared that he trusted the judgement of fellow members: 'We, who have not studied, for the longest time have not sought to learn our work properly.' Another asked the president to negotiate with the tax authorities for an amnesty of past dues. Most emphasised particular problems in the tax system. On behalf of his client, the accountant who had been contacted on the phone showed up in person for a few minutes to assuage fears about the worst-case scenario that could result.

After more discussion, the president summarised their conclusions. They worked in an economic environment in which unauthorised traders carried out more than two-thirds of transactions. He insisted that this placed them in an advantageous position. They needed to detach themselves from petty traders who lacked the means to become 'true professionals'. He assured them that bringing to the table the issue of an amnesty concerning past dues would be a tactical mistake. He suggested that their approach should be to champion a process of 'regularisation' of business licences. 'Can we all pay and get our papers straight?' he asked everyone present. Doing so would allow them to make demands rather than submit to pressure from the authorities. They could envisage arguing for a change in the discriminatory system of tax advances to which traders in other provinces were not subject. It would also allow them to press authorities to live up to their responsibilities in fighting corruption, market insecurity, and imports of foreign beef. But, before that, he needed everyone to realise that 'you cannot work without papers'. On this note, and after the customary *do'a* (religious invocation), the meeting was adjourned.

That same day, the ANCBC president took the step of informing the prefect about the DGI's letter. Because the initial correspondence had excluded him, the prefect asked the president to send him an official letter, warning him about the disruptive effects that the tax administration's initiative were likely to have on the national supply of beef. Thus, the prefect had the formal justification that he needed to call all interested parties to a *concertation* (consultation) meeting. On 10 September 2004, traders therefore sat at the same table with the tax authorities. The initial discussion on whether the drop in tax revenue from cattle trade was due to a downturn in commercial activity or to increased tax evasion paved the way for a two-hour-long give and take. While the *chef de centre des impôts* (head of the district tax centre or CCI) was intent on reminding traders of their tax obligations and their failure to meet them, the ANCBC president questioned the legitimacy and rationale of existing procedures for collecting tax. The prefect and the MINEPIA delegate also made major contributions to the discussion, more often than not striking a conciliatory note.

One of the demands contained in the DGI's letter referred to the business location map, an instrument of tax administration that readers have encountered in the earlier discussion of public contractors' tax obligations. On paper, establishing a *plan de localisation* involved conducting a *descente sur le terrain* (inspection visit), recording an address and drawing a map, and having the taxpayer sign the *attestation de localisation* (verification of location). At the time, despite the fact that the requirement had existed since 2000, tax officials themselves considered formalities like this one novelties, so the traders' lack of familiarity with them was to be expected. The issue was raised in the meeting. Lacking their own business premises, traders operate in public markets in broad daylight. Yet, as I noted earlier, markets do not offer obvious bases for individualised controls. The regulations requiring taxpayers to specify a business location refer to a 'place of activity', so both the prefect and the traders asked for further elucidation. What did this mean in the case at hand? Did the *plan de localisation* need to include a list of markets where the trader could be found? The CCI replied that, as far as cattle traders were concerned, the relevant place was their home address. In Adamaoua's population centres, where there are no street names or numbers and many family compounds are labyrinthine, the usefulness of this information is limited. Furthermore, in practice, verifications are often paper-based rather than made through actual inspections.

Making taxpayers 'locatable', however, was only a first step in the programme of action spelled out in the DGI's letter. At the time, while some traders paid licences and many opted for the *impôt libératoire*, a substantial number chose to stay under the radar of the tax authorities. While those who shipped cattle by train invariably paid income tax advances, only very exceptionally did any of them file an income tax return. At the end of the meeting, when pressed by the prefect, the CCI provided compelling evidence of the difficulties involved in holding individual traders accountable. In 2003, he admitted, only two cattle traders in the district had had their location verified, applied for a licence, and filed an income tax return at the end of the year. Most of the meeting's discussion centred on the fact that existing arrangements for the collection of income tax advances did not allow Camrail to know either who was shipping what cattle, or who was paying what tax advances. The MINEPIA delegate himself was keen to disabuse the CCI of the notion that there were realistic alternatives to this state of affairs. This was a result as much of the traders' proclivities ('Traders shy away from light; they love darkness') as of what was practicable from an administrative point of view. But the words of a hitherto silent Camrail manager proved the most compelling in this regard. After all, it was to the railway company that the tax authorities were delegating the proposed new tasks. The DGI's request that his company report on the number of cattle shipped per individual trader, the manager pointed out, was simply not feasible. He noted that the present system whereby Camrail distributed available freight cars equally between the two traders' associations was a great improvement over the previous system of atomised distribution, which had been rife with conflict. 'When each of the groups has been ascribed x number of cars, it is up to them to know which traders are loading those cars with their cattle. That problem is not of Camrail's concern anymore,' he concluded. As he had told a group of traders a few days before, the last thing Camrail wanted was to become 'the Ministry of Finance's errand boys'.

The prefect himself summed up the thrust of the meeting's protracted deliberations with an assertion of the authorities' dependence on the traders' cooperation: 'With [cattle] traders ... we cannot but count on their honesty, both towards themselves and towards the authorities. That is all. And the authorities, in turn, must be subtle enough in this regard.'

The commitment of the traders' leaders to 'work things out' with the tax authorities with which the meeting concluded was put into practice three days later on a visit to the district tax centre. After some negotiation, they reached an agreement whereby the CCI accepted to forgo that year's outstanding income tax payments. In exchange, the traders' representatives agreed to urge the members of their groups to pay for a business licence. The implication was that no one would try to continue operating under the *impôt libératoire*, which, in the CCI's idiosyncratic reformulation of the law, only concerned 'trade in sheep, goats and poultry'. The group leaders also committed themselves to ban anyone without a licence from shipping cattle by train.

During the next weeks, all the places where traders mingled buzzed with speculation on tax payments. Had so and so paid for his licence? Was that other trader, who stubbornly refused to pay anything but the *impôt libératoire*, going to be able to get away with it? Would the group leaders strictly enforce the exclusion of unlicensed traders from railway transport? Was there a mismatch between what traders were paying in terms of tax advances and what Camrail had actually paid the tax authorities? Did such irregularities also affect the handling of the funds raised through MINEPIA's *laissez-passers* before shipments? If so, who was pocketing the money? What were they to do if in practice they could not get individualised receipts for the sums they paid at the markets (municipal tax, veterinary certificate, farmers' union dues) or when loading cattle (VAT, *laissez-passer*, income tax advance)? Would it be useful to have their respective groups file their taxes or was it best to do it individually?[28] What would happen next year with the commercial income tax? Would they be forced to file a tax return, as the law required?

In mid-November 2004, once MINEPIA had finally fixed that year's list of authorised cattle traders, the list was published by the prefect. It contained the names of 34 traders. Of those, few had obtained their licence before the *concertation* meeting. A large batch of Comité licences was processed on 28 September. ELCOBCAM complied a week later. Even then, some traders took longer to pay for their licence. Less powerful traders paired up to get one between them. A few even decided

---

[28] On 28 September 2004, I went with the ANCBC president to the tax centre to obtain licences for several members of the Comité group. One week earlier there had been an incident that required his intervention. A trader who had decided to go there independently to obtain his licence was fined CFAF 14,000 for late payment. Instead of paying, he had enlisted the president's help. A long, acrimonious row ensued. The CCI insisted that he was simply enforcing the law. Although he had agreed to forgo outstanding balances of income tax, as far as licences were concerned he had to apply existing regulations and impose the appropriate penalties. The delegate reminded him that they were 'in a second stage of the law', so the terms negotiated at the meeting with the prefect should govern their relationship. The CCI did not raise the issue of possible penalties again.

to remain under the *impôt libératoire* in open defiance of the authorities and their own peers. In 2004, the list was eight traders short of the 42 in the previous year's list. The most significant change was the move many had made from the *impôt libératoire* to paying for a licence under the *régime de base* (basic tax regime). The sum at stake in switching from one tax status to the other was relatively small. For most traders, it meant only an additional CFAF 35,000.[29] The reluctance of some traders to switch was partly rooted in a preference to remain outside the reach of the tax authorities, since it is not them but rather municipalities that are in charge of managing the *impôt libératoire*. Some, however, simply did not have the additional money at hand, for they had not planned to set it aside. Their lack of savings demonstrates the narrow financial base of some traders.

In the end, a couple of months after the 10 September meeting, the majority of those who had paid the *impôt libératoire* the previous year had changed to a licence. In Vina District, this was the most tangible result of the process initiated by the DGI's letter. Yet, the letter did not concern cattle traders exclusively. It also sent a message to everyone involved in the collection of income tax advances that they were under scrutiny. Some traders argued that the letter's implicit target was '*le cafouillage* [the shambles] between Camrail, MINEPIA, and [the Ministry of] Finance'. Traders had compared Camrail's figures with their own records on weekly shipments dating back to January 2004 and detected significant discrepancies, which they attributed to misappropriation by Camrail employees and state officials. Furthermore, because the implications of the measures delineated in the letter were negotiated ad hoc at the local level, agreements reached in other places differed. Traders in Adamaoua's Mbéré District, for example, were told that they could stay on the *impôt libératoire* until the end of the year 2004. In 2005, they would all be shifted to a basic regime licence and would be expected to pay a quarterly *forfait* (lump sum) of CFAF 20,000 as income tax. The fact that many Meiganga-based traders who use the railway ship cattle from Bélabo (East Province), where the provincial ordinance that instituted the tax advances has no effect, may account for their agreement to pay income tax quarterly, although at a flat rate.[30]

In terms of revenue, payment for a few additional licences made only a small difference. When compared with the funds from tax advances that they collected through Camrail, the sum raised from those extra licences was negligible. All the same, the provincial tax authorities could present

---

[29] See note 26 on *impôt libératoire* categories.
[30] Cargo trains from East Province represent a substantial part of the flow of cattle to the south. According to official records, in 2002 over 12,000 head came from Bélabo, about 19 per cent of all cattle reaching Yaoundé's market by train (INS 2006: 255).

this to their superiors in the capital as a step in the right direction. It allowed them to have a slightly larger group of cattle traders 'located', with their respective files and identifying numbers. Under the circumstances, this seemed to be all they could aspire to. Other measures announced by the DGI, such as the individualised control of the traders' income, had little chance of implementation. As a market-goer put it in a casual conversation at the Dang cattle market on the outskirts of Ngaoundéré in October 2004:

No matter what they say about certificates of tax payment, location maps, or whatever else it is, they have no way of catching us ... There are too many ways [to confound tax controls]. They'd better be reasonable, entice people to return to the fold, try to talk them into organising things differently ... But if what they want is to find a way of blocking traders who do not comply, there is nothing they can do. Nothing!

* * * * * *

The governance of cattle trade has been a long-standing concern. Colonial authorities put in place a network of weekly markets converging around Ngaoundéré, which thus became a major cattle-trading centre. World War Two marked the beginning of ambitious policies aimed at ensuring constant supplies and low prices of beef in southern urban centres. These interventions included both short-lived experiments such as the single price system in Yaoundé and more enduring measures including the licensing of cattle merchants to restrict access to the trade, or the establishment of veterinary centres to modulate southbound cattle flows. Independence brought few immediate changes to the commercialisation of cattle, but the mid-1970s were years of important transformations, including the demise of foreign operators, the creation of state ranches, and the railway revolution in the transport of cattle. The late 1980s marked the beginning of a turbulent era. The state could no longer afford to achieve its ambitions of intervention, and the cattle sector was hit hard by the economic crisis. In the early 1990s, traders were quick to take advantage of the newly enshrined freedom of association. In its response to the crisis, the new ANCBC, which built on existing structures of representation (the traders' delegates and the cooperative organisations that had their roots in the colonial era), went against the grain of the liberalising stance promoted by the government's international funders. To replace the old government-imposed controls of cattle supplies, the traders' association enforced a system of quotas allocated to groups based in different trading centres. The system, however, soon proved unsustainable, and since 1995 there have been no quotas restricting supply to southern Cameroon. Unevenly enforced measures are certainly still in place to restrict cross-border trade and to ban foreign traders from operating in Cameroonian markets. The government also retains considerable leeway to impose protectionist measures on imports of beef and still runs several state ranches and slaughterhouses.

The train compartment, the bush taxi, the railway station parking lot, its cargo loading section, and, most palpably, cattle markets are some of the spaces that cattle traders inhabit. In them, knowledge is displayed and transmitted; information exchanged, fashioned, and retained; skills tested with varying degrees of success; claims made, contested, and upheld; promises uttered, fulfilled, and broken; deals closed, terms renegotiated, cattle bought and sold, money paid, and gains or losses made. At present, the most robust dynamics of exclusion/inclusion in the trade derive from infrastructural dimensions that militate against the formalisation of transactions and promote a reliance on ethno-religious networks for access to cattle, finance, and other services, and for the mitigation of risks of non-payment.

Only some of the traders' interactions in the conduct of their business involve state bureaucracies. Encounters with veterinary officials are the most common of these. Broad powers of *tutelle* (trusteeship) have historically been understood as part and parcel of a paternalistic 'assistance contract' that linked MINEPIA to cattle farmers and traders (Boutrais 1999b: 622). Many of those powers are now a thing of the past, as the commercialisation of veterinary drugs became liberalised and the provision of veterinary services privatised. Public goods such as animal health and food safety still inform veterinary officials' efforts to govern the circulation, commercialisation, and slaughtering of cattle. Their ability to do this is premised not only on legal texts but also on their quotidian presence on the ground and their linguistic competence in Fulfulde. Veterinary officials are also more likely than other civil servants to have religious and ethnic affinities with traders. On the other hand, cuts in personnel and the resources available to state veterinary services have had an undeniable impact on how effectively they can carry out their current duties. Thus, for example, although the fees paid when selling cattle in markets and shipping cattle by train are justified on animal health grounds, these days such payments are accompanied by, at best, the most summary veterinary inspection, or, at worst, no checks whatsoever. In such circumstances, the veterinary *laissez-passer* is mostly a revenue-raising exercise, a toll bearing little connection to animal health.

When going about their business, cattle traders must also deal with constant road checks by police and gendarmes, who in their daily search for a few extra thousand francs see the verification of all sorts of papers as lying within their remit. If, in the 1960s and 1970s, anyone travelling needed to carry the one-party card to make it through countless roadblocks (Geschiere 2009: 181–2, note 14), today those travellers whose ID cards identify them as professionals are often required by the security forces to show relevant tax documents. In this way, papers documenting payment of a licence or *impôt libératoire* also become *laissez-passers*, although traders willing to put up with the hassle and the small sums required to keep gendarmes and police at bay manage to do without them.

Other authorities have a more distant relationship with the cattle trade. Tax officials have little opportunity or inclination to rub shoulders with cattle professionals. From these officials' perspective, the cattle economy is a 'sector protected by the state' (as the head of Adamaoua's tax office put it to me in 2004), given the influence of cattle-farming interests in northern Cameroon's electoral constituencies. This adds a specific texture to the well-documented challenges of taxing any agrarian economy 'organised in small enterprises that lack formal, bureaucratic structure and operate without extensive use of banking systems and written or electronic records of economic transactions' (Moore 2009: 40). Unlike veterinary agents, tax officials do not have a regular presence where the trade takes place. Their contact with most cattle traders is indirect, through the municipal authorities that administer the *impôt libératoire* or the railway company that collects income tax advances. The rare instances of direct interaction make apparent both a lack of familiarity and a distinct cultural distance. The senior official who participated in the seminar organised by the ANCBC in February 2004, for example, was the only guest speaker to address the audience in French. As if reminders were needed, his name, his suit, and the golden crucifix on his tie signalled that Adamaoua's tax offices were – with few exceptions – staffed by Christian southerners. Similarly, traders' visits to the tax offices are annual occasions honoured only by the minority of traders who pay for a licence or file an income tax return (and, even then, some prefer to delegate the task to the leaders of their associations).

This chapter has drawn a picture of the very uneven levels of compliance with the official rules governing the cattle trade. Even minor requirements whose enforcement is entrusted to state agents in close interaction with traders are widely ignored. This is the case with the *agréments* (administrative authorisations). In an environment where veterinary officials in charge of specific markets have no practical ways of preventing non-compliant traders from operating, even the most prominent, better established traders see little point in applying for these authorisations. The opposite situation – where the observance of rules is linked to transactions that are central to the trade – is much rarer, but one example is the income tax advance established in 1999. The governor's ordinance made shipments of cattle by train contingent on tax payments. Traders wanting to use the railway to transport cattle to the south were thus left with no choice but to pay these advances. But this is the exception. Most of the time, traders are perfectly able to 'work without papers' (despite the ANCBC leadership's wishes to the contrary) and the authorities have few practical ways of preventing this. Yet, an account of how cattle trade is governed that stopped there would be misleading.

The preceding pages have shown the need to go beyond a simplistic opposition between elusive cattle traders and helpless authorities. For one thing, such a portrayal takes for granted the commitment of officials to bureaucratic rigour. The discussion of the PSREP, the programme to enhance revenue reliability in the cattle sector, shows how tenuous such a commitment can be. The programme's rationale was to address a situation in which traders (and butchers) were routinely paying veterinary fees at markets (and slaughterhouses) while officials were misappropriating a substantial portion of those fees. An even more extreme example is cattle exports from Adamaoua to Nigeria. As a matter of course, this cross-border trade takes place in violation of the legal requirement to obtain export permits. Veterinary officials and other authorities who are present at border-crossing points (customs, municipalities, and chiefs) not only allow this trade but subject it to a system of unofficial payments.

A further complication is that effective enforcement of legal provisions is often premised on cooperation between different government departments. This is not always easily achieved. The PSREP experience once more makes this apparent. Relations between MINEPIA and the tax authorities have long been marked by mutual mistrust. The head of MINEPIA's provincial office, for example, used the *concertation* meeting in September 2004 to vent a few grudges. He opened his remarks by lamenting that the tax authorities had adopted the measures contained in the DGI's letter without bothering to inform his ministry. Such disregard for MINEPIA's role was not new. As it was, he admitted, it had become the tax authorities' standard practice. Not only that, in recent years, they had also repeatedly accused his ministry of stoking farmers' and traders' *incivisme* (lack of civic behaviour). The *concertation* meeting also showed how enforcement is contingent on the helping hand of non-governmental actors. The tax authorities rely on Camrail's collection tasks on their behalf. The railway company is ready to oblige only as long as it does not further complicate the already highly contentious process of allocating freight cars and loading cattle. This delegation of tasks also creates opportunities for the diversion of public revenue.

Finally, the sweeping image of slippery cattle traders who 'shy away from the light' and 'love darkness' does not do justice to this group's range of practices and attitudes towards the law. Indeed, a significant minority among them see increased compliance with the law as part and parcel of the transformation of the trade, a transformation that they aspire to. Influential factions within the ANCBC share this vision of a trade in which only 'true professionals' can flourish. A constant message to their members is that reclaiming the position of law-abiding citizens is a condition for the effective defence of their rights and interests. In this vein, the ANCBC regularly involves the authorities in its events. The prevailing context in which routine violation of the law goes unpunished, however, holds no prospect for the realisation of this professionalisation agenda.

4 On and off the road

Émile Deschamps had worked since the 1980s as a manager for a company that specialised in the transport of timber. In 2000, lured by the prospect of getting freight from the Chad–Cameroon pipeline construction, he decided to move from Douala to Ngaoundéré and start a trucking company. In November 2004, he agreed to share with me his views on the challenges of running a profitable business in the transport sector. It was more than a year since the pipeline construction had come to an end. I was invited to take a seat in the living room, where I found a heterogeneous group of people who had come to see him for diverse reasons, all of them matters of more pressing substance than my need for enlightenment. When our host showed up after a few minutes, he was on the phone talking to a business associate in Douala. 'It's him who has laid hands on that shipment,' we heard him say, visibly angry. The shipment in question concerned some 50 railway wagons of imported produce for Chad's largest brewery. The wagons had arrived in Ngaoundéré earlier that week and needed to be taken to N'Djaména. Émile had just seen his expectations of transporting a sizeable part of the cargo vanish. The person whom Saga-SDV, the *transitaire* (freight forwarder), had preferred over him happened to be a well-known Chadian transporter.[1] For a Cameroonian national of French descent like our host, this seemed to add insult to injury: 'He is a self-professed Muslim – and yet he has no quibbles in working for a brewery!' The assurances about obtaining a share of the brewery shipment, which Émile had repeatedly been given over the previous days, had turned to nothing. He ventured that his competitor must have bribed everyone involved. Payments on the side were the only explanation he could come up with: '[Saga's manager in Ngaoundéré] must eat his part in this operation. Maybe [their man in

---

[1] *Transitaire* is the word most commonly used in Cameroon to refer to international freight forwarders or forwarding agents. It underscores the fact that a significant part of their business deals with freight in transit, i.e. freight that, due to the customs union existing between Cameroon and its neighbours in the Economic and Monetary Union of Central Africa (CEMAC), crosses Cameroon without paying customs duties. Because of their involvement in customs-clearing procedures, forwarding agents are also referred to as *commissionaires agréés en douane* (authorised customs brokers or CADs).

Douala] is also in on it. The authorities too, he must grease their palms.' In a few minutes, Émile had dealt with his visitors summarily. As for me, our conversation would have to wait for a better occasion. Before we had time to get into our respective vehicles, our host was on his way to the cargo terminal. He had no time to waste if he were to make the forwarder's manager reconsider his decision.

This is one of several similar incidents that I witnessed during my fieldwork in Ngaoundéré. Conflicts over the distribution of freight are the daily bread of interactions between trucking companies and freight forwarders, the two most prominent protagonists of this story. Émile's mention of 'the authorities' refers mostly to Cameroon's Bureau de Gestion du Fret Terrestre (Road Freight Management Bureau or BGFT) and Chad's Bureau National de Fret (National Freight Bureau or BNF), the agencies that oversee the allocation of freight according to the quotas agreed between the two neighbouring countries. Less obviously the target of my interlocutor's fury but nonetheless influential in shaping trucking companies' business prospects are the *syndicats de transporteurs* (truckers' unions).[2] In fact, that same day, after his visit to Saga, Émile went to the local offices of the Syndicat National des Transporteurs Routiers du Cameroun (Cameroon's National Union of Road Transporters or SNTRC), the dominant union nationwide, to discuss an impending strike. The union wanted to force CotonTchad and Saga to increase the proposed ton per kilometre rate for Chadian imports of fertiliser for the upcoming cotton season; this dispute repeats itself, with varying degrees of intensity, year after year.

Forwarders, freight bureaus, and truckers' unions – the three sets of actors that Émile mentioned more or less explicitly in his phone conversation – are key players with which trucking companies based in Ngaoundéré interact on a daily basis. This chapter explores how those relationships have been constituted historically and what factors shape trucking as a business activity. It devotes particular attention to evolving policies and measures that are aimed at organising and transforming the sector.

The emergence of a regional transport hub

The origins of motorised transport as a business enterprise in Ngaoundéré coincide with the construction of minimally functioning roads and

---

[2] *Transporteur* is the word used most often to refer to truck owners or, as I call them throughout this chapter, truckers. Although I have used 'union' to translate *syndicat*, readers should be aware that the French word has a broader meaning than the English trade union. Both employers' and employees' organisations are called *syndicats*. The resulting ambiguities are compounded by the fact that many drivers' unions (*syndicats de chauffeurs*) have members who own their trucks and are thus self-employed and, in some cases, employers.

the first experiences of cultivating commercial crops for export in the northern part of the territory under French mandate. Largely built using only human labour and small hand tools (Freed 2010: 208–9), the earthen roads linking Yaoundé to Ngaoundéré and Ngaoundéré to Garoua were completed in 1928 and 1929 respectively (Boutinot 1994: 65). Colonial designs for commercial agriculture in this 'poor province of a rich country', as René Dumont, at the time a relatively unknown agronomist, called it in the 1950s (Boutrais 1984b: 501), focused on groundnuts from the 1930s and on cotton and, to a lesser extent, rice from the 1950s (Hallaire 1984: 407–27). Garoua's port on the Benoué River, which offered a three-month window each year in which to navigate the 1,600 kilometres that separated it from the Niger Delta, was the main outlet for these exports (Roupsard 1987). Accordingly, the early days of commercial transport in Adamaoua were decidedly modest and generally linked to small commercial ventures. In 1942, for example, soon after arriving in Cameroon, the oldest of four Lebanese siblings who settled in Ngaoundéré bought a Chevrolet truck to service his newly opened store. Pioneering Muslim merchants in Ngaoundéré such as Alhadji Nana Hamajoda and Aboubakar Gagara bought their first trucks only in the aftermath of World War Two.

In the early 1950s, the few privately owned vehicles in Ngaoundéré were still devoted to *transport mixte*: that is, taking passengers as well as freight. It was in 1953 that the colonial administration tried to compel transporters to specialise in either passengers or freight and to banish unlicensed transporters – with limited success, to judge from oral testimonies and the complaints found in the archival record.[3] Officials enjoyed wide discretion to grant and deny licences as they saw fit, often to the detriment of 'native' operators. As we saw in the case of Bakary Bandjou, some of them had to surmount considerable obstacles when it came to purchasing vehicles and putting them to work. This restrictive approach towards new entrants in the transport sector was justified 'on the grounds of the absence of precise texts governing the practice of this profession'.[4] In early 1957, these legal lacunae began to be filled through a sustained effort that culminated in decree no. 59/227 of 3 December 1959, the first text that aimed to be comprehensive in regulating road transport.

After independence, expatriate operators largely withdrew from passenger transport and tried to maintain a foothold in freight transport. In

---

[3] See, for example, ANY 2AC 4108, 'Adamaoua, Transport, Lettre de 25 Mai 1954'; ANY 3AC 2308, 'Adamaoua, Transport, Réglementation 1956, Correspondance concurrence déloyale'.

[4] ANY 2AC 4108, 'Adamaoua, Transport, Procès verbal réunion des transporteurs, 8 Mars 1957'.

the early 1960s, Ngaoundéré saw no major changes other than a gradual improvement of road infrastructure and a moderate increase in the number of vehicles. The year 1967 marked a turning point. Nigeria's civil war rendered transport routes through its territory unviable – and dealt Garoua's port a death blow from which it never recovered, despite a resumption of activities in the 1970s.[5] With no other alternative to Cameroonian roads, all trade along the north–south axis now had to go through Ngaoundéré. In an interview in July 2004, a well-weathered Lebanese transporter recounted with a mixture of pride and nostalgia how the Total Oil manager had contacted him and his siblings in September 1968, after one of the company's ships was burned while leaving Port Harcourt. He promised them that, if they purchased a road tanker, Total would hire them permanently to transport fuel from Douala to northern Cameroon and Chad. 'The first thing I do is to go and see the [Cameroonian] Minister [of Transport]. He assures me that if I buy [a tanker], he makes me work without interruption,' he remembered a quarter of a century later as he showed me the receipt for the final payment for the truck. 'We paid a total of CFAF 5,570,000 for it. 5,570,000 francs!' He repeated the figure recorded in the receipt before putting it away with a care bordering on reverence. This was the foundational document of the prosperous business in fuel transport that his family has run ever since.

The drastic reconfiguration sparked by the conflict in Biafra crystallised in 1972 with the consolidation of a government-backed agreement between the foreign *transitaires* and the recently strengthened national truckers' union SNTRC.[6] As someone close to the union leaders of the time explained to me in November 2004:

A distribution of tasks was already in place. They had negotiated things so that the people from the metropolis closed their transport agencies down and occupied themselves with forwarding freight only. The war [in Biafra] only made more pressing the need to create a structure that ensured the link between railway and road ...[7] This was how Mory, Socopao, Soaem [the three companies involved], and the union put in place a freight bureau that they called Sogetrans.

The effects of the Nigerian civil war and the new developments in the organisation of the transport sector took time to be felt in Ngaoundéré.

---

[5] In 1965, the year when its activity peaked, Garoua's port processed 60,000 tons (Marguerat 1984a: 462).

[6] Created in 1963, the union was first called Syndicat de Transporteurs Routiers du Cameroun Occidental. In 1967, after absorbing its equivalent organisation in anglophone Cameroon, it became the SNTRC.

[7] In 1968, trucks still had to unload and load freight in Yaoundé, whose railway connection with Douala dated back to 1927. As the Transcamerounais railway line advanced northwards, Sogetrans offices moved – first to Bélabo in 1969, then to Ngaoundéré in 1974.

Relatively few trucking companies were based in the city, which remained a place of transit for another few years. As we saw, this was to change with the completion of the Transcamerounais railway in 1974. Ngaoundéré then became the northern terminus of the railway line. The city was thus transformed into an almost unavoidable place of passage for all goods traded to and from Chad. It also handled a significant portion of the Central African Republic's (CAR's) imports and exports, although the majority of those were channelled through Bélabo. The investment in transport infrastructure also involved the paving of the road from Ngaoundéré to Kousséri, on the Chad border, via Garoua and Maroua; this was completed by 1977.[8]

Trucking companies proliferated in an unprecedented manner. According to estimates provided by the last assistant general manager of Sogetrans, by the end of the 1970s around 800 trucks and semitrailers serviced the railway cargo terminal (350 of which were Cameroonian, 350 Chadian, and 100 from CAR). The majority of the Cameroonian trucks were owned by traders based in Garoua, a city whose 'preponderance as the distribution center of the North' (Marguerat 1984b: 493) was never threatened seriously during Ahidjo's presidency. Yet, the number of truck licences issued in Ngaoundéré grew sharply from 29 in 1969 to 153 in 1976 (Gondolo 1986: 313). Of those 153 trucks, 93 were owned by Greeks and Lebanese, including Theo Tiliakos, who at the time managed 30 Mercedes trucks, and the Zattar, Damien, Omaïs, and Dabaji families, whose descendants remain active in this and other economic sectors to this day (Fimigue 1999). The rest of the licensed trucks were owned largely by Fulbe, Hausa, and Kanuri, whose new but generally small investments had been funded for the most part with sales of cattle (Boutrais 1984a: 298, note 1; Gondolo 1986: 314).

By the end of the 1970s, two individuals stood out among Cameroonian truck owners based in Ngaoundéré and both had leading roles in the local chapter of the SNTRC. The union's president had arrived

---

[8] Chadian and Central African exports and imports could follow other routes. The two main alternatives were: from N'Djaména through Kousséri to Maiduguri and then to Lagos by road in the case of northern Chad; and from Bangui to Brazzaville by the Oubangui River and then to Pointe-Noire by train in the cases of CAR and southern Chad. Traffic from Bangui through Brazzaville to Pointe-Noire grew considerably in the 1960s under the authority of an intergovernmental agency called the Agence Transéquatoriale des Communications. By 1964, the Congolese route attracted about a third of the cotton exports and 59,000 tons of imports (Abakar 2010: 27). Although the Transcamerounais meant that Chadian exports and imports stopped taking this route for the most part, in the mid-1980s 75 per cent of CAR's foreign trade was still channelled through it (Slob et al. 2006: 85). However, in the 1990s, political troubles in Congo-Brazzaville and the decline of the Congolese railway made this option unviable. In recent times, these alternatives to the Cameroonian corridors have attracted smaller commercial flows (Bennafla 2002: 49–59).

from Nigeria in the early 1940s. He was a trader who, after independence, benefited from contacts with the national leadership of the union and thus obtained extensive credit facilities to purchase trucks. This 'favouritism', lamented by one of my interlocutors who at the time had tried his hand at road transport without much luck, also meant that he got priority access to freight. The other was the vice-president of the union's local chapter. He had been involved in transport activities since 1962 and, with the opening of the railway station, he had moved to Ngaoundéré, where his operations greatly expanded. A 'unitary' organisation such as the SNTRC was emblematic of the one-party system. Through its partnership with Sogetrans and with the blessing of the transit companies, the union monopolised business opportunities in the sector. Its members were captive in the sense that membership was a precondition to doing business. Nothing prevented the union leadership from reserving most of the available freight and credit for themselves and for those in their good books (Plat and Rizet 1989: 10). Many of those who owned or drove trucks during this period, however, are adamant that the situation compared favourably with what came later.

Sogetrans, the consortium formed by the three main freight forwarders present in Ngaoundéré (Mory, Socopao, and Soaem) and the SNTRC, was the cornerstone of the transport system during this period. As the former assistant general manager put it to me in September 2004:

Sogetrans' role was essential. Transporters were not specialists; they were simply traders who had purchased trucks. Since Sogetrans was formally a member of the union, it was in charge of managing everything from the internal functioning of [Ngaoundéré's] cargo terminal to the individualised follow-up of the [union's] members' work. Its remit went as far as issuing the truck owners' invoices, processing the payments [they received from forwarders], collecting [the truck owners'] taxes on behalf of the state, and producing their annual balance sheet. As well, Sogetrans played a financial role. The company provided advances and even loans for union members... Under this system there was a proliferation of transporters. All it took was to buy a truck, join the union, and put your truck at Sogetrans' disposal.

Sogetrans' prominent role relied on interlocking agreements with all the other actors involved. As a result, Regifercam, the parastatal railway company, obtained a virtual monopoly on all freight to and from CAR, Chad and northern Cameroon in the Douala–Ngaoundéré segment of the route. The postponement of a paved road connection between the port and the railway terminal was meant to ensure the financial viability of the railway line. The Coopération des Transporteurs Tchadiens (CTT) and the Bureau d'Affrètement de la Centrafrique (BARC), the organisations representing Chadian and CAR truckers respectively, entrusted Sogetrans with ensuring that the distribution of freight conformed to the established quotas.[9] Thus, for example, to get their cargo documents validated by the BARC and the CTT in Ngaoundéré, truckers had to go to Sogetrans' offices. Accordingly, Sogetrans, which had the legal status of a private *société anonyme* (public limited company), came to be regarded as a state agency by many Cameroonian, Chadian, and CAR truckers (Plat and Rizet 1989: 11).

'Disorder took hold'

After a decade of remarkable expansion for road transport, a severe national economic downturn unsettled the stability of the preceding arrangements. The volume of goods traded through Ngaoundéré diminished drastically. The drop in business experienced by the railway operator Regifercam offers a powerful illustration. The company's revenue from freight, which had peaked in 1985, fell by almost 40 per cent within only two years (Blanc and Gouirand 2007: 9). In the recollection of many of my informants, 1987 marked a watershed. In a November 2004 conversation, a SNTRC member offered a concise recapitulation:

In 1987, the crisis announced itself. Cameroon as a destination had been flagging. The port of Douala was no longer functional and ships had stopped docking there. This meant that Ngaoundéré did not receive sufficient cargo. Sogetrans had to close. The CTT disappeared, forcing Chadians to create their own small unions to fend for themselves. The BARC moved [from Ngaoundéré] to Douala. Disorder took hold ... President Biya issued a decree that allowed truckers go to Douala to get their freight. Everyone went all the way to Douala. Business in Ngaoundéré fell sharply.

Decided in December 1987, the closure of Sogetrans put a fitting seal on an *annus horribilis*. In the words of an employee who lost his job as a result: 'It was catastrophic for everyone. Sogetrans managed the truck fleet, took care of social security, taxes, and insurance. Truckers did not know how to do any of this. It was a debacle.' The shutdown caught most truckers unaware. Someone who would later become a national leader of the SNTRC reconstructed the logic of the decision taken by the partnering French forwarding companies in these terms:

The country is not doing well. There are political problems, the government has changed, investors are scared, the war in Chad is still going on ... What are we to do? We are going to liquidate the company. It's our only way to stay out of trouble. If things get better, we'll take up our business again.

---

[9] Berberati Agreement between CAR and Cameroon, signed 24 July 1969, and Ngaoundéré Agreement between Chad and Cameroon, signed 12 April 1975. Both bilateral conventions were revised in 1999.

The reference to changes in government is indicative of underlying factors other than the economic slump.

The political instability that Cameroon experienced after Paul Biya succeeded Ahmadou Ahidjo as president in 1982 made apparent the links between the regime and the SNTRC. Indeed, in the backlash against northerners that followed the attempted putsch of 1984, the union leaders from the north, who had been instrumental in forming and managing the partnership with the foreign forwarders, fell from grace. Those formerly excluded who now enjoyed good connections with the new government wanted a share in this profitable venture. Under new leadership, it did not take long for the SNTRC to clash with its former partners. It is in this light that we can read the hint that Didier Plat and Cristophe Rizet (1989: 11) give us in a study based on some 50 interviews with transport operators in Douala and Ngaoundéré in 1988. In their words, the demise of Sogetrans came about 'seemingly in the aftermath of [the freight forwarders'] problems with the union'.

The liquidation of Sogetrans in January 1988 was characterised by a lack of public oversight. In one of our conversations 15 years later, the company's assistant general manager made this point through a revealing anecdote:

I find it amusing how Sogetrans shut down as if it were a small shop. People [the French forwarding agents' representatives] came from Paris, they sat on the table and said: 'Well, it's closing time!' They all packed their bags and left. Sometime in mid-1989, while spending a few days in Ngaoundéré, somebody in a suit approaches me to inquire about Sogetrans. 'I've been told that you work for them. How is it that you have stopped paying your taxes?' [When told that Sogetrans no longer existed, he replied:] 'You say the company is closed, since when?' [I tell you this story,] so that you get an idea of how far the neglect went. A company that would pay [CFAF] 200 million in taxes on behalf of truckers every quarter ... It shuts down without the government even knowing!

The terrain was favourable for the opportunistic stripping of the company's assets. Its 150 permanent employees in Ngaoundéré lost their jobs. A proper liquidation was never conducted. Several of my informants, for example, wondered who sold Sogetrans' premises in Ngaoundéré's cargo terminal to Saga, which established itself there in the early 1990s, and under what terms. The recovery of Sogetrans' credit against its debtors – some CFAF 500 million, according to the former assistant general manager – was never attempted.

In short, faced with bleak business prospects, the freight forwarders operating in the Cameroonian rail–road interface saw the power struggles within the SNTRC over control of the union's monopoly on the distribution of freight as an opportunity to abandon the commitments they had undertaken during the previous decade. The most immediate consequence of the freight shortage and the disappearance of Sogetrans was that many truckers went out of business. Those who remained active evolved towards increased informality. 'In 1988, the union was in disarray,' a trucker who managed to stay afloat during this period explained to me in October 2004. 'Truckers went into *le maquis*. Before, it was Sogetrans that collected our taxes. All we did was stop by to pick up our cheques. With the crisis, we no longer took the trouble to file our taxes. It wasn't our problem.'

In 1990, as in many other West and Central African countries, the World Bank was already working on the design of a major transformation of all branches of the Cameroonian transport industry, with 'liberalisation' the overall objective. A World Bank evaluation of road transport was conducted in June 1992 but the reticence of the government and constant changes in the teams of expatriate consultants delayed the approval of a Project for the Preparation of the Transport Reform (PPRT) until 1995 (Meyo-Soua 1999: 45). However, on the path to liberalisation, other developments were equally consequential, if not more so.

As already noted, the end of the railway monopoly on the Douala–Ngaoundéré section led to a reorganisation of trucking services that had previously been based in Ngaoundéré. Douala replaced Ngaoundéré as the transport platform for goods in transit to and from CAR, which explains why the BARC office in Cameroon moved from the railway terminus to the port. This measure also allowed much north–south long-distance transport within Cameroon to bypass the railway altogether. Other changes that had liberalising effects were directly linked to the disappearance of Sogetrans. In this new setting, forwarders could subcontract freight to non-SNTRC members. Furthermore, no one in particular was overseeing adherence to the Chadian and CAR trucking quotas, a task that Sogetrans had carried out until then. Finally, the effects of political unrest on the conduct of business and on the regulatory role of the state also need to be highlighted. The *villes mortes* campaign in April 1991, a forceful show of defiance against the government, seriously disrupted road transport, and, indeed, the national economy. As the manager of a then emerging trucking firm explained in April 2004: 'Everyone was brought to a standstill during the strikes. Why would you put your drivers at risk and have your trucks burned?' The general strikes aimed at halting economic activity, which in Adamaoua necessarily involved blocking any traffic to and from Ngaoundéré's cargo terminal. However, the broader goal was to question the foundations of the political regime. Government services and officials were attacked. The provincial offices of the Ministry of Transport were 'the first administrative target to be burned down' by the strikers, one of the ministry's senior managers recalled in 2004, and they did not reopen their doors in a safer location until two years later.[10]

The end of the railway monopoly, a weakened union, the non-observance of national quotas, and the erosion of governmental legitimacy in the context of the advent of multiparty politics were all factors that featured prominently in the equation that some of the truckers I interviewed made between liberalisation and disorder in the late 1980s and early 1990s. In practice, the elimination of regulatory constraints was soon watered down. First and foremost, this was achieved through an ostensibly 'harmless' (Gaïbaï 2009) decision by the minister of transport to create the Road Freight Management Bureau (BGFT) on 26 August 1993. The context was one in which the government was reasserting its public authority once it felt that it had safely left the challenge of the *villes mortes* behind. On account of the need for a mechanism to ensure the observance of freight-sharing agreements between Cameroon and, respectively, Chad and CAR, the BGFT was awarded extensive powers over truckers involved in international transit. Additionally, by acknowledging the SNTRC as the only representative of Cameroonian truckers in Ngaoundéré, the BGFT supported the national union's de facto position as the *interlocuteur valable* (recognised partner) of most freight forwarders.

If liberalisation and the pervasive sense of disorder were countered by these measures, the decline in road transport was harder to reverse. The 1994 CFA franc devaluation altered the cost structure of the trucking business, dramatically increasing the national currency prices of trucks, petrol, and spare parts. These worsening business conditions resulted in two major transformations, which a comparison between two surveys conducted in 1988 and 1996 highlights (Rizet and Gwet 2000). First, the increasing difficulty in replacing old vehicles and the abrupt expansion of imports of used trucks resulted in the average age of the truck fleet increasing.[11] Second, higher costs also led to more general overloading and its attendant effects on the condition of the roads. In October 1995, the Cameroonian government made a series of concessions to embattled truckers, which amounted to an endorsement of the rationale for overloading. Not only did the authorities suspend weight controls on the Douala–Yaoundé road for three months but, 'as an exceptional measure

---

[10] The provincial offices, located next to the railway station, had only existed since 1985, once Adamaoua had gone from being a district within a larger North Province to become a province in its own right. The provincial archives were also lost at this time.

[11] Rizet and Gwet (2000: 14) provide the following aggregate figures for Cameroon and Côte d'Ivoire's international trucking: vehicles older than ten years went from representing 8 per cent in 1988 to 32 per cent in 1996; vehicles less than five years old went from 54 per cent in 1988 to 12 per cent in 1996. For internal trucking, the ageing of the fleet was even more pronounced.

and despite the additional strain that this puts on our roads', they decided to authorise 'a gross vehicle weight of 50 tons instead of the 35 tons set by the Traffic Code'.[12] Two other phenomena that were always present in my discussions with truck owners and that date back to the late 1980s were the proliferation of informal intermediaries and the intensification of *tracasseries policières* (road-level police harassment) at checkpoints.

Freight forwarders adapted to these changes. Certainly, the crisis did not reverse the concentration that existed. In 1988, four companies controlled 85 per cent of international transit (Plat and Rizet 1989: 17). This became more pronounced in the early 1990s, when Saga established a virtual monopoly in Ngaoundéré's cargo terminal. The demise of Sogetrans, the scarcity of freight, and a moribund truckers' union left the few forwarders that remained in a 'position of strength' (ibid.: 13), which in many ways they have preserved to this day. Yet, in the 1990s environment of decline, freight forwarders and owners also had a tough time finding viable trucking companies to work for them. For example, Sodecoton, the Cameroonian cotton parastatal, which had relied on Sogetrans until its disappearance, was forced to create its own trucking department. Its approach was what in the sector's jargon is called *écrémage du marché* (market skimming). The 'skimming' in this case involved reserving for its own trucks the transport services that lent themselves to a more efficient use of the vehicles and relying on a preselected pool of outside truckers for seasonal peaks and less profitable trips (ibid.: 14). The post-devaluation era also saw the reappearance in Cameroon of foreign trucking companies. The return of foreign companies, which had left the Cameroonian market in the aftermath of independence, was premised on privileged links with freight owners. They were seen as a partial remedy to 'the lack of reliable local truckers in such a difficult economic context', as the manager of United Transport Africa, an Italian trucking firm, told me in a November 2004 interview.

In short, the legacy of the years of economic hardship experienced in Cameroon and Adamaoua in the late 1980s and throughout the 1990s proved to be burdensome. A deteriorating road network, an aged trucking fleet (increasingly coming from the international second-hand market), the prevalence of overloading, and intense road-level police corruption all contributed to the reputation of Cameroonian transport

---

[12] MINEFI/Ministry of Transport joint press release, 10 October 1995 (Ngabmen 1996). The 50-ton limit was subsequently adopted by law no. 96/07 of 8 April 1996 for the protection of the road network. However, the enforcement of its provisions took time. The first weight stations were only operational in 1998. The lengthiest delay concerned oil tankers, which had until July 2001 to comply. Even then the measure motivated a four-day strike that caused serious fuel scarcity in Douala (Chomba 2001).

corridors as slow and expensive, a reputation that the World Bank would use to gain leverage in pushing its reform designs in the late 2000s (*The Economist* 2002; Teravaninthorn and Raballand 2009).

Times of pipeline-induced plenty

The Chad–Cameroon Petroleum Development and Pipeline Project is one of the largest infrastructural projects undertaken in recent decades in West and Central Africa. Carried out by a consortium formed by ExxonMobil, Chevron, Petronas, and the Chadian and Cameroonian states, this project aimed to develop more than 300 oil wells in southern Chad and to construct a 1,070-kilometre pipeline to offshore oil-shipment facilities on Cameroon's coast. Funding for this US$3.7 billion project included a World Bank loan to enlarge the equity participation of Chad and Cameroon. After years of protracted discussions and negotiations over alternative arrangements, the project created high expectations of profitable opportunities in the transport sector. No organisation was better placed than the Bolloré group to take advantage of these opportunities. In the years running up to the start of the pipeline construction, the French multinational had made substantial progress in realising its vision of becoming Africa's leading 'integrated' logistics network (Debrie 2001). In 1986, it bought SCAC, the French freight-forwarding firm that controlled freight routes to Africa through its Socopao network. Bolloré's expansion continued into the early 1990s with the acquisition of the ailing Delmas-Vieljeux, a shipping company whose presence in sub-Saharan Africa dated back to the 1910s (Barrier and Gugenheim 1990). Bolloré's merger with SCAC resulted in the creation of SDV. In 1997, Bolloré stepped up its freight and logistics operations with the purchase of Saga. Two years later, the group was the main beneficiary of the new railway concession that completed the privatisation of Regifercam, which the government had agreed with the World Bank in the above-mentioned 1995 PPRT reform project.[13]

The steady transport of materials and equipment was a key element in the smooth progress of the Chad–Cameroon pipeline construction works. The oil consortium worked closely with Camrail (Regifercam's successor) to ensure that rail tracks could cope with the very high levels of traffic and tonnage to be expected along the Douala–Yaoundé–Ngaoundéré line for the duration of the project. Storage yards were built at strategic railway stops to guarantee the connection between rail and

---

[13] Bolloré's objective of controlling the entire logistics chain was achieved in 2004 with its successful bid for the concession of Douala's port container terminal (Debrie and De Guio 2004). However, soon afterwards, in 2005, the group withdrew from the maritime shipping business with the sale of the Delmas shipping lines to CMA-CGM.

road along the route of the pipeline. Segments of the northern regional road network were upgraded. From the business point of view, a key issue at stake was who would benefit from the reactivation of the trucking sector the project was going to set in motion. Any hopes that national operators may have had were dispelled when the consortium announced that Saga-SDV was to become its main logistics contractor. This choice was widely interpreted as a concession to French economic interests by the US-led consortium. With this and other contracts (besides Bolloré's Camrail, other French companies carried out pipeline-related road upgrading and construction works), ExxonMobil was purportedly making up for having intruded in the 'home turf' of the French.

As a result of the World Bank's involvement, the pipeline project incorporated a series of 'development' goals, including a commitment to promote Cameroonian business participation in the economic benefits of the project. This, however, took effect only a few months before October 2000, when the construction phase proper started. This meant that the consortium had to take steps to sign additional 'socio-economic action plans' with its largest contractors. Among other provisions, these action plans contained a rubric on 'local business development'. To take on its work for the consortium, Saga-SDV created an ad hoc subsidiary named Doba Logistics. In light of the project's new goals, Doba Logistics could make a virtue of necessity and present its subcontracting arrangements with 'host country' truckers as development-oriented. Indeed, Doba Logistics' actions featured in the project's first published progress report to substantiate claims that the consortium and its contractors were 'identifying opportunities to build up local capabilities'. Doba Logistics, readers were told, 'has worked with small local trucking companies to ensure they will have a piece of the haulage work' (CCDP 2000: 26).

According to the oil consortium, decisions taken relating to the project's transport needs observed the principle of maximising host country business opportunities, namely by 'breaking jobs into smaller increments when possible' (CCDP 2000: 26). The underlying assumption was that no Chadian or Cameroonian firm was in a position to absorb the consortium's logistics needs. Nevertheless, the foreign contractor would promote local business interests by dealing with a myriad of small and medium-sized firms. Moreover, since most local truckers had deficient vehicles, in order to ensure that nobody was excluded on these grounds, Doba Logistics would take it upon itself to bring them up to safety standards, and would do so at a minimum cost. However, the majority of Chadian and Cameroonian truckers whom I interviewed were not convinced – they were not, at any rate, the main target audience of these reports, which at the time had a position of prominence on ExxonMobil's website. Truckers overwhelmingly thought that Doba Logistics had neither the interest in nor the means of undertaking road transport by itself.

It needed Chadian and Cameroonian truckers to do the job. The oil consortium's contractual arrangements meant that the job was done on Doba Logistics' own terms rather than the truckers'.[14] Most truckers were not particularly impressed when they became acquainted with the company's dubious managerial practices and violations of workers' rights, which in the end became an embarrassment for the consortium and led to the termination of Doba Logistics' contract in late 2003 and its replacement by Geodis, another French logistics multinational.

Many of the trucks active in Adamaoua did not meet the project's requirements, such as having trailers with brakes. Anticipating the enormous increase in freight that the pipeline was going to bring about, those transporters who were financially able to do so adapted their trucks and purchased better vehicles in order to ensure that they received a share of the pipeline work. In most cases, banks did not finance these purchases. In many instances, the trucking companies' owners, who often have diversified interests in cattle and trade, disinvested in these other sectors to advance their transport operations. Others received private loans from wealthier relatives or patrons. As has become the practice in the sector since the 1990s, the 'new' trucks were bought in the international second-hand market. For all the truckers' discontent with the consortium's contracting arrangements, transporting pipeline freight turned out to be an extremely attractive proposition for those whose trucks met the project's specifications. In order to comply with its socio-economic development commitments, the consortium tried to ensure that its logistics contractors set out favourable terms for the truckers. The local chapter of the SNTRC, which during the whole project mediated Doba's relations with truckers, also played a role in negotiating better rates. All the same, the determining factor was the sheer scale and urgency of the consortium's transport needs. In order to make the construction phase a success, the consortium needed to make sure that its rates were higher than those paid by competing freight owners in the cotton and timber sectors.

One of the pipeline project's most celebrated contributions was its enforcement of strict road safety standards. Most truckers agreed that they had made a big difference. The drivers I knew were very appreciative of the training they received from the oil consortium. Some truckers claimed to have adopted project rules (the avoidance of night driving, for example) as standard practice when working for other clients. Due to

---

[14] There were a few exceptional cases in which the oil consortium contracted Cameroonian and Chadian truckers directly, some of them based in the north of the country. Rayba, a Sudanese company said to have privileged political connections in Chad, also benefited from a large separate contract. In recent years, Rayba has resurfaced in the Douala–N'Djaména corridor under the name of Trans-Afrique.

the project's safety standards, the loads transported per truck were considerably lighter than those customarily carried in the region. More often than not, the return trip was made without any cargo. This made working for the project particularly appealing. A former driver from Ngaoundéré, who in the 1980s started his own small transport venture and today owns five trucks, expressed the view of many of his colleagues: 'If Doba is around and they have abundant freight, there is no one like them'. This, however, was a retrospective comment made when Doba Logistics had already been replaced by the Geodis subsidiary Tchad-Cameroun Logistique (TCL) and, more importantly, the transport needs of the project had become smaller and less urgent. Indeed, by the end of the construction phase, the volume of freight sharply diminished and TCL significantly reduced the rates it paid.

Both Doba Logistics and TCL also offered credit facilities to their truckers. Credits against future transport financed improvements needed in order to bring vehicles up to the project's specifications, such as adding brakes to the trailers or replacing tyres or engine parts, and also the charges for the required technical inspections. Initially, Doba Logistics attempted to supply the tyres that it helped finance but truckers successfully pushed for choosing their own supply sources – which allowed many of them to avoid paying value-added tax. Payment advances were nothing new for freight forwarders and truckers working on the Cameroonian north–south route. While it existed, Sogetrans had provided union members with such advances. After its disappearance, freight forwarders offered advances to individual truckers. Given the chronic undercapitalisation that characterised the sector after the 1994 devaluation, advances had become standard. Saga-SDV offered them as a matter of course. However, first Doba and then TCL could offer very substantial advances of up to 50 per cent – even more substantial if we bear in mind that they paid higher rates than other companies. Most of the remaining payments were promptly made by cheque from banks with local branches. Doba Logistics' terms (two weeks after delivery) were more favourable than TCL's (one month or even longer), a difference that resulted from the project's diminished transport needs as the construction phase came to a close.

Despite their appreciation of these aspects of the project, many of my interviewees perceived Doba Logistics' margins, and later those of TCL (i.e. the difference between what these companies received per tonnage/mileage from the consortium and what they in turn paid to truckers) as excessive. Even if they found the remuneration of their services adequate (at least in the initial stage of the construction phase), they were painfully aware that it was the foreign logistics companies that got the lion's share of the consortium's expenditure on transport. These negative perceptions of the consortium's contracting arrangements were only reinforced when, at different points, the logistic companies were shown to be paying local truckers less than they had agreed with the consortium.

Freight volume decreased sharply once the pipeline construction phase was over. The oil consortium's spending in Cameroon peaked in mid-2002 and fell after the end of construction in early 2003: it went from CFAF 32.6 billion in the second quarter of 2002 to 17.2 billion in the second quarter of 2003 and then to 8.5 billion in the second quarter of 2004. Some found what a consortium food supplier called the 'return to the civilian economy' (CCDP 2002: 73) particularly challenging. Some truckers had invested their profits in expanding their fleet with the purchase of more vehicles. Such was the case of Émile Deschamps, who some identified as the foremost beneficiary of pipeline contracts among Ngaoundéré-based truckers. Others had been more cautious. In anticipation of the foreseeable downturn after the pipeline construction, they had channelled their profits into trading or cattle ventures – a trend that conforms to diversification strategies in the past during periods when transporters have needed to adapt to the sector's ups and downs. The project had also attracted trucking companies based in southern Cameroon to come north and the increased competition in times of diminished freight put many trucking companies under strain. Even if the pipeline project contributed to minor infrastructure improvements and to the renewal of the available trucking fleet, its aftermath left many truckers ill-prepared to face the sector's excess capacity and attendant low rates of pay. The tensions that surfaced during my first visit to Émile Deschamps in 2004 were symptomatic of this post-pipeline construction environment. Indeed, Émile could not keep the business afloat and three years later he was forced to sell all his trucks and leave the country.

Access to freight

Chadian and, to a lesser extent, CAR freight constitutes one of the distinct specialisations of trucking companies based in Ngaoundéré. Inspired by the international legal principles that govern the rights of landlocked countries to access the sea (Upetry 2006), two bilateral conventions have instituted a system of national quotas for the distribution of road freight. Chadian truckers are entitled to 65 per cent of Chadian freight, leaving 35 per cent to Cameroonian truckers; for CAR freight, the allocations are 60 per cent for truckers from CAR and 40 per cent for Cameroonians. For 15 years, the private consortium Sogetrans, in collaboration with the Central African Republic's BARC and the Chadian CTT, monitored adherence to the agreed quotas. In 1987, the economic downturn brought about the disappearance of Sogetrans and the CTT. Although the BARC survived as best it could and the

Chadian government replaced the defunct CTT with a Bureau National de Fret (National Freight Bureau or BNF) in 1989, the institutional vacuum was not filled until 1993, when the Cameroonian government created the BGFT.

Over time, the Cameroonian freight bureau has become a formidable actor. Its large budget derives from a 3 per cent commission on the value of transport services supplied along the Douala–N'Djaména and the Douala–Bangui axes. It has offices in all key Cameroonian nodes of the international transport corridors. Its powers go well beyond the monitoring of compliance with national quotas. All available international freight must be advertised (and its allocation approved) by the BGFT. This enables the bureau to fulfil another of its missions: to keep comprehensive statistics on transport flows along the corridors. It is also entrusted with fixing minimum and indicative transport rates and issuing documents such as the *lettre de voiture international* (international waybill) and the international safe conduct certificate, which are essential for trucks in transit.

From a legal standpoint, the BGFT is certainly a governmental agency. Moreover, its funds come from compulsory levies imposed by the government. Yet, the make-up of its governing body, the *comité de gestion* (management committee), points to a more hybrid character. Only one of its five members represents the Ministry of Transport, the other four standing for the railway company, the shippers (importers and exporters), the truckers, and the forwarding agents. In fact, the most widespread version of the bureau's origins locates them in a collective decision by truckers to reorganise themselves in a period of economic and political difficulty. A Chadian trucker who arrived in Ngaoundéré in the early 1990s, for example, contrasted the Chadian and the Cameroonian freight bureaus in the following terms: 'In Chad, it was the state under the dictate of the World Bank that founded the BNF. Here, it was the truckers themselves who created the BGFT. It is their business. The Cameroonian state has nothing in it.' This explains the paradoxical conclusion reached by Sanda Maliki and mentioned in the opening pages of this book: the BGFT is not only an informal arm of the state but also an employers' organisation.

The closeness between the BGFT and the SNTRC is a related aspect that surfaced in numerous conversations. One of my interlocutors went as far as to dub the BGFT 'the truckers' boss'. Indeed, as the report of his exchanges with the anti-corruption commission in 2012 show (CONAC 2013: 129), Oumarou Dandjouma, the BGFT's unflagging director, regularly acts as a spokesperson for trucking companies. The 'we' that he invokes in his frequent public addresses tends to refer to truckers. It is also often pointed out that Pierre Simé, the president of the BGFT's management committee, happens to be the long-serving president of the

SNTRC. All of this is consonant with the BGFT's role in mediating evolving public and private interests. It is, after all, not an entirely new phenomenon, since in the past Sogetrans also blurred the distinction between public and private. This private consortium made sure that truckers transporting freight for them had a licence and respected the inter-state quotas. Sogetrans issued the truckers' invoices, processed the payments they received, kept their books, and collected their taxes on behalf of the state. As mentioned earlier, in this context truckers did not make much of a distinction between governmental authorities, generically designated as *ngomna* in the pidgin term used by Fulfulde speakers, and Sogetrans. For many, Sogetrans was *ngomna*.

The BGFT fulfils its tasks alongside a series of other actors. The BNF and the BARC share with it responsibility for enforcing national quotas, a collaboration that goes through periodic ups and downs. The BGFT is routinely accused of allocating freight to Cameroonian truckers in excess of their national quota. By all accounts, this is a well-founded contention (Bennafla 2002: 53), but it is one that is difficult to verify independently, since the Chadian and CAR freight bureaus have tended to rely on the BGFT's statistics instead of producing their own. As one of the staff in the BNF's Ngaoundéré office admitted: 'The BGFT distributes freight and the BNF follows.' The BGFT's role is also premised on close working relations with freight forwarders. In order for the national quotas to be monitored, forwarders must declare all the cargo they handle to the freight bureaus before the paperwork authorising its transport can be generated. Without this paperwork, trucks cannot circulate, and so no freight negotiated between forwarders and trucking companies can bypass the freight bureaus. A perennial bone of contention with transit companies is the BGFT's power to set minimum and indicative transport rates '*en accord avec les parties concernées* [in agreement with stakeholders]'.[15] These official rates acquire salience in heightened moments of collective bargaining but are otherwise not systematically enforced or observed. There remains an underlying tension between a sector that sees itself as liberalised and one built around the market-coordinating function of a freight bureau.

Since the BGFT's inception, its relation with trucking companies has been strongly mediated by the SNTRC, which is still the only truckers' union represented in the bureau's governing body. When Cameroonian law incorporated the principle of freedom of association in 1990, small truckers' unions proliferated all over the country, but not in Ngaoundéré. In June 2004, during one of our interviews, the president of the SNTRC's local chapter underscored this oddity himself: 'Truckers got

---

[15] Article 2, decision no. 1107/MINT/DT, of 26 August 1993.

together and created their union. Those were the times of the single party. An act was issued [establishing that] a single party [should be matched by] a single union. With democracy, numerous unions were created. Yet, in Ngaoundéré, it's only us. Nobody has created another.' This was all the more perplexing in light of the general dissatisfaction expressed by virtually everyone concerned. 'There's a lack of consensus; there's no order within,' explained one of the board members. 'It is not a union that enjoys recognition and defends the interests of transporters. Freight owners and forwarders are the ones who decide the terms. The union's voice remains irrelevant,' opined the owner of one of Ngaoundéré's largest transport companies. To this subordination to their clients, a young transporter, whose company had expanded during the pipeline construction, added the SNTRC's submission to public authorities: 'The union is controlled by the state. It cannot be expected to defend truckers' interests autonomously.'

Why had no other association challenged the SNTRC? Historically, a source of strength for the union was its management of a queuing system known as *tour de rôle* (order of loading), which allocated freight to affiliated companies following the order of arrival of their trucks. Forwarders had distributed freight through the union since the opening of Ngaoundéré's railway terminal. The system was maintained after the creation of the BGFT, but with time its importance had dwindled. When I began my fieldwork in 2003, although it still remained important at peak times in the cotton season, the *tour de rôle* system controlled only a small part of international freight. It was mostly kept alive by Saga's reliance on it to hire Cameroonian truckers to transport Chadian freight ranging from cotton and fertiliser to sugar and flour. Large trucking companies regularly working for Saga could afford to ignore queuing constraints altogether. Similarly, truckers with privileged relations with union staff or who were willing to bribe them would manage to jump the queue. In July 2004, Alhadji Yero captured the discontent of many fellow truckers:

The *tour de rôle* does not always work as it should. The [trucker] who has just arrived and got the last number, you are going to find that he's all of a sudden moved to the top [of the blackboard]. If you keep your eyes open, you can contest it on the spot. That is, if you are present. They are going to say: 'Ah, yes! It was a mistake.' And they will take him back to the bottom. But you need to be always there.

After years of gradual erosion, the SNTRC's *tour de rôle* in Ngaoundéré received its final blow in 2008, when Saga stopped channelling freight through the union and began to work with individual trucking companies. In 2010, there was an attempt to revive the union's *tour de rôle* for transport demands from smaller importers, but, after a couple of weeks of little activity, it died out (Figure 4.1).

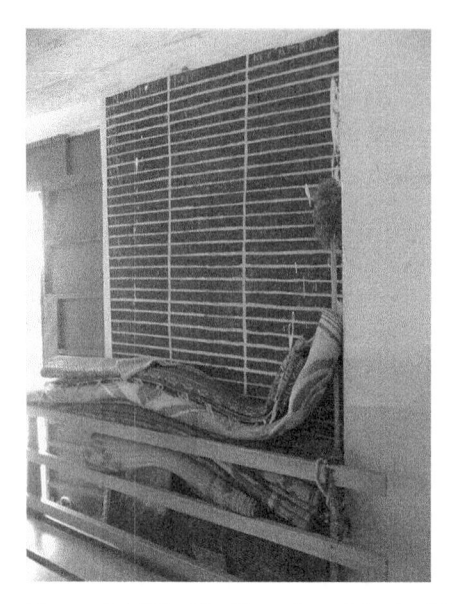

Figure 4.1 The blackboard used in the SNTRC's attempt to revive the *tour de rôle* in 2010, Ngaoundéré cargo terminal, July 2014

What other factors worked against the emergence of rival truckers' organisations? Perhaps the single most important one was the BGFT's requirement of SNTRC membership in order to access international freight. This requirement was more than a simple formality, since the bureau collects from truckers a *contribution syndicale* (union contribution) amounting to CFAF 500 per ton. As the only recognised Cameroonian truckers' union in Ngaoundéré, the SNTRC monopolised these funds. The BGFT rescued the union from its almost fatal weaknesses in the post-Sogetrans era; or, as some of my informants would rather put it, the SNTRC ensured its survival through the creation of the BGFT. The SNTRC's position was not seriously contested until 2009, when reduced volumes of freight, particularly acute in the timber sector, pushed prices down drastically.[16] This proved a propitious environment in which to question the status quo. In January 2009, three new small unions began to publicly demand a share of the Cameroonian quota of international freight going through Ngaoundéré. After months of acrimonious controversy that was reported in the national press, in March 2009 the BGFT agreed to grant these unions freight on the basis of their declared truck fleet. In spite of this, the appeal of the new unions has been very limited,

---

[16] In 2008, about two-thirds of the trucks servicing the logging industry were refurbished to transport containers (Karsenty et al. 2010). According to SNTRC's estimates, rates experienced a 60 per cent decrease within a year (Chendjou 2009).

since they are widely seen as personal platforms for their founders, some of whom have few or no trucks. To this day, the overwhelming majority of Cameroonian truckers active in the Ngaoundéré terminal are SNTRC members. At the national level, not only does the SNTRC remain the leading truckers' organisation but it is also considered to be the dominant voice within the BGFT.[17]

Although the BGFT is unavoidable for truckers wanting to access international freight (as was membership in the SNTRC until 2009), there is substantial domestic freight passing through Ngaoundéré's road–railway interface over which the freight bureau has no jurisdiction. Regardless of whether freight is international or domestic, ultimately freight owners and forwarders have the final say on who transports what. The cement company Cimencam, the cotton parastatal Sodecoton, and oil marketers such as Total and Mobil[18] are examples of businesses that transport large annual volumes of freight and deal directly with trucking companies. To the regret of Cameroonian trucking companies, for decades Cimencam relied exclusively on the trucks of United Transport Africa (UTA), an Italian multinational.[19] After an attempt at keeping a large truck fleet from the late 1980s to the mid-1990s, Sodecoton has relied on small trucking companies for the bulk of its transport needs. Every year its truckers undergo a strict *procedure d'agrément* (approval procedure), which involves exhaustive legal documentation and a visit to the company's headquarters in Garoua for a thorough vehicle inspection. Oil marketers also require truckers to provide proof of compliance with all sorts of regulations. Given the risks entailed, they are interested only in trucking companies that are financially sound and able to supply tankers meeting stringent technical and safety specifications. These exceptional cases aside, most freight owners involved in international trade contract logistics services out to forwarding companies, thus saving themselves the requirement to manage the considerable administrative

---

[17] In 2016, a group of disgruntled SNTRC members allied with the former leader of the largest drivers' union launched a rival organisation under the name of Organisation des Transporteurs Terrestres du Cameroun (Cameroon's Ground Transporters' Organisation or OTTC). This latest attempt to unseat the SNTRC from its privileged institutional position has not succeeded yet. Interestingly, OTTC campaigns have targeted the BGFT rather than the SNTRC.

[18] In October 2007, ExxonMobil sold its network of depots and petrol stations to Libyan investors. Mobil thus became Libya Oil. The fall of the Gaddafi regime in 2011 has had a negative impact on the company's management and its market share in Cameroon has been eroded by smaller marketers such as MRS (former Texaco), Tradex, and Bocom.

[19] UTA's decline led to Cimencam diversifying its trucker portfolio. Its main transport contractor today is the Sudanese-owned Trans-Afrique. The national cement market in Cameroon has undergone significant transformations in recent years. Between 2014 and 2015, three new foreign investors (Morocco's Cimaf, Nigeria's Dangote, and Turkey's Medcem) opened factories in the country. Unlike its competitors, Dangote has controversially chosen to rely on its own large fleet of trucks.

processes involved in international shipments and the need to hire customs brokers.

In her research on cross-border trade between Cameroon and its Central African neighbours, Karine Bennafla remarked on the way in which large forwarding companies 'carve a large freight share for themselves on account of their renown and the *garantie de sérieux* (reliability) that they represent in the eyes of distant trade partners. These firms operate alongside small national companies labelled "informal", whose calibre is lesser and whose prices are more affordable' (Bennafla 2002: 115). This is an accurate characterisation of the diverse landscape of forwarders operating in Ngaoundéré. Humanitarian agencies, armies, large construction companies, and breweries and soft drink companies rely on the better established forwarders. For such clients, firms such as Bolloré (Saga) and Geodis are also appealing in that they oversee the physical passage of cargo through different links in the logistics chain. Merchants and businesses operating in Chad or CAR with either less sizeable or more sporadic transport needs tend to depend on smaller companies. All forwarders, large and small, multinational and national, rely on basically the same pool of truckers.

As the previous pages make apparent, competition among truckers in search of freight can be fierce. Volumes of available freight are highly variable. Farming cycles result in seasonal fluctuations of imports and exports. The effects of the economic slump of the mid-1980s and the impact of the pipeline construction offer examples of other sources of variability. When freight is scarce, truckers struggle to find clients. The outcome of their efforts is the subject of uncertainty, speculation, and intrigue, as exemplified by Émile Deschamps' attempt to get a share of a large brewery shipment to Chad. The opening vignette shows how such situations lend themselves to close scrutiny of the decisions taken by the forwarding agents' managers. In this regard, it is significant that, for many truckers based in Ngaoundéré, for example, the temporal markers favoured when recounting their own business trajectories are the tenures of different Saga/Bolloré managers rather than calendar dates. Alhadji Yero, for example, identified the departure of a Saga manager who seemed to place particular trust in him as one of the key moments in sealing his fate in the trucking business.

Even changes in the forwarders' management approach or style are read in highly personalised terms. A Chadian-Cameroonian trucker who had moved to Ngaoundéré in the late 1990s, for example, explained how he stopped working for Saga/Bolloré:

It was so-and-so who came and got us into deep shit. He chose their three or four [approved] truckers in very opaque fashion. These truckers, with one exception, only have a few trucks. They would then come towards you and tell you: 'Bring your trucks and I'll get you cargo.' They would offer you some ridiculously low price and, even that sum, they wouldn't pay on time. Since so-and-so began that system, I refuse to work for Bolloré.

The heir to one of Ngaoundéré's trucking dynasties similarly accounted for Bolloré's decision to put an end to partial advance payments in 2009 in the following terms:

> When a white person arrives as a new manager, she wants to make savings, so that her bosses see what she is capable of. So-and-so came and said: 'No! From now on, we don't give advances. If you can, you transport the stuff, you return and I pay you on the spot.' [Her bosses] looked at their monthly accounts and noticed that this way [the new manager] had made enormous *économies de gérance* [management savings, in French in the original Fulfulde speech].

Another important set of actors in determining who obtains what freight are the intermediaries known as *démarcheurs* (literally, door-to-door salespersons). They can be found peddling freight in the cargo terminal or killing time around the forwarders' offices in order to be the first to learn of any opportunities that may arise. Like brokers in other fields of activity, they are regarded with ambivalence. They stay in business because they are useful to forwarders needing to expedite abundant freight. Most truckers also have their own intermediaries of choice with whom they work regularly to avoid their trucks lying idle. Accordingly, many downplay the impact of intermediaries on prices and underscore the fact that they provide a necessary service. Yet, some see intermediaries' profit margins as excessive and earned at the truckers' expense. In one of our conversations of July 2004, Yero eloquently moved from the second to the third person when talking about intermediaries:

> When somebody entrusts you with cargo, so that you find trucks to transport it, you become a seller. [In periods of scarcity,] cargo is for sale. You find a trucker who tells you that [if you have him transport the cargo] he gives you [CFAF] 30,000. Someone else, whose truck is paid in full [and has fewer financial constraints], is going to show up and tell you: 'I give you twice as much, take 60,000.' The *démarcheur* is on the winning side. *O jaali* [he is sitting pretty; literally, he laughs]. He runs no risk and he does not pay for petrol or anything else. His name does not even feature [anywhere in the resulting paperwork]. Whatever happens to the truck [on the road] is at the owner's risk.

Since Chadian truckers lacked as much access to Saga's freight as the Cameroonians until 2008 under the SNTRC's *tour de rôle* system, they felt particularly victimised by intermediaries. In the words of a Chadian truck driver: 'If we go to [the forwarders'] offices ourselves [requesting cargo], we get nothing. Saga's employees and the intermediaries, *c'est entre eux qu'ils bouffent* [they keep the food for themselves].' In ways that parallel some Cameroonian truckers' nostalgia for the days of Sogetrans, the manager of a small Chadian group of truckers regretted the disappearance of the CTT and the ensuing proliferation of truckers' unions since the 1990s:

> Even people with no trucks, they are going to create truckers' groupings, so that they can attract people and make money. After liberalisation things changed completely and the changes have benefited neither people who own trucks, nor foreign companies, but intermediaries. For us [Chadian truckers] *la liberalisation a dramatisé les choses* [liberalisation exacerbated things].

Accusations directed at intermediaries often touch on their duplicity. The BGFT, for example, has repeatedly denounced one among many intermediary figures in the trucking business, the so-called *commissionnaires clandestins* (clandestine forwarding agents), who present themselves to importers or to forwarding companies as owners of trucks, while claiming to represent forwarding companies when dealing with truckers (Enbond 2009).

The discretionary power of local managers and the influence of intermediaries notwithstanding, much like Émile Deschamps in this chapter's opening vignette, truckers are aware that high-stake decisions about freight allocation cannot be made without the approval of the company's headquarters in Douala. As a Chadian trucker told me in November 2004: 'Everything happens in Douala. You go take a look [at Ngaoundéré's cargo terminal] and you see [something that interests you]. You say you want to transport it and they tell you: "No, that's been sent to [another trucker's name]."' Similarly, a month earlier, in October 2004, when in a conversation I brought up the role of intermediaries, the manager of a trucking company noted:

> Those you call intermediaries, they start *à la souche* [at the point of origin], at the top. It's not here in Ngaoundéré [that the job is done]. Them, they go to Douala to negotiate. Once they are back here, when the shipment arrives, it's under their name. The [Ngaoundéré] manager has no power. It's his boss in Douala who decides.

Bolloré's position in the Ngaoundéré cargo terminal has itself changed over time. The virtual monopoly it established over *gros fret* (large importers' and exporters' freight) after 1997 with the purchase of Saga was dented when it lost its contract with ExxonMobil to Geodis in 2003. Developments in the oil sector in Chad since 2010 (new oil fields and the construction of the Djarmaya refinery) and their spillover effects have reactivated freight levels for brief periods and have increased competition among forwarders in Ngaoundéré. Bolloré has captured part of this freight but the (mostly Chinese) corporations undertaking these projects have also shown themselves willing to work with other multinationals such as Danko/Maersk and with Chadian and Cameroonian forwarding agents.

Enforcement on the road

Since independence, transport by road of goods in Cameroon has been subject to four main legal regulations: decree no. 59/227 of 3 December 1959; law no. 77/24 of 6 December 1977; law no. 90/30 of 10 August 1990; and law no. 2001/15 of 23 July 2001. For most of the period during which these regulations were in force, many officials and professionals found them wanting in various ways. They often pointed out that their scope was far too narrow and left many aspects unregulated. Such was the case of the 1959 decree, which dealt only with traffic rules and established four types of licences for passenger and freight transport. Similarly, the 1977 act suffered from numerous gaps and omissions. Among other things, it did not even mention the national truckers' union, which had become a key element in organising the sector a decade earlier. Another much-lamented feature of these regulations was that their applicability was uncertain. Most of the vague provisions of the 1977 act, for example, were never developed through *décrets d'application* (implementation decrees) to make them operative. In 1989, two French economists summed up the resulting uncertainty: 'At present the question arises as to which legal arsenal should govern road transport in general and freight transport in particular' (Plat and Rizet 1989: 8). Significantly, they answered their question by noting that, for all intents and purposes, road transport was still regulated by the 1959 decree, despite the fact that this decree had been explicitly abolished by later regulations in the 1970s. Their choice of the word 'arsenal' is also particularly apposite. Relevant provisions were dispersed in a myriad of legal texts, ranging from multilateral and bilateral treaties, acts of parliament, and several decrees to ministerial, provincial, and district ordinances.

The reforms of the 1990s did not remedy the dispersed nature and inconsistencies of applicable legal texts, despite the stated goal of their foundational document to 'align existing regulations with the reform programme'.[20] In 2003 and 2004, for example, a few of the better established trucking companies in Ngaoundéré made use of an already dated official compendium (Ngabmen 1996). In its preface, Issa Tchiroma, the minister at the time, explained that:

Hitherto scattered, most of these legal texts are not accessible and thus remain little known by the public, including even the government staff who have the task of enforcing them and the economic operators (transporters, shippers, drivers, etc.) who have a direct concern and interest in them. This ignorance of their rights and obligations is unquestionably one of the reasons behind the amateurism that characterises the road transport sector in Cameroon.

---

[20] 'Déclaration de Stratégie Sectorielle des Transports', 16 April 1996.

More than a decade later, the formulation of clear, consistent, and accessible rules for the transport sector seems to be beyond reach. In 2009, the Ministry of Transport hired consultants with the goal, among other tasks, of establishing 'an appraisal of the road transport's regulatory framework'. Thus, '[the formulation of] the legal apparatus in a simple language to make it accessible' has now fallen within the purview of government contractors (Tchapmi 2010), a clear indication of the persistent difficulties that both the authorities and transport professionals experience when navigating the rules.

However, the clarity and accessibility of evolving rules are only two of several relevant aspects of the process of governing road transport. As in other areas of economic life in Cameroon, many written rules in the domain of transport are seen as ancillary at best and simply irrelevant at worst. Echoing widespread views that many of my informants shared, an interviewee told a group of researchers evaluating the European Union's assistance to Central African countries in this sector: 'We're really good at drawing up legal texts; when it comes to enforcing them, that's another story' (Slob et al. 2006: 98). These researchers, however, juxtapose such a statement with their own pronouncement that 'none of [the Central African Economic and Monetary Community (CEMAC) codes and regulations] are actually enforced by any of the [member] states'. This is a gross exaggeration, which also fails to capture what their interviewee had told them. That enforcement is 'another story' does not mean that there is no story to speak of.

Consider the 2003 *règlement* that established the conditions that have to be met to engage in inter-state freight transport within CEMAC.[21] This regulation, which was issued during my fieldwork, introduced an *agrément CEMAC* (CEMAC approval) that all truckers based in Cameroon transporting goods to and from Chad and CAR needed to obtain in order to continue operating. By mid-2004, police and gendarmes had added this document to their already lengthy checklist of items requiring verification. Obtaining approval entailed submitting a voluminous application to the CEMAC Executive Secretariat through the Ministry of Transport and paying a CFAF 100,000 processing fee. Once the ministry confirmed that the application was complete and forwarded it to the secretariat, truckers received provisional approval that covered them until a decision on their application had been made.

One morning in July 2004, while driving round one of the city's busiest roundabouts, I came across Abdoulaziz, an acquaintance who worked as a manager of a trucking company. We stopped to greet each other and he took the opportunity to tell me how the police had seized one of his

---

[21] Regulation no. 15/03-UEAC-612-CM-11 of 12 December 2003.

trucks' papers on account of some missing documentation, thus preventing the truck from continuing on its journey. Since he had managed to get only one of the two missing items, their most recent VAT return, a small payment had been necessary to recover the papers and get the truck back on the road. The document he had been unable to conjure up was the CEMAC approval. The company had applied for it four months before and had yet to hear from the Ministry of Transport. He had contacted the ministry in person and by telephone several times without success. He lamented that the *lenteur administrative* (administrative slowness) left them at the police's mercy. That same day, in the afternoon, I had an appointment with the manager of another, larger trucking company. Like many of his colleagues, he was sceptical about the constant addition of new instruments to facilitate economic integration among neighbouring countries. To make his point, he invoked the CEMAC approval: 'It's just another piece of paper. Fulfilling the requirements is not a problem for us. We have all that's needed. The real problem is the police hassle you are bound to experience until you get the document.' As it turned out, they had obtained the temporary approval a couple of weeks before and their tanker trucks could now circulate with a photocopy of the fax they had received from the Ministry of Transport. 'Even these photocopies don't do the trick! In two weeks we have already had a couple of incidents with gendarmes who refuse to acknowledge their validity,' he complained.

Once this particular CEMAC *règlement* was issued, the timing and methods of its enforcement were the compound result of decisions at the ministerial level of different national governments, the discretion of commanders and of police and gendarmerie officers, and the efforts of truckers' unions and individual trucking companies. Those who questioned the CEMAC approval's rationale did not lack arguments: it duplicated the approval process that truckers already underwent at the national level; it overlapped with the sticker for transit issued by the government freight bureaus; it did not offer its possessors any additional advantage but instead imposed yet another unwarranted expense ... These arguments failed to win over the authorities. Nonetheless, the authorities proved somewhat responsive to collective and individual voices calling for a period of grace that would give companies time to comply. Although the Cameroonian Ministry of Transport did not issue a circular spelling this out, as some of the unions had demanded, the first months of 2004 went by without gendarmes and police requesting the CEMAC approval at checkpoints. This flexible attitude came to an end in May, when trucks on the Ngaoundéré–N'Djaména road began to be inconvenienced for not having it. From then on, those trucks not covered by an approval whose drivers were not able to 'negotiate' their way through checkpoints could be stopped indefinitely, thus forcing the trucking company's owner or a representative to intervene. Even in such a situation, someone such as Abdoulaziz could raise the fact that his company had already applied for approval as a mitigating factor. The argument that *lenteur administrative* should be matched by an equal dose of *tolérance administrative*, as Abdoulaziz put it, could be convincing.[22]

The regulatory dynamic that emerged around the CEMAC approval makes apparent the specificity of the trucking business. Since transport and mobility go hand in hand, enforcement agencies have a powerful weapon in their ability to prevent circulation. Indeed, the role routinely adopted by police and gendarmes working on Cameroonian roads in verifying compliance with existing regulations is extensive. It involves the inspection of vehicles and cargo as well as all sorts of documentation. To mitigate the negative impact of such verifications on transport and trade, the bilateral conventions signed between Cameroon and its landlocked neighbours establish a fixed number of checkpoints. However, the security forces' prerogatives are frequently abused and trucks in transit are regularly stopped at many other points. Apart from limiting the number of checkpoints, in their revised versions of 1999, the conventions created two instruments to ensure unimpeded circulation along the transport corridors: a free special *vignette* (sticker) for vehicles in transit and safe conduct for every trip that involved international transport. After the introduction of these instruments designed to facilitate trade, most truckers noticed a significant reduction in average delays and money spent at checkpoints. For the BGFT in particular, in its early years of existence, the issuing of safe conducts was a way of asserting its claims to be working on behalf of truckers, many of whom saw the BGFT mostly as a source of added taxation.

However, the improvements brought about by the *vignette* and the safe conduct were short-lived. 'After eight or ten months, the agents stopped showing any respect for it and began taking more money from us than they did before the safe conduct was created,' a driver who had worked on the Ngaoundéré–N'Djaména route since 1976 explained. The Cameroonian manager of a Chadian trucking consortium similarly underscored how the efficacy of the safe conduct vanished over time: 'At first, it worked brilliantly. It lasted less than a year, though. Then it became useless. It's gotten to a point where it's best not to show it. If you do,

---

[22] This line of reasoning acquired greater traction when it became apparent that the CEMAC Executive Secretariat was unable to process applications within the established five-month period. Eventually, after a six-year wait, in an example of what socio-legal scholars call the recursivity of law, the initial *règlement* was amended to extend both the duration of the renewable temporary approvals from three to six months and the time within which the secretariat had to make a decision from five to ten months. See *règlement* no. 12/09-UEAC-612-CM-12 of 11 December 2009.

Enforcement on the road   159

you're creating problems for yourself.' As could be expected from a union leadership known for its closeness to government circles, in an interview of July 2004, the president of the Ngaoundéré SNTRC chapter emphasised the impotence of the authorities in curbing corruption on the roads:

> There's nothing the government hasn't tried to do to help us. Even the prime minister received us [the SNTRC]. At his own house, we met him! But the policemen and the gendarmes have reverted to their old ways. '*Les papiers, on ne mange pas* (Papers don't put food on the table).' '*Allez dire à Deby ou à Biya* (You go and tell [President] Deby or [President] Biya).' These are the sort of things they tell truck drivers. What can drivers do? The [Adamaoua] governor is aware of the problem and has ordered an inquiry to be conducted.

Indeed, ministerial circulars and ordinances issued by governors and prefects often reminded officials and agents that controls should be restricted to the official checkpoints, but such instructions have very limited impact on checkpoint practices.[23]

In addition to police and gendarmerie checkpoints, trucks are also controlled at weigh stations and customs posts. Weigh stations are a frequent source of delays and added costs. Excess weight leads to the immobilisation of vehicles until the cargo is reduced and the ensuing fines are paid. Truckers complain about the consistency and reliability of scales and the abuses of controllers.[24] Customs officers' discretionary powers over the circulation of trucks are also extensive. Customs work involves controls in cargo terminals and at border crossings as well as verifications performed by mobile brigades. Additionally, in 2009 Cameroonian customs introduced Nexus, a GPS-enabled system that is designed to combat fraud by tracking goods in transit to Chad and CAR. Nexus has involved setting up new customs checkpoints along these transport corridors.

An administrative category that appositely captures the role of documentation in governing transport is the *laissez-passer* (let pass),

---

[23] Thus, for example, in October 2010, the heads of the police and the gendarmerie at the national level agreed to suspend those checkpoints known as *contrôles intempestifs*: that is, all road checkpoints not listed in the regional texts establishing the transport corridors (Nouwou 2011). But the measure was implemented very unevenly and its effects did not last. In January 2012, Chadian truckers addressed a letter through the BNF to the secretary of state in charge of the gendarmerie, reporting that the number of checkpoints on the Douala–N'Djaména route had reached an all-time-high of 146 and denouncing the gendarmes' routine attempts to extort money from them (Fouhba 2012). As recently as 2012, the Cameroonian–Chadian permanent technical commission on transport called for an official text to 'state clearly' that the only document to be presented at checkpoints by trucks in transit is the international safe conduct (CTMPT 2012: 4).

[24] In 2013, the European Union funded a project to modernise the eight weigh stations on recently paved roads. The Ministry of Public Works has repeatedly acknowledged the corrupt practices taking place in weigh stations. In 2010, its magazine *Génie Civil*

which, as we have seen, refers to the documents that allow people, livestock, vehicles, and goods to circulate. In the domain of transport, even documents not directly related to the vehicles, the cargo, or the licensing of drivers and of professional transport activities are required to pass through checkpoints. As my encounter with Abdoulaziz shows, tax returns are a case in point. The fact that his company's driver had to produce recent VAT returns in order for the truck to proceed was far from unusual. In fact, there are ordinances issued by the Ministry of Finance (ordinance 84/MINEFI of 2 August 1995, for example) that expressly authorise police and gendarmes to undertake verifications of tax payments. Thus, the effects of tax returns go beyond their manifest function of establishing truths about economic activity (i.e. commercial turnover, VAT paid to suppliers, and VAT collected from clients) from which liabilities (VAT remitted to the tax authorities) derive. In this sense, since they make circulation possible, tax returns are also *laissez-passers*.

This dimension of tax returns is also illustrated by an incident experienced by Nouhou, a wealthy trucker whom I befriended. In June 2004, he asked me to accompany him to see the gendarmerie brigade's commander. One of his drivers had had the truck's papers taken away from him at a checkpoint some 20 kilometres from Ngaoundéré on account of missing VAT returns. The added irony was that, because he specialises in transport to and from Chad, Nouhou's transactions are exempt from VAT, so that his returns are simple formalities that do not document any payments. After a short wait, the commander received us and asked one of his subordinates to bring the truck's documentation. 'Who on earth checks for VAT returns?' he asked without expecting an answer. He handed us the papers and, with a smile, added: 'It must be a young recruit, so you'll understand I cannot be tough on him.' On our way back to his house, my friend phoned his driver. The incident had interrupted Nouhou's weekly television viewing of French league football, so his angry tone did not surprise me at first. Yet, the conversation rose to a tense crescendo. 'An old man like you! You keep doing things that shame you and shame me. Find your way back to Ngaoundéré!' he ordered his employee before hanging up. It struck me that he sounded more upset with his driver than with the gendarmes. When I mentioned this, Nouhou explained that the driver had already called him the day before requesting that he send extra money for fuel. If the driver had managed his money better, he would have had CFAF 1,000 to pay at the checkpoint and would have avoided any incidents. 'He had more than enough

estimated that fraud at weigh stations caused annual revenue losses of CFAF 7 billion. Recent measures to tackle this phenomenon include the issuing in 2014 of a 'Professional and Ethical Code of Conduct for Personnel Manning Weigh Stations'.

money [for the whole trip]. He must have spent it in some nightclub or other,' Nouhou concluded. The driver had not only handled the checkpoint situation clumsily, he had also used the money for the trip unwisely.

While missing documents are obvious grounds for stopping a truck at a checkpoint, having all the required documents does not guarantee unimpeded travel. This was explained to me vehemently by a senior official at the provincial tax centre in a February 2004 interview:

> The police and the gendarmes are of no use to us. Quite the contrary! A police checkpoint has never helped the tax authorities. Never! People do not come to us to pay their licence or file their VAT returns because of the police. The reason is simple enough. Whether they file their returns or not, the police bother them all the same.

This goes without saying for everyone involved in road transport. No matter how complete their documentation might be, the money truck owners give drivers for travel expenses always factors in funds for payments at checkpoints. That said, some documents are more important than others and their importance can also change over time. The safe conduct, which is meant to be a proxy for all other documents and to ensure the expedient passage of cargo in transit at checkpoints, proved remarkably effective in the first months after its introduction, only to become virtually useless in less than a year. Most truck owners and drivers judge *deereji* (papers) according to their potential to make it easy to pass through checkpoints. There is, as a result, an undercurrent of secondary elaborations on the changing effectiveness of specific documents.

Of course, the kind of scrutiny vehicles and documents receive at checkpoints is not uniform. Trucks owned by the largest companies in the sector (like the oil tankers owned by the veteran Lebanese trucker I mentioned earlier in the chapter, for example) are bothered only in exceptional cases. For small companies, the person who happens to be driving has a bearing on the prospects of unimpeded passage. As Alhadji Yero noted, in the eyes of gendarmes and policemen, driver-owners have greater moral authority and resourcefulness than mere drivers. Differential treatment can also be premised on nationality. Chadian truckers have long-standing grievances about the way in which they are treated on Cameroonian roads. Similarly, the difficulties Cameroonian drivers experience when in Chadian or CAR territory are coloured by their vulnerable standing as foreigners. To make up for the double burden of being both small-sized and foreign enterprises, in the last decade some Chadian associations have opted at various times to travel in convoys when in Cameroonian territory. These have to be accompanied by an escort vehicle (with an added cost) but travelling in convoys spares drivers much inconvenience (and reduces overall road expenses).

Beyond these underlying factors, there are also variable situational dynamics that, as Louisa Lombard (2013) in her work on CAR puts it, test drivers' 'navigational tools'. Drivers need to read particular situations and decide accordingly. Should they keep silent or talk back? Should they joke and seek complicity or vent their anger to garner respect? Should they pay and, if so, how much and when? Truck owners value their drivers' ability to handle checkpoint crossings and resent the delays and the bother of having to get involved themselves in sorting out conflicts with gendarmes and police. This explains Nouhou's annoyance when his driver was not able to get the truck to Ngaoundéré on account of a missing VAT return. Owners also know that a particularly skilful driver can minimise payments at checkpoints. Indeed, the practice of pocketing the funds saved in this way is widespread and many truck owners see it as a reward commensurate with a driver's performance.

* * * * * *

This chapter has tried to reconstruct the parameters within which trucking companies based in Ngaoundéré operate. It is a line of business subject to substantial fluctuations, whose underlying factors range from trends in global markets of export products such as cotton and timber to large infrastructural projects led by foreign investors such as the Chad–Cameroon pipeline project. Political instability in the region, which has been particularly pronounced in Chad and the Central African Republic at different points, has also been a cause of changing business prospects. These histories have also entailed shifts in policies and regulations, although these have been less straightforward and more gradual than labels such as liberalisation would imply. Trucking companies have tried to anticipate, influence, and adapt to changes in regulation, infrastructure, costs, freight volume, and transport rates. The last decade's overall trend of increased costs and drops in freight and rates has proved difficult to weather. From large ventures like that of Émile Deschamps to small operations like that of Alhadji Yero, numerous companies have gone out of business.

On the road, trucking companies are at their most vulnerable. Checkpoints are the sites where such vulnerabilities become most apparent. Encounters at checkpoints pit truck drivers against state agents, who have it within their power to halt vehicles for substantial periods of time. Other encounters take place away from the road and in the offices of different agencies concerned with transport. They may also transcend the specific activities of a single trucking company and involve established representatives of collective interests such as the truckers' unions. Yet, this chapter has shown how an exclusive focus on dyadic interactions between rulers and ruled would offer an oversimplified view of enforcement processes. These involve a constellation of public and private actors whose roles and actions interlock in complex ways.

First, while we should not rule out that state agents are invested in enforcing existing rules with rigour, neither should we take this for granted. At checkpoints, agents of the Ministry of Public Works, customs officials, gendarmes, and the police verify compliance with countless regulations. Their zeal is highly variable and depends on factors such as nationality, social class, ethnicity, kinship, friendship, or acquaintance. Rules that are particularly impractical or difficult to comply with may call for suspended enforcement. The margins of this administrative tolerance, as Abdoulaziz called it, can also be expanded with relative ease by providing financial inducements. When gendarmes and the police detect irregularities, the result is hardly ever the imposition of an official penalty (a fine, for example) and a requirement that the violation be remedied (the problems with the cargo or the vehicle fixed, or the missing documents supplied). Instead, officials are willing to turn a blind eye in exchange for a payment commensurate with the gravity of the violation. Time and bargaining may be required to reach such a settlement and sometimes it has to be achieved beyond the checkpoint, with the involvement of the officials' superiors. Whatever the case, officials' commitment to enforce regulations can be trumped by their willingness to receive money to supplement their more or less meagre salaries. Such scenarios are also common in other government agencies, including the BGFT and the tax authorities. Voicing views that were widespread among truckers, for example, Alhadji Yero did not mince his words when talking about the tax authorities:

The guy at the tax office, he is not interested in ensuring you pay your dues. He doesn't want to do a *kuugal laaɓdum* [clean job]. What he wants is to take advantage of you. So you pay the *impôt libératoire* or a licence and other things that cannot be avoided [income tax and VAT withheld by your established clients] and you find ways of hiding [part of] your turnover. Then, you give a little something to the tax official if need be and minimise your payments at the end of the year. Some truckers are ready to go to greater lengths. They find a receptive official in a remote place where nobody knows them, who issues them a licence documenting a low turnover, and then they don't even bother to file [an income tax return].

Second, public authorities have considerable difficulties in collaborating with each other. Interdepartmental blockages and rivalries among different agencies are widespread. For instance, in recent years Cameroonian customs and the BGFT have competed against each other for powers over the introduction and management of a programme to track via GPS all imports to Chad and CAR. After customs got the go-ahead and launched such a programme under the name of Nexus, the BGFT became a vocal critic. CEMAC institutions have worked for years on a rival system that, unlike Nexus, which is confined to Cameroonian territory, would track freight all the way to its final destination in Chad or CAR. Cameroonian customs' support for the CEMAC initiative has been at best lukewarm. Taxes from the trucking business provide another example of the limits of collaboration between different government departments. As mentioned earlier, the tax authorities in Ngaoundéré think that the gendarmes and police verifying truckers' licences and tax returns (and the payments they exact in the process) actually undermine tax-collecting efforts. But the tax authorities do not complain only about the police and gendarmes. They also decry a lack of cooperation from other government officials, including the local representatives of customs, the Ministry of Transport, and the BGFT. For example, the ruse adopted by some truckers that consists of applying for a licence in a sub-district or a small municipality to avoid taxes, which Alhadji Yero described and tax officials often lamented, is premised on this strategy being facilitated by a sub-prefect or a mayor. As in customs administration, barriers to inter-state cooperation in the domain of taxes can prove even harder to overcome. Thus, in spite of the significant business of Chadian trucking companies based in Cameroon, their effective tax burden is generally thought to be extremely low, thanks partly to the lack of information exchange between tax authorities in Cameroon and Chad.

Third, private businesses can also have a decisive impact on degrees of compliance. This is not so much because of frequent calls by larger, better established trucking companies for the government to combat smaller companies' flaunting of the rules, which, they claim, is a source of unfair competition. Such calls have few tangible effects on enforcement. More consequential is the role of freight owners and forwarders. The control exercised by Sogetrans over the tax status and social security contributions of trucking companies between 1972 and 1987 is a case in point. In more recent times, companies such as Sodecoton have similarly required of their truckers that they comply with rules and regulations. It is also worth noting that large freight owners and forwarders are entrusted with the collection of income tax and VAT advances, which they withhold when paying trucking companies for their services and remit to the tax authorities. The potential of big businesses to push smaller ones towards increased formalisation and compliance with regulations, however, is not always realised. Saga's long-term cooperation with the SNTRC is a good example of this. Within the framework of the SNTRC's *tour de rôle* system, trucking companies could work for Saga while choosing to disregard all sorts of regulations. Even after Saga/Bolloré put an end to the *tour de rôle* and introduced a system of trucker approval in 2008, it has remained common practice for its approved truckers to subcontract freight with truckers whose legal standing Saga/Bolloré does not monitor. This is also the case for most forwarding agents, regardless of how meticulous they are in selecting their truckers. With a few exceptions, forwarders do not have mechanisms in place to control their truckers subcontracting jobs to others.

5 Under the NGO label

In November 2004, I was invited to attend a meeting of what for the last few weeks some of my acquaintances in Ngaoundéré's NGO scene had somewhat mysteriously been calling Le Collectif (The Collective). This was the still embryonic attempt of three NGOs based in the city to work together on a project-by-project basis. The meeting concerned a one-year contract to run a campaign on sexually transmitted diseases and HIV/AIDS prevention in the northern Cameroon section of the Chad–Cameroon pipeline corridor (from Goyoum, East Province, to Mbaïmboum, North Province). Another local NGO had been selected in 2003 to perform these tasks but had subsequently seen its contract terminated. When a new call for bids was launched in October 2004, the three members of Le Collectif had submitted a joint proposal. It had now come to their attention that the agencies overseeing HIV/AIDS-related activities within the framework of the pipeline project were scheduled to visit Bélabo (East Province) in late November on an unrelated fact-finding mission. The team of experts included representatives of COTCO (the Cameroonian subsidiary of the oil consortium), the World Bank, and the Comité National de Lutte contre le SIDA (National Committee for the Fight against AIDS or CNLS). Some members of Le Collectif thought that they should seize the opportunity to meet the team of experts in person in order to increase the chances of their bid being selected. Here is a paraphrased excerpt of the debate that ensued:

BELLO: We are well placed. One of our organisations has already worked for the pipeline [consortium]. It is simply a matter of multiplying our chances of obtaining this job. Even if we are likely to be selected all the same, how could it hurt to get in touch with them before the project resumes?

ALPHONSE: What if what they are looking for is transparency? Shouldn't we rather show that we are serious about what we do? What I fear is that an attempt to contact them does not turn out to be our downfall. We should not forget the difficulties that [the NGO that first obtained this contract] experienced.

BELLO: Precisely! That first call for bids was never a concern of the [Adamaoua] GTP [the CNLS Groupe Technique Provinciale/ Provincial Technical Group]. They merely collected the bids

ARABO: that were submitted. The decision was taken by the GTC [CNLS Groupe Technique Central/Central Technical Group] in Yaoundé. Now, once more, it's a national-level decision. This is a problem case; that's why we need to position ourselves. This time around, unlike before, when it was only us and a few other small NGOs, there are serious competitors ...

ARABO: I have to say I agree with M. Alphonse. Is it appropriate to send someone to meet this team of experts in Bélabo? Personally, I don't think so. It would be considered an attempt either at moral corruption or at hiding one's incapacity. On this particular topic, I've had a phone conversation with [a GTC official]. He explicitly told me that he would not like to meet up because we are both from the same province. If people learned that he and I met, all sorts of interpretations would be possible. There is a substantial contract at stake. Let's wait! There's a chance we may get it ...

BASILE: If it were up to me, if I were to decide this as village chiefs do, I would tell Aminou: 'Let's take the bus and go to Bélabo.' If I have suggested the idea, it is because I am persuaded it can be done without feeding any suspicions of corruption. If we do it well, it is to Le Collectif's advantage. This is a national call for tenders. It is the only time these people are coming anywhere near us ...

AMINOU: We're talking about going to Bélabo ... To tell them what? Once we manage to talk to them, if we get that far, what is it we need to sell them? This is the part that I'm not entirely sure I get.

ARABO: If it concerns the pipeline corridor contract, I don't think we should go. Our bid has been made. We wait for the resolution. If we're talking about meeting them with some other projects in mind ...

AMINOU: If it's about this [contract], I don't see the need to go.

BASILE: I must say I'm disappointed. Our work in this file started three months ago, when I met these same people on a trip to Yaoundé. I asked the GTC why Adamaoua's population was being left out. That's when I was told that in fact the process to recruit another local NGO was about to start. That's how we learned that the call for bids was imminent ...

BELLO: It is a situation in which we already have personal connections because of the work we've done for the pipeline. Everyone should know what it is we want to tell them ... I guess we'll do as always. We'll put together a bid and hope that God brings us a favourable resolution ...

This dialogue offers a window into the predicaments of NGOs based in Ngaoundéré. Le Collectif itself was a reflection of the recent expansion of the sector. As international donors and NGOs launched numerous programmes and projects in Adamaoua, opportunities for contract work abounded. These were particularly prized in a context of persistent economic downturn and massive unemployment. Accordingly, the number of organisations had also grown substantially and competition among them had intensified noticeably. The previous year, for example, the three organisations grouped within Le Collectif had competed against each other for contract opportunities that ranged from the construction of schools and health dispensaries to the setting up and support of different types of neighbourhood and village committees. In the informal conversations and meetings that had led to their coming together, the members of Le Collectif had always underscored the rationale of 'eliminating competition'. In trying to outdo the remaining competitors, Le Collectif faced a dilemma. The procedures involved in awarding contract work are ostensibly geared towards transparency, fairness, equal opportunity, and, at times, preference for 'the local'.[1] However, in practice those procedures are tainted with countless irregularities. In discussing their views, the members of Le Collectif show an acute awareness of the difficulties inherent in trying to strike a balance between conveying professionalism and commitment to transparency and rigour, on the one hand, and establishing privileged connections with decision makers, on the other. Such difficulties have not passed unnoticed. A major European Union programme, for example, has highlighted 'the ambiguous positioning of certain [Cameroonian civil society] organisations between NGO and contractor' (PASOC 2009b: 11). This is typical of a widespread phenomenon that, in their work on Tanzania, Claire Mercer and Maia Green (2012: 107) have called 'the rise of the NGO as contractor'.

In the late 1990s, NGO work was one of the few activities in Ngaoundéré that attracted financial support and generated employment opportunities. This, added to the sector's relative novelty, made it a logical focus for a study of economic governance in the city. Early on, my approach to NGOs as part of the city's *milieu des affaires* (business world) flew in the face of claims to NGO distinctiveness. This chapter explores how NGOs' charitable claims and the visions and positions that inspire them coexist with significant flows of money. If NGOs can serve as platforms through which entrepreneurial trajectories are launched or reimagined, the definition and management of 'profits' are bound to become sensitive tasks. Here, I reflect more broadly on the effects of legal provisions governing NGOs, which, unlike the contractual terms imposed by funders or clients, are at best only loosely enforced. The resulting irregularities make these organisations distinctly

---

[1] Examples of this preference for 'the local' are numerous. Consider two cases that are mentioned in the chapter: the Chad–Cameroon oil pipeline project and the National Programme for Participatory Development (PNDP). In its agreements with the World Bank, the pipeline consortium committed to 'giving priority to host country subcontractors'. In Adamaoua, these included several NGOs (Muñoz 2008). To help communities draft their 'local development plans', the PNDP hired only NGOs that had been 'long and permanently established in the zone of intervention' (PNDP 2004: 79).

vulnerable in the increasingly common scenario of government hostility towards them.

A 'flourishing' of associations

After independence, the regime that consolidated around President Ahidjo maintained a tight grip on associational initiatives, aided by the restrictive 1967 Freedom of Association Act.[2] The emergence of groupings outside the one-party framework (the party, its female and youth wings, and the unions) was effectively blocked (Bayart 1985: 250–1; Geschiere 2009: 44). Established churches, particularly those with international backers, were the most significant exception. As long as they stayed clear of anything 'political', they were authorised and tolerated. For example, around 1968, the Evangelical Lutheran Church of Cameroon founded an organisation called the Oeuvre pour le Développement Rural (Initiative for Rural Development), which had three agricultural centres in Adamaoua. Also in place in Adamaoua was the state-sponsored network of cooperative associations known as *sociétés coopératives pour la production et le développement* (cooperative societies for production and development or SOCOOPEDs), which in many regards were the postcolonial successors to the *sociétés de prévoyance* (provident societies) found across colonial French Africa (Mann and Guyer 1999).

In 1990, under President Biya and in the context of an increasingly troubled political and economic environment, the National Assembly passed two acts that marked a break with the one-party system: the first regulated the freedom of the press and the media; the second regulated freedom of association.[3] A so-called declarative system for the creation of associations replaced the previous one based on administrative authorisation. Whereas in the past prefects had to authorise new associations, now an association could acquire legal existence by simply depositing its by-laws with the district authorities. This resulted in a proliferation of associations – *une floraison* (a flourishing), as the government's National Governance Programme (PNG) described it.[4] Reforms did not stop there. In 1992, new laws created three additional organisational forms: *groupes d'initiative commune* (community initiative groups or GICs), cooperatives, and *groupements d'intérêt économique* (economic interest

---

[2] Law no. 67/LF/19 of 12 June 1967.
[3] Laws no. 90/52 of 19 December 1990; no. 90/53 of 19 December 1990.
[4] The first PNG had identified the legal vacuum in which NGOs operated. The revised PNG discussed further measures required to strengthen non-profit organisations. It estimated that, in 2003, there were around 55,600 'civil society organisations' (Republic of Cameroon 2005).

groups or GIEs).[5] These forms also proved extremely popular, particularly in the case of GICs.

In Ngaoundéré, the creation of these numerous organisations coincided with the World Bank-sponsored Fonds d'Investissement des Micro-réalisations Agricoles et Communautaires (Investment Funds for Agricultural and Community Micro-projects or FIMAC). Through FIMAC, the Ministry of Agriculture disbursed CFAF 1.8 billion in loans nationwide in the 1991–8 period and many GICs and cooperatives were set up with the sole purpose of attracting such loans. The establishment of cooperatives later became subject to stringent conditions, when a 1998 prime minister's decree introduced the requirement that they be authorised by the Ministry of Finance, but registering a GIC remained remarkably easy. It is simply a matter of producing the minutes of the group's constitutive meeting and its by-laws, which are almost always copied from widely available models, and submitting them alongside an official form to the Ministry of Agriculture's local offices. That first massive wave of new GICs of the early 1990s has been followed by smaller but frequent spurts, as new projects and funding have reached Adamaoua.[6]

During my fieldwork, I lost count of the number of times I was surprised by people of all walks of life, including civil servants, who casually mentioned having created a GIC at some point or other. In October 2003, for example, during a visit to some friends who were discussing the prospects raised by an internationally funded urban renewal programme, Alhadji Djibrilla, the building contractor, revealed that he had a GIC of his own. The decision had come about because of a neighbour of his, who had specialised in creating GICs and 'would do them by the dozen'. 'You do not need to do anything but pay him CFAF 5,000 and he takes care of everything. I did mine a couple of years ago in order to apply for an interest-free loan from the Islamic Bank of Development,' he recounted. Since he failed to get the loan, the GIC had never been active. This is a fairly common situation. Despite nominally being groups of at least five people, many GICs are purely individual initiatives. Many also exist on paper only. Dormant GICs may be resurrected if the opportunity arises. Readers will remember how, in

---

[5] Law no. 1992/006 of 14 August 1992; *décret d'application* (implementation decree) no. 1992/455/PM of 23 November 1992.
[6] In 2013, the Ministry of Agriculture announced its intention to phase out the GIC as an organisational form, opening the door for interested GICs to become cooperatives, which are now notionally regulated by a 2010 Organisation pour l'Harmonisation en Afrique du Droit des Affaires (Organisation for the Harmonisation of African Business Law or OHADA) Uniform Act. Recent years have been marked by numerous uncertainties surrounding this transformation (Seh and Ndemen 2013), which, with few exceptions, has not taken place.

order to become a supplier of foodstuffs to the catering companies working for the Chad–Cameroon pipeline project, Bello had repurposed an old GIC his father had created with a different goal in mind.

Development programmes and projects are themselves invested in the proliferation of GICs. Their 'logical frameworks' often list quantitative targets for newly created organisations as indicators of key outputs. The African Development Bank-funded Programme d'Amélioration du Revenu Familial Rural (Project for the Improvement of Rural Households' Income or PARFAR), for example, aimed to create 500 revenue-generating units (most of them GICs) in the country's three northern provinces. In July 2004, I accompanied a Ministry of Social Affairs official working for PARFAR for several days while she met potential beneficiaries in need of encouragement and advice. Sometimes, she would even take it upon herself to submit paperwork to the Ministry of Agriculture on behalf of GIC promoters. She noted that, no matter how much help it received, Adamaoua lagged behind when compared with other provinces such as the Far North, which were 'more advanced' as far as associations and NGOs were concerned. 'On average, for every ten funding requests PARFAR receives, only two are from GICs in Adamaoua,' she lamented. Similarly, the Projet Intégré d'Appui aux Acteurs du Secteur Informel (Integrated Project for the Support of Informal Sector Operators or PIAASI), a Ministry of Employment project that drew its funds from debt relief granted within the IMF and World Bank's HIPC initiative, envisaged forming groups of youngsters as one way of facilitating their transition from the informal to the formal sector. In an interview with the *Cameroon Tribune*, the project's technical supervisor for Adamaoua boasted of having been instrumental in forming 40 new GICs in two years (Djarmaïla 2008).

The NGO scene was also particularly active in the early stages of my fieldwork. I first noticed this in September 2003, when the wife of one of Adamaoua's members of parliament gave a friend of mine the task of founding an NGO on her behalf. After some enquiries, he decided that the first step would be to form an association. This required the drafting of the association's by-laws and, in order to avoid any potential mistakes, my friend decided to base these on successful examples. So, I found myself accompanying him in his quest to get hold of the by-laws of several organisations that he had identified as worth copying. We spent a whole day following different leads until in the late afternoon we located the president of a small NGO that did 'community mobilisation' for UNICEF. She and my friend happened to know each other from the sports club they both belonged to. In spite of their former acquaintance, however, she was visibly annoyed both by our intrusion in her family compound and by what she perceived as my friend's amateurism. She tried to make him see that it made little sense to launch an NGO without first having a critical mass of people who shared a vision and were ready to work towards realising it. Copying somebody else's by-laws was not a good enough basis on which to build a new NGO, she told us. My friend was unfazed and his persistence ended up paying off, as the NGO leader allowed him to copy a file with their by-laws onto a flash drive. A couple of months later, once my friend's efforts culminated in the submission of all the required documents to the relevant prefect, a new association for the defence of women's rights saw the light.

Like the partner organisation of UNICEF whose by-laws my friend copied, I encountered several other Ngaoundéré-based organisations that dated back to the 1990s and considered themselves pioneers of the local NGO movement. Two of Le Collectif's members saw themselves in this light. Their associations had both been created in the mid-1990s. One of them originated in another partnership with UNICEF, and had the aim of remedying the widespread lack of birth certificates among school-age children in rural Adamaoua. The other had been created to channel the funds made available to members of parliament in order to promote development projects in their constituencies. It was also in the 1990s when the Lutheran Church decided to close down its Initiative for Rural Development after a negative evaluation of its accomplishments and to replace it with the Programme d'Appui au Développement Intégré (Programme for the Support of Integrated Development or PADI). Established in 1997 with its central office in Ngaoundéré, PADI was a more flexible organisation than its predecessor. As its director, who later embarked on a very successful humanitarian career abroad, explained to me in June 2004, PADI had adopted the autonomy and more secular look that the new times called for.[7]

For all these changes, according to the available nationwide estimates, by 2000 Adamaoua and the South West were the two provinces with the smallest number of registered associations (UNDP 2000: 14). At the turn of the decade, there were two important sources of renewed impetus to the creation of NGOs: the broadening and intensification of the struggle against HIV/AIDS and the construction of the Chad–Cameroon pipeline. During the 1990s, the country's response to HIV/AIDS had remained under the control of a 'biomedical oligarchy', which was concentrated mainly in Yaoundé and, to a lesser extent, Douala (Eboko 2005: 791; see also Eboko 1999; Eboko and Mandjem 2011). In 2000, with the launch of the first national strategic plan against HIV/AIDS and support from international donors and NGOs, a 'new associational wave'

---

[7] The Lutheran Church has also been behind the establishment of Réseau de Lutte contre la Faim (Network for the Fight against Hunger or RELUFA), one of the NGOs that has most actively addressed the impact of extractive industries in southern Cameroon (Lickert 2011).

(Otayek 2004: 82) reached other parts of the country, including Adamaoua. For example, the Association des Jeunes de Ngaoundéré pour la Lutte contre le SIDA (Association of Ngaoundéré Youth for the Fight against AIDS or AJLC), which had won and subsequently lost the pipeline contract that the members of Le Collectif were vying for in October 2004, was in many regards the fruit of this process. It had been started in 2000 by a group of friends in their last years of high school, who, as one of them put it, 'heard the echoes of the disease of the century, saw how people were creating associations everywhere and asked ourselves: "Why don't we create one too?"' By mid-2001, they had already registered as an association. In August 2002, they took part in a CARE-sponsored five-day seminar on 'the participatory process of the fight against AIDS'. Shortly afterwards, they got their first contract work from the newly active GTP, the provincial arm of the CNLS, joining nine other associations in the task of setting up *comités locaux pour la lutte contre le SIDA* (local committees for the fight against AIDS or CLLSs) across Adamaoua. From 2002 to 2004, there were several other opportunities to engage in this line of work by training *pairs éducateurs* (educator peers) and revisiting urban neighbourhoods and villages for the *redynamisation* (reactivation) of CLLSs. HIV/AIDS campaigning in this period, however, turned out to be a precarious basis on which to consolidate nascent organisations. Financially, the rewards were much smaller than anticipated. Adamaoua's GTP first delayed and ultimately failed to pay significant portions of the sums agreed. Moreover, accusations of corruption cast a long shadow over the government bodies in charge of these campaigns. In the eyes of the presumed beneficiaries, the reputation of the collaborating associations became tarnished by extension (Boyomo 2006).[8]

Because of the international attention it received right from the early planning stages, the Chad–Cameroon pipeline project became the focus of much NGO mobilisation. The origins or expansion of important Cameroonian organisations that specialised in monitoring the impacts of extractive industries can be found in the transnational protest movement against the pipeline project.[9] Yet, such Yaoundé-based organisations had

---

[8] Payments were initially frozen in early 2004, when a control mission was sent from Yaoundé to look into potential cases of embezzlement. In September 2004, Adamaoua's GTP coordinator was dismissed for *mauvaise gestion* (poor management), alongside 11 other high-ranking officials in the struggle against HIV/AIDS across the country. He was later accused of embezzling CFAF 133 million during his tenure. In March 2008, the Minister of Health, who had led the accusations against his subordinates four years earlier, was arrested on corruption charges.

[9] This was the case of FOCARFE (Fondation Camerounaise d'Actions Rationalisées et de Formation sur l'Environnement), CED (Centre pour l'Environnement et le Développement), and the above-mentioned RELUFA (Petry and Bambé 2005; Lickert 2011).

practically no presence in Adamaoua. For NGOs located in the province, the project acquired most relevance somewhat later, once the substantial development agenda that the consortium undertook in exchange for the World Bank's backing was defined. In the end, only a small number of those development projects were entrusted to Adamaoua organisations. Most of these opportunities fell under the consortium's regional compensation programme, which was conceived as a supplement to its provisions for individual compensation. Of these regional compensation funds, CFAF 144 million were allocated for educational, health, sports and other facilities and equipment (wells, pumps, and mills) in Adamaoua and North Province in 2002 and 2003. Organisations based in Ngaoundéré and Meiganga won these bids, but about half of them were construction businesses rather than NGOs. For the few NGOs that benefited from the contracts, they represented important injections of funds as well as providing valuable experience in following bureaucratic management procedures and accounting standards. Their work for the pipeline consortium also enhanced their credibility as potential partners for future development initiatives. Beyond those few NGOs that landed contracts, the inflated expectations that surrounded the pipeline project contributed to the growth of the NGO sphere in Adamaoua. Mobilisations around the project also furnished inspiration for the organisations that led the response to the revival in 2005 of an old mining project targeting the bauxite reserves of Minin-Martap and Ngaoundal in southern Adamaoua (Boyomo 2007a).

The proliferation of NGOs in Ngaoundéré in the early 2000s prepared the ground for externally driven efforts at *structuration* (organisation). This is a process that has been well documented in other countries. Writing about Tanzania, for example, Claire Mercer and Maia Green note: 'As the civil society sector grows it is organised through donor-funded workshops into a hierarchy of geographically distributed "networks" that connect civil society at the local scale to civil society at the regional, national and international scales' (Mercer and Green 2012: 107). A first step in this direction was taken in Adamaoua following a workshop organised in Ngaoundéré in April 2005 by the Programme Concerté Pluri-Acteurs (Consultative Multi-Actor Programme or PCPA). This programme envisaged a partnership between French and Cameroonian organisations in 'civil society building' (Amougou and Lambert 2008; Cumming 2009; Onana et al. 2009). The rationale was to promote accountability in the Cameroon government's use of the substantial funds freed up by France through the conversion of multilateral and bilateral debt into aid. Aimed at overcoming the amateurism and *cloisonnement* (isolation) of civil society actors, the PCPA's workshop provided the impetus for the creation of a Collectif des Organisations de la Société Civile de l'Adamaoua

(Coalition of Adamaoua's Civil Society Organisations or COSCA), which, from 2005 to 2008, was to channel funds for a number of training events, participatory forums, and advocacy campaigns in the province. With a much larger budget than the PCPA (€5.6 million as opposed to €2 million), the European Union's Programme d'Appui à la Structuration de la Société Civile (Support Programme for the Structuring of Civil Society or PASOC) also worked towards the institutionalisation and professionalisation of Cameroonian civil society from 2007 to 2011. The template, which was tried in a number of European aid recipients in Africa and elsewhere, incorporated the policy agenda set out in the 10th European Development Fund (Courtin 2011). PASOC operated in Adamaoua through an *organisation relais* (representative organisation) based in Ngaoundéré, which gave the programme a local anchoring and which became empowered as the arbiter of decisions with funding implications.

Le label ONG (the NGO label)

In February 2004, after my landlord rented out the adjoining premises to a grilled meat parlour that attracted more noise and flies than either my visitors or I could bear, I decided to move out of the small storage room in Ngaoundéré's city centre that I had been using as an office for about six months. I was lucky enough to find an alternative space within a few days. A wealthy merchant had just built a row of street-facing shops in a quiet but conveniently located side street in the Tongo-Bali neighbourhood and, thanks to the good offices of a mutual friend, he deemed me reputable enough to be his tenant. I was the first one to move into the new building but several other tenants joined me soon after. We were an odd assortment, including a short-lived luggage shop, a travel agent specialising in trips to Mecca, and an NGO I had heard about but had never come across until then. The NGO in question was AJLC, and one of the first things it did when it moved into its new office was to put up a sizeable metallic sign. The sign's heading read 'ONG AJLC', and the lines below spelled out the acronym and provided telephone numbers and an email address.

At the time, there were dozens of organisations in the city that operated *sous le label ONG* (under the NGO label), as a MINEPIA civil servant doubling as development consultant put it to me. AJLC had become an association in 2001 by depositing its by-laws with Vina District's prefect. Ever since then, it had been referring to itself as an NGO and had been treated as one by its partners. Cameroonian law had created a specific legal framework for NGOs only in late 1999 and the implementation decree that was required to make the NGO Act effective was not issued until mid-2001.[10] The first ordinances officially authorising associations across the country to operate as NGOs were issued in 2003, when the technical commission in charge of approving requests became operational (Kimaka 2009: 11). Nonetheless, despite authorisations being extremely hard to acquire, 'ONG' is an acronym that has been used liberally in Cameroon since the 1990s. It is present in everyday speech and inscribed in the built environment of towns and villages, written on signs and painted on walls. Like AJLC, many entities have been using the label and are thus recognised as NGOs not only by ordinary citizens but also by different kinds of international development actors and (unofficially) by the Cameroonian government.

Even after 1999, when the NGO Act was passed, adding a new layer of complexity to the legal framework, it was not uncommon for self-declared NGOs to operate without any legal cover. AJLC itself had been active for several months before deciding to approach the district authorities and complete the formalities required to become an association. Consider also the example of Synergies de Développement (Development Synergies or Sydev), an organisation that I saw emerge as a prominent player in Adamaoua's NGO sphere during the early period of my doctoral fieldwork. Sydev was a coalition of several organisations, whose heterogeneous membership included northerners and southerners with diverse religious and ethnic identities. Among its leading figures, Sydev counted a former civil servant who had international experience and had transitioned into the NGO world upon his return to Cameroon, a former employee of an international NGO, and the national vice-president of an ethnic association. Although its members were either associations or GICs and the consortium had been fully operational since August 2003, Sydev itself lacked a legal identity. This, however, had not been an obstacle to Sydev becoming one of several privileged partners in Ngaoundéré of an internationally sponsored programme. This and other activities, including contract work in Adamaoua's public campaign against AIDS, raised Sydev's profile to the point where the district authorities noticed its irregular circumstances. As one of its consultants explained to me at the time: 'The prefect has made us understand that we must legalise our organisation here [in the Vina District].' Accordingly, Sydev complied with the required formalities and officially became an association in September 2004.

The reverse situation could also be found. Many associations came formally into being well before they developed any meaningful activity. The leader of another Ngaoundéré-based NGO that expanded greatly in the 2010s, for example, explained to me on our first meeting in July

---

[10] Law no. 99/14 of 22 December 1999; *décret d'application* no. 2001/150/PM of 3 May 2001.

2004 how 'our NGO has existed for two years on paper and for seven months in the field'. As has been described elsewhere in the country (Jiogue and Demanou 2015: 33), some associations reported having experienced blockages from prefects or their staff, who had refused to issue a receipt for the deposit of an association's by-laws unless facilitation payments were made. Yet, overall, the procedure for constituting an association legally was widely perceived as straightforward and expedient. It should also be noted that a number of organisations that saw themselves as NGOs had chosen not to become associations and opted for other legal forms instead. GICs and cooperatives were the most common alternatives but I also came across the exceptional but significant case of an NGO that had been created as an economic interest group (GIE). A GIE is 'a subtle structure, where everyone can come in and leave as required', one of the organisation's managers explained. It is worth mentioning that the GIC, the GIE and the cooperative structure prevent these organisations from obtaining recognition as NGOs, since the law establishes that only associations can opt for such a status.[11]

The NGO Act was preceded by expectation and controversy. When it was finally passed by parliament in December 1999, it attracted considerable criticism. One of its critics' many targets concerned the procedure for the creation of NGOs, which entailed obtaining an *agrément* (authorisation) from the Ministry of Territorial Administration and Decentralisation (MINTAD). Applications were to be submitted to the provincial authorities, which in turn would send them to a technical commission entrusted with assessing them and issuing the recommendations on which the Ministry would base its final decisions. The commission, which consisted of 15 members, including four civil society representatives, became operational in 2003. Since its inception, however, the commission has met only infrequently and has adopted a very restrictive stance towards granting authorisations.[12] This meant that, by 2011, no organisation based in Adamaoua had succeeded in achieving legal status as an NGO, although this did not prevent them from

---

[11] It is also worth adding that international actors tend to see the usage of the NGO label by GICs and cooperatives as a feature of Cameroonian civil society's confusing landscape, which 'structuring' programmes such as PASOC are designed to remedy. From their perspective, 'NGO' is an ill-fitting designation for GICs and cooperatives; instead, categories such as grassroots or community-based organisations should be favoured when referring to them. Cristophe Courtin (2011: 122), who worked as PASOC coordinator, has reflected on how this 'prescriptive architecture' was inscribed in European Union programmes.

[12] From October 2003 to April 2009, the commission held five sessions. In this period, it reviewed 290 applications, only 26 of which received a favourable recommendation (Kimaka 2009: 10). In more recent years, sessions have been more frequent but have still been irregular: two in 2011, none in 2012, three in 2013, and two in 2014 (Jiogue and Demanou 2015: 139).

presenting themselves and being treated as such by partners and third parties. Most explained their failure by referring to the favouritism that characterised the treatment of requests for authorisation. As a university student who worked for two different NGOs at the time told me in July 2004: 'Those eight NGOs [that had obtained authorisation nationwide at the time] are organisations behind which there are powerful persons, including influential ministers, for whom all sorts of concessions are made.' This was also a justification given by associations using the NGO label that had not even bothered to apply for an authorisation. In June 2011, AJLC's managing director had the following to say about why, after a decade of NGO activism, he had never applied for an authorisation: 'I have colleagues who have prepared several applications with utmost care and they never succeed. The governor, he sends it to Yaoundé. But, once there, it depends on the willingness of the minister. We have seen him favour associations in which current members of government or a former minister are involved. It's deplorable!'

Lacking authorisation could exclude organisations from getting access to certain contract opportunities. However, contract work that was contingent on having an authorisation was the exception. In fact, no organisation in Adamaoua enjoyed a competitive edge because it was an authorised NGO. AJLC, Sydev, and numerous other active organisations knew that programmes and projects in search of partners based in the province had little choice but to work with them. Often, those associations that had gone through the motions needed to obtain legal recognition had done so at the request of their international partners. In 2004, for example, a pioneer organisation that collaborated with a United Nations agency applied for authorisation as *ONG unipersonelle* (one-person NGO), a format that the NGO Act (article 2) had introduced and that critics saw as 'an opening for all sorts of adventurers and opportunists' (Mpon Tiek 2004: 69; Jiogue and Demanou 2015: 135). Its partner's reservations about this choice eventually pushed the organisation's founder to withdraw the initial application and submit a new one as a standard NGO. Cameroonian ministries would also offer long-established partner associations their help and endorsement in submitting an application to MINTAD – although in the cases I followed the results were equally disappointing.

The vulnerability associated with operating under a label to which one had no legally sanctioned claim had greater consequences for organisations that embraced causes pitting them against governmental agencies. An example that received coverage in the national press (Boyomo 2010a) involved Action pour la Promotion de la Santé et la Protection de l'Environnement (Action for Health Promotion and Environmental Protection or APROSPEN). In 2009, this NGO launched a project aimed at improving the organisation of the hadj for Cameroonian pilgrims; this was one of the two projects funded by the European Union through PASOC that year in Adamaoua (PASOC 2010). By questioning the arrangements put in place by the government-controlled National Commission for the Hadj, APROSPEN upset the authorities. In March 2010, the sub-prefect of Yaoundé II forbade a national workshop for the dissemination of the project's findings and recommendations from taking place. The decision, which came from a sub-prefect who, in the preceding weeks, had authorised an earlier scheduling of the same event, was motivated on the grounds of 'threats to public order, illegality, lack of entitlement, and *défaut de qualité* [lack of status]'. In May 2011, looking back on the incident, one of APROSPEN's founders whom I had known since 2003 commented on the seemingly unattainable prospect of obtaining official NGO status:

> We have tried [to get an authorisation] to no avail. When we've been operating [as an association] for [the required number of] years and we have a track record that justifies our capacity, we want NGO status. But you submit your file and nothing happens. The commission does not hold sessions. This is one of the concerns voiced by PASOC. They wanted to identify [the source of] this mystery. Why are certain [applications for authorisation] blocked?[13] The more you put your finger on real problems, the more difficult they make your life. When PASOC began its struggle around this, we thought things would begin to work well but the authorities would not budge. MINTAD, for one, has circulated the notion that PASOC was funding people to *les emmerder* [piss them off].

Indeed, the Cameroonian government had not always welcomed PASOC's encouragement and funding of a series of advocacy initiatives. In July 2008, the then head of MINTAD had issued a press release listing all authorised NGOs (21 at the time), which many interpreted as a warning directed at PASOC's management team. In it, the minister 'invited' Cameroonians and foreigners alike 'to exert more vigilance regarding the proliferation of associations and other groups that today claim [the NGO] status'.[14] Yet, for all the vulnerability deriving from its precarious legal position, APROSPEN has prospered in recent years. In 2013, it went on to become Adamaoua's representative organisation of PASOC's successor programme (Programme d'Appui à la Société Civil/ Civil Society Support Programme or PASC).

Complying with the letter of the law does not become any easier for organisations that succeed in obtaining authorisation to operate as NGOs. The NGO Act and its accompanying decrees stipulate a series of additional obligations such as the deposit of minutes with the authorities

---

[13] The informant is here referring to several activities that PASOC funded on the legal framework within which civil society organisations operate, including a study on the organisations' perceptions of this framework (CREDDA 2008; PASOC 2011).
[14] *Communiqué radio presse* (press release), no. 00078/CRP/MINTAD/DAP/SDLP of 11 July 2008; see also Boyomo (2010b).

and the auditing of accounts, which many fail to meet. Furthermore, authorisations are valid only for five-year periods and the obstacles and delays experienced by those applying for renewal are similar to those suffered by first-time applicants. None of this prevents NGOs from operating normally, but their precarious legal situation can weigh on them when problems arise.

The quest for contracts

How do NGOs in Ngaoundéré go about identifying funding sources and securing contracts? Timely access to information is a key variable. Contacts with officials in relevant ministries, representatives of international donors in Cameroon, and members of other NGOs in Adamaoua and beyond can all prove useful. Although information may be relayed in their home region, it is advisable to have a regular presence in nationwide NGO forums, often held in Yaoundé and Douala. Basile emphasised the importance of this when he reminded other members of the short-lived Collectif how, thanks to his participation in an unrelated meeting in the capital, they had learned about the pipeline consortium's call for tenders even before it was announced publicly. Similarly, looking back on missed opportunities, the founder of another NGO recalled how in 2008 he had not been aware of PASOC's call for expressions of interest in becoming the programme's representative organisation for Adamaoua: 'Many NGOs applied. If only I had known, we would have had a chance. We are among the longest-standing ones. But communication does not work well here ... The last thing [a rival organisation] would want to do is to spread the news about available opportunities.' Organisations that have only intermittent activity are more likely to let opportunities pass by. In June 2011, the leader of an association whose dedication has waned in recent years on account of his increasing involvement in various commercial ventures regretted having missed the chance to bid for a contract to prepare the municipal development plan of a village near his home town: 'It was [the representative of a rival NGO] who obtained the information and kept it to himself.' The importance of accessing information in a timely fashion as well as developing close relationships with key decision makers has pushed the managers of several NGOs to move their main residence to the national capital. Bello's is a case in point. In 2010, he moved to Yaoundé because, in Ngaoundéré, he felt isolated from those decision centres that most affected the prospects of his NGO.

In addition, NGOs need a modicum of familiarity with the technologies of document production, both material and conceptual. In-house skills in this area are typically developed gradually. Unlike nascent or small organisations, better-established ones depend on their own equipment and expertise to produce the documents required to bid for a contract. International NGOs and government agencies themselves offer workshops on *montage de projets* (conceptually and physically putting together a project proposal). The older the organisation, the more likely – and the more extensively – its staff will have benefited from such training sessions. External assistance may also cover computers and printers, and even ink cartridges and paper. PASOC made this an explicit focus of the support it provided to its provincial representative organisations. In 2010, Sydev, the organisation that PASOC selected in Adamaoua, created *la mutualisation*, a shared office space where associations in Ngaoundéré could use computers, access the internet, and print documents at below-market prices. It is also common for international NGOs to pass on office equipment to their partners when projects come to an end.

Applying for funding requires elaborate documentation. Applications are normally divided into an administrative and a technical file. The administrative file includes elements such as contact details for the NGO managers, the receipt issued by the relevant prefect showing that they have constituted themselves as an association (and that certifies how long they have officially existed), the association's by-laws, a map showing its location, and proof of having a bank account to receive payments. The technical file varies greatly depending on the type of intervention. It comprises evidence of relevant experience, availability of human resources and equipment, and financial sufficiency, but also, crucially, a suitable, feasible, and persuasive proposal. While familiarity with the administrative component tends to be more widespread, a competitive bid may require hiring a consultant to write up the technical aspects, particularly if the contract relates to a domain in which the organisation lacks previous experience.

A decisive aspect of this documentation is the language used and its conformity with donors' changing expectations. It is often during workshops and other encounters with national and international development professionals that NGO promoters become acquainted with the buzzwords of the moment. Thus, it is no coincidence that the two projects that PASOC funded in Adamaoua during its first call for bids in January 2009, in which 32 projects received funding nationwide, hinged on keywords such as *veille citoyenne* (civic watch) and *plaidoyer* (advocacy), with which the NGO leaders behind these projects had acquainted themselves through training sessions organised by PASOC itself.

Less subject to such shifts in terminology but equally oriented to meeting funders' expectations is the need to get across 'an autonomous and long-term strategic vision' (PASOC 2009b: 10), the absence of which is often pointed out and lamented. For example, the first venture undertaken by Le Collectif, which preceded its joint bid for the pipeline consortium's health campaign, involved contacting a minister who was coming to Adamaoua on an official visit. To that end, the members of Le Collectif had prepared a document that was crafted to convey the impression that they had a long-term programme in specific development domains that arose from a sustained assessment of the needs of the populations with whom they worked. The extent to which such visions are genuine – something that outsiders often wonder about – is in many regards beside the point. Those who have their 'own' vision and find themselves starved of funds soon mould that vision to make it more accommodating. Specialisation tends to operate as a marker of an autonomous vision.[15] Yet, regardless of their expertise and their variable efforts to stick to that vision, the main organisations in Ngaoundéré have all had a share in the area's major development programmes and projects. Thus specialisation tends to be a rhetorical effect tailored to specific funding opportunities, and 'chameleon' organisations are the rule rather than the exception, as observers conducting research in other parts of the country have also noted (Mpon Tiek 2004: 72).

Although conforming to the required conventions and touching on fashionable formulas are considered essential, the documentary support of a contract bid is also seen as an opportunity to distinguish oneself from other organisations. Those who can afford it do not economise on paper and colour printing. One of the NGOs that seemed to have gone further in the use of impressive documents to denote competence astonished me during a 2011 visit to their office. I was welcomed with a 47-page document entitled *Réunion de concertation avec M. José M. Muñoz dans le cadre de la relance de la collaboration avec X* (Consultation meeting with Mr José M. Muñoz within the framework of resuming his collaboration with X). A few NGOs offer their *montage* services to the general public. For example, when in early 2004 the well-connected owner of a modest and problem-ridden hair salon in Ngaoundéré was encouraged by a national celebrity to 'think big', she approached a local NGO for support. She needed them to help her put together a convincing project for a private elementary school for girls. After almost a year of regular visits, a series of money advances that failed to generate anything substantial, and her failure to meet further requests for exorbitant sums, she finally gave up. In a few cases, when the people in need of assistance in conceptualising a project were in a particularly strong position (i.e. their connections with the contracting authority made their success very likely), the

---

[15] Specialisation is certainly not such an obvious asset for programmes that in recent years have tried to support 'civil society' structuring and professionalisation more broadly. Therefore, it is hardly surprising that the organisations that were chosen to represent programmes such as PCPA, PASOC, and PASC in Adamaoua boasted about rather than hid their many areas of interest.

NGO offering help might agree to wait until the contract was finished to be paid its fee.

Areas in which technical expertise is particularly prized can turn into lucrative strands of NGO activity.[16] Sometimes rival organisations may share the same source of expertise, at times mobilised to produce remarkably different documents. For instance, in the national programme for malaria control that began in 2010 under the sponsorship of the Global Fund, the association that was selected to carry out communication and educational tasks in one of Adamaoua's districts had its bid prepared by employees of another NGO, which was also among the competing candidates.

However, as the discussion among members of Le Collectif underscores, a finely tuned and impressive-looking application file is necessary but not sufficient. Before and after contracts are awarded, competence may also be signalled in other important ways. Consider Aminou's words when voicing his doubts that he, or anyone else, could pull off a successful performance if and when they managed to meet the team of experts visiting Bélabo: 'To tell them what? ... What is it we need to sell them?' A convincing performance of competence involves not only confidence and certain social skills – which, in fact, some of his colleagues thought a panic-stricken Aminou might lack – but also, as Bierschenk, Chauveau, and Olivier de Sardan (2000: 27) have underscored, crucial choreographic dimensions. These dimensions are captured well by 'donor dancing', a phrase used in Nigeria to which Kamari Clarke (2009) has drawn our attention.[17]

NGO choreographies require a stage, often in the form of an office. NGO operators in Ngaoundéré are very conscious of this requirement. For example, when questioned by a reporter about the use of support received from the French-sponsored PCPA, which was its very first injection of outside funding, COSCA's coordinator singled out the organisation's office as one of the project's outcomes (Boyomo 2008a). This office contributed to COSCA's continued success in securing

---

[16] An extreme example of this can be found outside Adamaoua in the area of forest resources. The 1994 Forest Law granted residents of timber-rich areas the possibility of creating 'community forests'. A few consulting firms and NGOs, which enjoy close links to (and share personnel with) the Ministry of Forests, have specialised in preparing and compiling the different elements of the 'simplified management programmes' (SMPs) that these 'communities' need to submit to see the rights to their forests acknowledged. At the time, the price of a SMP ranged from CFAF 7 million to 12 million (REM 2006: 8–9; Topa et al. 2009: 106).

[17] In 'donor dancing', 'members of NGOs attract sponsors willing to support particular aspects of an organization's activities and then must submit ongoing reports using the organization's reporting guidelines, mechanisms for documentation and service, and narrative structure to maintain the program' (Clarke 2009: 81). As the quote makes explicit, its requirements do not disappear once the contract has been signed and the project begins.

contracts. The case of AJLC losing its contract for health campaigning on behalf of the pipeline consortium also illustrates the importance of staging. During a monitoring visit in early 2004, the GTC found AJLC insufficiently prepared to handle a contract of CFAF 51 million. To remedy this, it was decided that they should work under the financial supervision of a consultancy firm based in Yaoundé. It is significant that, at the time, many interpreted the GTC's negative evaluation as the direct result of AJLC's lack of an office, although the audit only referred to the 'limited capacity' of its human resources. AJLC's leaders confirmed this interpretation by leasing an office soon after their funders communicated the revised terms to them. Ultimately, they were not able to use the new office to any effect since their failure to reach a working agreement with the designated consultants led to the termination of the contract.

Several other examples indicate that NGOs' anxieties about deficiencies in terms of office space are not groundless. In the years since I began my fieldwork, I have witnessed how a well-advertised office, clearly marked off from adjacent residential spaces, gradually became indispensable to meet the expectations of outside funders who took the trouble to visit Ngaoundéré. At the time of its appointment as PASOC's representative organisation in Adamaoua, Sydev occupied a large compound in one of the city's most coveted neighbourhoods. Subsequent changes in the organisation's relationship with its landlord and the failure to honour rental arrears, however, meant that it had several months without proper accommodation. This had a negative impact on its standing with PASOC, whose auditors reported 'reduced working space' and 'visibility problems' due to poor location and signage (PASOC 2009c: 9) (Figure 5.1). APROSPEN's staff connected their success in securing funding from PASOC to their opening of new office space separate from the veterinary activities of the organisation's leading figure: 'The way PASOC worked, they would visit your premises. The absence of an adequate office is precisely what relegated the proposals of many associations. You have an association and you don't have an office! How is that possible?'

Offices are just one of several potential elements through which NGOs try to persuade funders that they deserve their trust. Persistent NGOs also seek other less obvious platforms for productive encounters with those who allocate funds and award contracts. Some of the members of Le Collectif, for instance, were keen on trying to create such propitious events. The unscheduled visit to the hotel where the minister was lodging during a brief stay in Ngaoundéré and the delegation to welcome the pipeline's team of experts upon their arrival at Bélabo's train station are two such examples. No matter how unconventional, NGO representatives prepare more or less subtle scripts, props, and attire for these encounters. In putting them together, with varying degrees of calculation

Figure 5.1 Sydev members with the author at the NGO's office in Ngaoundéré's Tongo-Bali neighbourhood, June 2011

and consistency, they make assessments as to what aspects of their identity should be privileged. Educational background, technological adeptness, closeness to the grassroots, gender sensitivity, embrace of ethnic or religious diversity, thematic specialisation, probity, and organic ties to the peasantry were some aspects that I saw being foregrounded during my fieldwork. Of course, such assessments are inherently tentative and the associated performances are adjusted as the assessments change. Thus, for example, one of AJLC's leaders interpreted the termination of their contract with the pipeline consortium as a result of a miscalculation. The youthfulness that he and his closest collaborators exuded was what had seduced both Exxon and the World Bank representatives when they awarded them the contract. In hindsight, he thought that they had failed to adjust their performance when dealing with the bureaucrats in the Ministry of Health and the GTC, for whom youth was a liability rather than a guarantee of dynamism. Indeed, people working in the organisations I got to know are well aware of the need to deploy different registers in different venues, often concurrently.

It is worth underscoring the experimental character that these choreographies may adopt. The *déjeuner de presse* (press lunch) that I attended in June 2004 in Ngaoundéré offers an apt illustration. Hosted by an NGO based in the city, it gathered a diverse audience comprising the sub-prefect, a representative of the *laamido*, members of a national ethnic association, public contractors, local media, and other interested citizens. The tracksuit that the sub-prefect chose to wear, so unlike his attire when acting in an official capacity, was symptomatic of the pervading casual atmosphere. The ostensible reason for the gathering was to present the NGO's recent and future involvement in urban renewal work conducted within the framework of the Programme d'Appui aux Capacités Décentralisées de Développement Urbain (Support Programme for Decentralised Capacity Building for Urban Development or PACDDU). In the previous week, there had been discussions among the NGO members about the advisability of organising this event. Some were reticent, arguing that PACDDU had not explicitly sanctioned any such promotional initiatives and that showcasing their role in the strengthening of the new 'neighbourhood development committees', which were likely to leave all kinds of expectations unmet, could backfire later. Those who favoured the idea countered that this was an excellent opportunity to make the most of their prestigious association with a European Union-sponsored programme and to have the authorities publicly give their stamp of approval to their activities. The press lunch would also allow them to outshine other organisations partnering with PACDDU and to recruit to their cause local notables who might facilitate the NGO's task of energising the neighbourhood development committees.

Once it was over, even those who had opposed the press lunch experiment voiced their satisfaction. As they feared, the Q&A had made apparent the flaws of the committees, which, for the most part, existed only on paper and on the signs painted on the metal rubbish bins that the programme had distributed all over the city. Another comment from the audience had drawn attention to the fact that PACDDU's treasurer was also a member of the NGO, a potentially awkward situation that, paradoxically, some members relished because of the closeness to powerful institutions that it signalled. Despite all this, however, those who had been most sceptical were won over by the impressive number of attendees and the congratulatory remarks of several distinguished guests. In the view of one of the organisers, the climactic appearance of the sub-prefect, who earlier in the day had warned that he might not be able to attend, was a tangible measure of their success. More importantly, the NGO had later been able to present this success to PACDDU as evidence of the dedication it put into its work. In fact, this initiative was explicitly mentioned in the letter of congratulation that the organisation received from the PACDDU administrator at the end of the programme.

In short, as the commonly used French word highlights, the *contractualisation* of NGO work is a process that requires elaborate assemblages of information, expertise, documentation, and interaction. The organisations behind well-funded, multi-year programmes and projects try to enhance transparency and avoid the risk of getting stuck with an incompetent or unscrupulous contractor by formalising this process into two stages: first, a call for expressions of interest; and second, an invitation to selected candidates to bid for contracts. However, in many cases, contracts are awarded through an open call for bids. Whichever approach applies, anxious anticipation and a suspicion of foul play on the part of competing organisations often suffuse attitudes to the process. This chapter's opening dialogue among members of Le Collectif illustrates this well. While Arabo and Alphonse thought it advisable to stick to the formal procedures and to rely on the merits of their bid, Basile and Bello perceived a need to 'position' themselves better than other bidders in relation to the officials who would make the decision. The question of what this positioning would entail in the specific encounter in Bélabo – a question that Aminou raised – received no conclusive answer. Partly because of my presence, something was left unsaid. In the preceding days, some of the members of Le Collectif had suggested that the trip to Bélabo should be an opportunity to provide monetary incentives to the officials concerned. The idea of the trip was dropped altogether in the end, but, a year later, one of those present at the meeting shared his annoyance with me: 'We were being asked to show our expertise in conducting a health awareness campaign and all they could think of was giving a [money-filled] envelope [to influence the outcome]!'

In the end, the effectiveness of the two contrasting approaches articulated in Le Collectif's discussion could not be tested in a conclusive way. A decision on the award of the contract was postponed as a result of a complaint by AJLC to the Ministry of Health once it learned that its previous contract had been terminated halfway through without compensation and that a new call for bids had been launched. Eventually, a fact-finding mission was sent to Ngaoundéré to meet AJLC's representatives and those of the NGOs that had submitted bids in response to the second call. The problems were found to be so intractable that the contract was never awarded. Or that is what people thought until a rumour, which I was never able to confirm, began circulating about the contract having been opaquely awarded to a Yaoundé-based organisation that only pretended to perform the assigned tasks. When all was said and done, in the minds of the informed observers who discussed the case with me, many doubts persisted. Could AJLC have avoided the contract termination if it had offered some financial inducement to the consulting firm that was appointed to monitor it? Was it advisable to remain committed to not paying bribes, as Le Collectif had chosen to do, and thus run the risk of being beaten by less scrupulous organisations bidding for the same contract?

Internecine battles for contracts between rival leaders and organisations can also be linked to attempts at creating umbrella organisations and collective platforms, such as those that programmes such as the PCPA or PASOC have orchestrated. In 2005, when COSCA emerged as the PCPA's broker in fostering collaboration among existing civil society groups, it also became the channel through which PCPA money was distributed in Adamaoua. An organisation known as Coalition Nationale des Jeunes pour le Développement (National Youth Coalition for Development or CNJD) received funding from COSCA for a project that was found to fit the PCPA's agenda of promoting civil society involvement in public policy implementation and monitoring. In 2007, disagreements over the use of funds led the COSCA coordinator and the CNJD president into a dispute that became public when CNJD was expelled from COSCA. When CNJD complained to the PCPA's managers in Yaoundé, the two parties exchanged hostile correspondence and incendiary statements to the press, which described the situation in typical hyperbolic terms such as 'pitched battle between NGOs' and 'civil society smashed to bits' (Boyomo 2007b). The PCPA's decision to send a financial control mission to Ngaoundéré, which identified a series of problems but exonerated both COSCA and CNJD from embezzlement, failed to defuse the tension. The irony was that the project for which CNJD had received funding was designed to expose 'corruption, extortion, and impunity' within Adamaoua's government agencies and community organisations involved in the struggle against HIV/AIDS.

For these organisations, whose staff are largely freelance and poorly rewarded, and which are so dependent on external funding, periodic controversies and short-lived scandals can acquire a routine character. For example, soon after its confrontation with CNJD, COSCA attempted to lead social mobilisation around the bauxite-mining project in Minin-Martap and Ngaoundal. It used PCPA funds to support one of its partner NGOs' efforts to sensitise the affected populations and to become their advocate vis-à-vis the mining company and the Cameroonian government. This placed COSCA in opposition to Développement sans Frontières (Development without Borders or DSF), an NGO that was also invested in shaping the terms of the mining project. In 2010, DSF and COSCA publicly accused each other of lacking representativeness and integrity (Mpele 2010; Nguele 2010). Once the mining project stalled, the customary media crossfire fizzled out.[18] These two controversies surrounding COSCA follow a familiar script. Once choices of

---

[18] In 2005, Hydromine, a company registered in Delaware with no known experience in the mining sector, obtained an exploration permit for the bauxite reserves. The consortium behind this project, which benefits from good connections with the Cameroonian

contractors are made (by PCPA and COSCA in this instance) and contracts completed, doubts, speculation, rumours, and accusations linger. The resulting climate, which can become markedly hostile among competing NGOs, cannot help but have an effect on what Bello would refer to as their *jeu de positionnement* (positioning game), as new funding and training opportunities become available.

NGOs and profits

In April 2004, I visited the offices of one of the oldest NGOs in Ngaoundéré. I had anticipated that this would be a particularly propitious opportunity. Their *technicien* (technical expert), a young engineer whom I had tried to get hold of several times, was going to be there. I was expecting an informal chat with him and with the couple of university students who worked for the organisation and whom I knew well. From the outset, the expert admitted that he failed to see how an organisation like theirs fitted my research interests. 'I think that you are chiefly concerned with businesses ... Here, you are dealing with an NGO. It is neither a company nor an economic organisation,' he told me. In earlier conversations, the expert's boss and founder of the NGO had situated its creation within his lifelong interest in *faire du social* (engaging in social issues), which he contrasted with his professional activities. 'This is a matter of philanthropy and self-esteem, whereas those other things I do to earn a living. [To the NGO], I direct the little money I have to spare; there is no return [on this money],' he explained. Assertions of the difference between business enterprises and NGOs like this one were not isolated instances. They were not unlike the contrast Bello established between his work as a foodstuffs supplier for the pipeline construction contractors ('simply about making money') and his NGO work ('a matter of the heart'). I came across such remarks constantly throughout my conversations with NGO activists in Ngaoundéré.

Yet, these assertions of difference coexisted with strong claims to the contrary. For example, as I mentioned when I introduced Bello in Chapter 1, a 'local community contact' (LCC) of COTCO, the Cameroonian subsidiary of the pipeline consortium, complained to the audience of a university symposium that the consortium's contractors in the regional compensation programme were 'only a bunch of businesses in NGO disguise'. His was not an argument about their efficiency (or lack

government, later expanded to include economic interests from Dubai and India. The feasibility and environmental impact studies were completed by 2009. Its financial implications, however, have delayed the project, which, over time, has developed substantial industrial, energy, and transport components alongside the planned mining activities.

of it). In fact, he was appreciative of their performance and tended to blame some of the shortcomings of programme implementation on the pipeline consortium's budgetary constraints rather than on the contractors' failings. Nor was he making the point that they were not truly non-governmental. Although, needless to say, governmental NGOs, such as the ones Daniel Jordan Smith (2007) has written about in his work on Nigeria, are also fairly common in Cameroon.[19] In the LCC's view, the NGO label was a disguise that hid these organisations' true nature. They were businesses, which in his view entailed a clear profit orientation.

While informed by first-hand experience of working with organisations based in different parts of Adamaoua and East Provinces, the LCC's remarks are consonant with widespread opinions about NGOs in Cameroon. Indeed, well-placed observers have not failed to notice the business orientation of many organisations. Thus, Séverin-Cécile Abega (1999: 181) regretted the existence of NGOs created 'to profit their founders [financially]'. René Otayek (2004: 106) noted how some have seen their 'business ambitions and desire for social mobility well served within the realm of associations'. Garga Haman Adji, former minister, veteran opposition politician, and NGO president, singled out financial motivations as a driving factor: 'Many Cameroonians think there is a lot of money to be made in the NGO sector. This is why they create them *à la pelle* [by the dozen]' (Boyomo 2010b). As these statements emphasise, the relative appeal of NGO work has increased in a context where other professional activities have become more scarce and less viable. Yet, in spite of their currency, such pronouncements on the primacy of the profit motive fail to go beyond the formulaic.

The trajectories of different actors involved in NGOs can help us analyse the motivations that are often glossed over with sweeping references to a profit orientation. As Julia Elyachar's ethnographic research in Cairo in the late 1990s shows, NGOs can serve the aims of a variety of individuals with varying success. In her account, emerging NGOs could become both a breeding ground for youngsters encouraged by international programmes to become entrepreneurs and conduits for weathered business owners in need of reinventing themselves to counter their tarnished reputations or to obtain tax benefits (Elyachar 2005: 66–95). In Ngaoundéré, NGOs can also become platforms for individuals with diverse outlooks. Consider the expert who questioned my choice of approaching NGO activities as economic. He already held a remarkably senior position in the civil service for his age, but he also regularly worked for two NGOs. This *jobiste* (literally, part-timer) – a

---

[19] Along these lines, René Otayek (2004: 80) has spoken of some Cameroonian NGOs as 'navel-gazing extensions of the state'. See also Fred Eboko's (2004) discussion of the role of Cameroon's first lady, Chantal Biya, in the country's NGO landscape.

term commonly used for enterprising civil servants – certainly drew a welcome supplementary income from these jobs.[20] But he claimed that they also provided him with additional stimulus for professional growth outside the rigid structures of the ministry he worked for, thus preparing him for bigger and better things.

As the account of Bello's trajectory since creating his own organisation shows, founders of NGOs are not necessarily devoted to them full time. For many, their NGO becomes one of several competing foci of attention, absorbing variable amounts of time and effort and shaping the changing nature of their involvement in the NGO sphere. Such an involvement may be predicated on the perception that they have the social status and relationships to attract contract work, with the potential to become both lucrative and reputation-enhancing. In less hierarchical organisations, the contrast between the status of the founder or member and that of staff is less significant.

NGO foot soldiers, who perform the bulk of the routine tasks required, tend not to receive a regular salary. Often, their contribution is phrased in terms of volunteering or apprenticeship. When less hierarchical arrangements are in place, they not only contribute labour but also pool their scarce financial resources. Many are postgraduate students getting by with meagre and intermittent payments while they finish their degrees, try their luck at the entry exams to the civil service, or wait for elusive opportunities of better employment. A university graduate who had briefly worked for one of the pipeline consortium's foreign building contractors articulated the lowering of expectations involved in his subsequent work for an NGO based in Ngaoundéré: 'When my contract [with the pipeline partner] came to an end, X [a well-placed acquaintance] told me: "If you have nothing better to do, you can go kill some time there."' The nature of the payments received varies. They may comprise per diems offered by donors hosting participatory forums, training sessions, and other events (to which their NGO work gives them access), as well as consultancy fees paid by private clients they themselves have attracted. They also include fixed sums for specific tasks performed within the framework of projects for which the NGO is a contractor. Contacts and experience are two additional rewards to be obtained from the otherwise precarious position of most of these NGO workers. Alphonse, the youngest participant in the conversation that opens this

---

[20] As mentioned in the Introduction, this possibility received legal endorsement in Cameroon at the height of structural adjustment policies (Article 37, Decree 1994/117 of 7 October 1994, *Statut Général de la Fonction Publique de l'Etat*). In fact, the moonlighting civil servants who are most sought after (for their expertise as well as for their influence on decisions over the awarding of contracts) are among the few NGO workers who are in a position to charge set fees, which are paid, at least partly, in advance.

chapter, is a telling example. At the time, he divided his energies mainly between university studies and NGO work. He later landed a job with a UN agency thanks to his NGO experience and his completion of a postgraduate degree. Similarly, Bello was able to create his own NGO by relying on contacts he had made during the three years he had worked for one of Adamaoua's most active NGOs. Not all NGO personnel, however, are able to lay the foundations of a long-term career in development. Many end up switching to civil service jobs or various commercial activities, at times with the support of the same relatives or patrons who encouraged them to do NGO work in the first place.

If the profit orientation of NGOs needs to be denied, denounced, or justified, as the case may be, this is partly because of NGOs' ambiguous legal status. The 1990 Freedom of Association Act defines an association as 'a convention through which people pool their knowledge or activities with a goal other than sharing profits' (Article 2). The act also imposes severe restrictions on associations receiving outside funds (Article 11), although such restrictions are rarely enforced in practice. The law, however, acknowledges the possibility that profits might result from the activities of not-for-profit associations; the Tax Code, for example, exempts such profits from income tax under some circumstances (Article 4.5). The 1992 Cooperative and GIC Act excludes the possibility that these organisations make commercial profits (Article 10.1), and, accordingly, declares such organisations exempt from income tax (Article 77). When a GIC or a cooperative distributes funds to its members, it is the members' income that is subject to taxation. The 1999 NGO Act defines them as associations that 'participate in the conduct of general interest missions' (Article 2.1) and establishes a 'rule of exclusive allocation of its resources to the NGO activities' (Article 12.1.b). The Act also explicitly mentions their capacity to hire salaried personnel (Article 17) and the possibility of enjoying various tax exemptions set out in the Tax Code (Article 18). Since only associations can become NGOs, the Act implies that NGOs are non-profit organisations. However, some observers have lamented that the non-profit nature of NGOs has not been asserted more explicitly (Wafo n.d.).

These complex, dispersed legal provisions do not always find a straightforward, uniform translation on the ground. Ideally, NGOs would keep track of their income and expenditure. When the former exceeds the latter, the difference would either be saved or reinvested. In the exceptional circumstances when these organisations decide to distribute profits among members, those sums would be taxed as the individual recipients' income. Yet, things are not that simple in practice. To begin with, the notion of profit is inseparable from a series of accounting concepts and practices that do not necessarily prevail within these organisations. Then, there are often no clear lines demarcating roles such as member, employee, or consultant. No one keeps count of the highly variable working hours, and much work is provided with no expectation of systematic pay. Funds advanced by members, employees, and consultants are paid back without calculating and compensating for financial costs. One of the founders of an NGO in Ngaoundéré, for example, explained how they addressed cash shortfalls:

Often, when we happen to be short of funds, there is one of us who pitches in. A technical expert who collaborates with us may contribute by drawing on his salary to advance money to pay the office rent or to buy ink cartridges. Everyone knows about it. When we get paid, he receives his money back. That's part of our internal operations. When we begin working on a project, we hardly ever know in advance how much we will need to spend. We raise money among us as needed.

An additional factor that complicates the nature of various payments is that terms of reference for contract work often exclude salaries for NGO personnel, thus inviting NGOs to inflate other costs and pocket the difference between budgeted and real costs. This reliance on inflated budgets to reward different combinations of labour and capital contributions is reminiscent of the over-invoicing that is common in public contracts and underscores the similarities between NGOs and contractors. Consider in this light the remarks of the manager of one of the NGOs that worked as a contractor for the pipeline consortium's regional compensation programme. He was particularly appreciative that the consortium's terms of reference allowed for a 20 per cent overhead for 'management expenses': 'This way, we were not forced to inflate construction materials and labour costs in order to be properly remunerated.'

Funders have the ability to introduce and shape formal accounting practices. Several of the NGOs that worked for prestigious international partners expressed their appreciation of the increased level of accounting sophistication they had achieved while working for such partners. However, these changes are not necessarily enduring. The Bertoua office of Coordination Diocésaine de Développement et des Activités Sociales – Caritas (Diocesan Coordination for Development and Social Activities – Caritas or CODASC), for example, which in the 2002–5 period was awarded a large share of pipeline regional compensation contracts in East Province, was praised at the time for doing exemplary work. In 2010, however, an audit commissioned by its main funder, the Dutch Catholic development organisation CORDAID, found numerous accounting gaps deriving from an almost complete disregard for the financial management software CODASC had committed itself to using. The consequences were drastic: CORDAID-mandated suspension of its activities, firing of its coordinator after 18 years of service, and termination of its tenure as PASOC's representative organisation for the East

Province. That said, only NGOs that receive regular income streams from their funders are held to such rigorous accounting standards. The large majority of Adamaoua-based NGOs do not conduct any formal accounting that would categorise the distribution of funds among members, consultants, and employees as salary, fees, repayment of loans, or profit.

Funders have an uneven impact not only on accounting practices but also on the logic that should prevail when purportedly non-profit organisations generate profits. There was an illuminating contrast between two important sources of contracts for NGOs in Adamaoua during my research: the Chad–Cameroon pipeline project and the Programme National de Développement Participatif (National Programme for Participatory Development or PNDP). Both caused much debate around the tension between the philanthropic and the lucrative in NGO activities. As noted, the remark by the oil consortium's employee about NGOs being 'a bunch of businesses' in disguise came from his experience running the pipeline's regional compensation programme. The consortium hired a number of contractors to construct classrooms, dispensaries, boreholes, and other facilities at village level. Contractors included both construction firms and NGOs. Although the work of these two types of contractor did not differ in any significant way, the tax authorities did not treat them equally. The tax liabilities of businesses working as contractors for the consortium were scrutinised closely, some of the construction firms subsequently being fined and compelled to pay tax arrears and to obtain more expensive business licences. By contrast, the NGOs that did construction work for the pipeline consortium were largely spared this closer tax surveillance. The presumption of their non-profit orientation exempted them from tax payments and no one took the trouble to look at how the contract earnings were distributed among NGO members. In informal conversations, the managers of several construction companies complained about being discriminated against. 'What makes the work of those NGOs any different from ours?,' one of them asked rhetorically.

The PNDP, a World Bank-sponsored initiative that became one of the centrepieces of Cameroon's *Poverty Reduction Strategy Paper* (Republic of Cameroon 2003: 38), took a contrasting, pre-emptive approach to the possibility of income derived from NGO activities going untaxed. During its phase I (2005–9), the programme spent CFAF 1.5 billion in Adamaoua (Lamissa Kaikai 2010). The contracts covered tasks ranging from drafting participatory community development plans to carrying out microprojects. A handbook for administrative, accounting, and financial procedures governed the relations between the programme and its NGO contractors. The handbook's intimidating 594 pages included a requirement that all contractors should have a taxpayer number and a business licence.

While some NGOs found it worthwhile to approach the tax authorities in order to meet the requirements and qualify as eligible bidders, others thought that taking such a step would jeopardise their non-profit status and thus chose not to bid for contracts. The former group included an organisation that had always seen itself as a for-profit entity, and, as I noted earlier, constituted itself legally as an economic interest group (GIE). For every contract they obtained, the members signed a *protocole d'opération* (operating protocol), in which they agreed on their respective contributions and shares in the ensuing profits, on which they would supposedly be taxed individually. This organisation saw no difficulty in obtaining a taxpayer number and a licence. But there were other NGOs operating under the more conventional form of association that were also ready to accept in principle that 'when your activities involve providing paid services, then you should be taxed', as the leader of an NGO that was awarded several PNDP contracts put it. For this particular organisation, working for the PNDP meant a first experience in filing tax returns and paying close to CFAF 4 million in income tax. Officials in provincial tax offices, however, were not necessarily in a position to accommodate 'the complications of the PNDP business', as one of them dismissively referred to them. To get around this, representatives of several NGOs based in Ngaoundéré had to travel to Yaoundé to see their tax status sorted out for PNDP purposes. As one of the PNDP contractors put it: 'The rules are the rules and they say that whomever works for the PNDP has to pay taxes.' A minority of NGOs showed less readiness to accept that. The manager of one of Ngaoundéré's longer-standing NGOs forcefully articulated this minority position: 'If you go [to the tax office] to apply for a *carte de contribuable* [taxpayer ID], that means you are no longer a non-profit association. You are now a businessperson. You run an enterprise ... It's not a good system. [The PNDP] might as well have hired companies to do that work.'

Therefore, various approaches to the possibility of NGO profits and the treatment they should receive coexist. In some cases, the generation of profits by NGOs is normalised and explicitly embraced, even by public programmes such as the PNDP or by the central services of the tax authorities. Nonetheless, NGO profits remain a muddled issue on account of the ambiguous legal status of most organisations and the incommensurability between standardised formal accounting and actual financial management within most of these organisations. Furthermore, discourses on the logics that should animate NGO work are still dominated by what Bill Maurer (2008: 160), in another context, calls a 'rhetoric of charitable obligation' – so much so that accusations of an overt profit orientation remain a favoured choice of those intent on denigrating specific organisations.

* * * * * *

In the last two decades, the proliferation of development initiatives in search of 'local' partners has led to a remarkable expansion of the NGO sphere in the city of Ngaoundéré. This period has also been one of changing legal frameworks, from the organisational free-for-all of the early 1990s to the more recent restrictive outlook that turned official NGO status into an elusive privilege and advocated the transformation of GICs into cooperatives. When I began my fieldwork in 2003, all organisations claiming the NGO label operated in defiance of various legal requirements as a matter of course. By and large, their lack of compliance often passed unnoticed. Their vulnerability became apparent, however, when they failed to be in the good books of different government officials or, more rarely, in the event of open conflicts with the government. In recent years, as the government has struggled to deal with the Boko Haram insurgency and the protest movement in anglophone Cameroon, the precarious legal status of many Cameroonian NGOs has become more consequential.

What shapes NGOs most decisively are the contracts that define their relationship with funders, ranging from multilateral organisations and governmental departments to foreign development agencies or NGOs. These contracts matter not only for their written terms of reference or the explicit procedures for bidding, awarding work, and monitoring performance. They also matter for the evolving set of mutual expectations that underwrite those terms and procedures, and, at times, have allowed for significant departures from them. Those terms, procedures, and expectations can differ considerably from funder to funder, and great effort on the part of NGOs is devoted to appraising them. For most funders, legal status is not an essential consideration. NGOs' ability to conform to the evolving language, formats, and protocols of international development is widely valued and rewarded. Most funders do not verify their contractors' compliance with labour and tax regulations, although there are significant exceptions. Evaluation of NGO performance is rare, and, when it happens, it ranges from lax to selective. This chapter has shown how the results of these variable contractual dynamics are assemblages of human and financial resources; of stages, performances, and props; of project design, document production, accounting practices, and other forms of expertise. As in the case of Le Collectif, whose internal debates opened the chapter, such assemblages can be transient and malleable. Even the more enduring ventures are characterised by a pronounced flexibility. Contracts are thus key in governing NGO activities but they are also time-bound. The end of a contract tends to mark a hiatus. Other contracting cycles, with new sets of rules, stipulations, and expectations, await those NGOs that manage to stay in business.

Conclusion: letting pass, letting go

This book began with a set of questions about how economic activities are governed in present-day Cameroon. In the preceding chapters, I have explored the experiences and trajectories of public contractors, cattle traders, truckers, and NGO promoters based in the city of Ngaoundéré. In recent decades, these actors' businesses in pursuit of monetary gains and ethical projects – both collective and individual – have unfolded in a context marked by turbulence and unpredictability. Such a context has proved propitious for flexible, dynamic repertoires of practice that nonetheless retain traces of the recent and not-so-recent past.

The advent of the economic crisis features prominently in the narratives of officials and business people with whom I engaged over the course of my research. In a few cases, my interlocutors mentioned specific memories of radio and television coverage of what in retrospect they saw as turning points: President Biya's acknowledgement on national television that '*la crise économique est là* [the economic crisis is here]' (19 February 1987), his address to the National Assembly announcing a package of measures to combat the crisis and reassuring Cameroonians that IMF assistance would not be necessary (20 June 1987), and the signature of the first standby arrangement with the IMF that began a 21-year cycle of financial assistance (19 September 1988). Those narratives also included vivid memories of events that took place closer to home. Readers may recall, for instance, the Sogetrans assistant general manager's account of the consortium's liquidation in January 1988. Fifteen years later he was still struck by the way in which the French shareholders had arrived in Ngaoundéré and packed their bags without fuss. Reflecting on what followed the demise of the institution that, until then, had been a cornerstone in the governance of the trucking business, a veteran transporter pithily remarked: 'In 1988, the [truckers'] union was in disarray. Truckers went into *le maquis*.' His words are revealing in their juxtaposition of disarray and *maquis*. In this and similar accounts, the crisis marked a moment when tracts of the economic landscape that lay beyond the reach of state bureaucracies expanded, not least because cuts in public spending resulted in severely diminished capacity for those bureaucracies. In my interlocutors' narratives of crisis, the transition to multiparty politics also plays a key role. The *villes mortes* represented for them a high-water mark in the questioning of prevailing modes of economic governance, a point that the work of Janet Roitman (2005) has made convincingly.

The late 1980s and early 1990s also saw the emergence (or a reactivation in many ways) of a trope as pervasive as that of crisis, but one that influential academic voices such as Roitman's have taken less seriously: reform. This book's footnotes are filled with details of policy frameworks and legal texts adopted in the name of various reforms. From major overhauls to the incessant stream of small modifications to laws and administration, reforms have been a constant source of challenges and opportunities for officials and business people alike. Drawing from formulas in vogue at various moments, these reform initiatives have attracted funding from United Nations agencies, international financial organisations, the European Union, and a long list of bilateral donors. They have mobilised the energies of foreign and national consultants, found more or less receptive or reticent publics (including government departments and factions within them), and fizzled out in due course as the networks, interests, resources, and devices that they brought together lost cohesion and consistency. Their relative success or failure aside (a topic on which much ink has been spilled), an aspect of the reforms that was central for many of my interlocutors was the uncertainty they generated. Reforms contain not only new rules and procedures that have to be adopted but also promises of better enforcement. Instilling 'best practices', as many of these reforms have set out to do, involves combatting prevailing 'bad practices'. In the task of reform, the line between persuasion and pedagogy, on the one hand, and threats and coercion, on the other, is easily crossed. Consider the sensitisation campaign for the reform of public contracting that reached Ngaoundéré in May 2006. The reformers came to introduce the new system and its new set of rules but also to foster a new 'culture of respect for rules and of systematic punishment of every case of rule violation' (ARMP 2006: 3). Their message included a warning: the 'time of penalties' was around the corner (Eloundou Bidjogo 2006). Even when officials and business people do not take such warnings at face value, reforms sow doubts about the continuation of a state of affairs where enforcement is at best sparse and selective.

The turbulence and unpredictability that have characterised economic transactions in West and Central Africa in the *longue durée* (Guyer 2004) have manifested themselves in these twin tropes of crisis and reform over the last three decades in places such as Cameroon and Ngaoundéré. Not surprisingly, this has been presented as an unfavourable context for the exercise of power by the myriad ministerial departments and other state agencies for which 'encompassment' (Ferguson and Gupta 2002) is the privileged mode of addressing economic sectors and actors. The activities of cattle traders, which are widely presented as particularly inscrutable, illustrate such dynamics.

Cattle traders operate in rural spaces where property rights over land, pasture, and animals are not easily legible and where, in any case, the presence of government officials is costly and unrewarding. The mobility of cattle and traders represents an additional challenge. Moreover, given the influence of cattle-farming interests on electoral constituencies in northern Cameroon generally and in Adamaoua specifically, the cattle economy is presented as a politically 'protected' sector. In this light, crisis and reform appear as breeding grounds for the evasion and circumvention of rules. The reforms of the 1990s in particular undermined the numbers, resources, and morale of veterinary agents who historically exercised *la tutelle* of these traders. As the head of MINEPIA's provincial services was willing to concede: 'There is much talk about cattle trails ... Well, frankly ... there is little we can do [to prevent the unauthorised circulation of cattle].' Lacking the socio-cultural proximity that most veterinary agents share with traders, the tax authorities do not fare any better. Even though they have been one of the segments of state bureaucracy that the reforms have favoured and empowered, cattle trade is a tough nut for them to crack. Organised around ethno-religious networks, the trade is extremely fragmented and subject to wide fluctuations. Traders are constantly on the move and hardly ever own *pignon sur rue* (bricks and mortar) businesses. Their transactions are overwhelmingly effected *bee hunduko* ('with the mouth' or verbally) and they do not keep conventional accounts that would be meaningful to outsiders.

Nonetheless, an undue emphasis on distance and the lack of legibility can make us lose sight of what transpires in encounters between business actors and state bureaucracies. While established cattle markets invariably feature municipal clerks and veterinary officials, railway shipments of cattle also provide occasions for regulatory encounters. Marketplaces are quintessential spaces of *encadrement* and provide a frame for commercial transactions. At markets, the same traders who are said to 'love darkness' rub shoulders with government officials in broad daylight. At markets, the names of sellers and buyers and the sums of the fees paid are inscribed in an official ledger. When someone such as the provincial head of the veterinary services declares that 'to trade without an authorisation, that is *le maquis* ', his words can be read as a call for increased compliance from traders. But they are also an attempt to construct the proximate (market transactions) at a distance (*le maquis*). Such words, which seem to admit that *le maquis* has taken root at cattle markets, betray the authorities' own permissive attitude towards practices that violate the law. In railway shipments, the tax authorities have identified a funnel through which large flows of cattle pass. The authorities make themselves present in these weekly events through the railway company, which withholds on their behalf income tax payments from the traders. As well as revenue, the shipments generate data on head of cattle traded and a receipt of tax payments per freight car. But even this group of traders with whom the tax administration has regular contact – albeit mediated through others – is not dealt with in a way that allows for the monitoring of individual compliance with legal obligations. The *concertation* (consultation) meeting discussed in Chapter 3 showed how an attempt to reverse this situation ultimately failed. The prefect's words in the closing moments of that meeting reiterated the need for a permissive stance: 'With [cattle] traders, [the authorities] cannot but count on their honesty.'

In stark contrast with the cattle economy, public contracting is a field of activity premised on close proximity to the authorities. When dealing with their clients, contractors are invariably subject to the rigours of bureaucracy. As contractor Alim Pierre made a point of reminding me: 'In public contracts everything to the last detail is put in writing.' Regulations make it a requirement for any public contract bidder to submit copies of a long series of official documents, including a valid business licence, verification of their place of business, a taxpayer card, and a recently issued certificate of tax payment. Even *bons de commande* and *lettres-commande*, which avoid bidding procedures, must be registered with the treasury before they are undertaken. This registration procedure is only the beginning of a series of formalities that trace the different stages of a contract until its completion and remuneration. Payment for the contractors' work itself comes from the treasury, which in principle should make obtaining a comprehensive picture of their turnover unproblematic.

The challenges of distance and limited legibility, which appear to hinder the governance of the cattle trade, are therefore absent in public contracting. In this line of business, what seems to facilitate the violation of rules and regulations is proximity to the authorities. The assiduous contact between contractors and officials renders possible the subversion of formalities. In extreme circumstances, the results are completely fictitious contracts or, as in one of the examples discussed in Chapter 2, networks of fraudsters profiting from the systematic recycling of old registration numbers to avoid paying contract registration fees. Often, underlying agreements between officials and contractors have the potential to empty formalities of their intended implications in a less drastic manner, for example when the award of a contract becomes a foregone conclusion well before the bidding process takes place, or when deficient works are certified as completed satisfactorily.

It is important, however, to dispel the opposite idea that the proximity of officials and contractors eliminates the possibility of rule enforcement and renders formalities meaningless. Formalities have a potentiality of their own, which enables the activation of what might be conceived as the law's 'recall effect' (Latour 1996: 45), thus forcing people and things, money included, to fall in line with the truths contained in official scripts. In exceptional cases, such as Alim Pierre's dispute with the paymaster general, parties may choose to cling to formalised truths to disown unwritten agreements. Even in more normal scenarios, formalities matter in ways that cannot be overridden by closeness between contractors and officials. Formal errors are routinely invoked as grounds for disqualifying bidders, delaying procedures, incurring penalties, or postponing payments. The formalities of public contracting are unavoidable (even when honoured in the breach), and, over the years of reforms that have entailed constant changes to such formalities, staying on top of the changes is vital; this helps us understand the pride that contractors such as Alhadji Djibrilla take in their mastery and meticulous fulfilment. So, what we face in public contracting is not really a matter of verbal agreements replacing bureaucratic procedures and written documents. Instead, I prefer to speak of a dialectic between procedures and documents, on the one hand, and their informal and unwritten counterparts on the other. Even in a domain such as public contracting, where the state is directly involved in the transactions at stake, officials and contractors find considerable room for the negotiated suspension and subversion of legal rules and procedures. For them, Jane Guyer's suggestive formulation that 'a coral reef of separate formalities' can 'coexist with – and shade into – conversionary modes of exchange' (2004: 159) rings particularly true.

Trucking and NGO work offer similar examples of the mutual constitution of repertoires of practice and modes of governance. As a tax official reminded me, and at the risk of stating the obvious, 'Truckers don't stay put.' Truck drivers used their routine of crossing (and presence in) different subnational and national jurisdictions to take advantage of the shortcomings of tax administration. The tax authorities in turn tried to find ways of responding to those practices. Truckers' mobility, however, does not spare them constant visits to the counters of forwarding agents, freight bureaus, and customs officials at cargo terminals before every shipment. Nor is there any way of eluding passage though checkpoints and weigh stations. In turn, NGO promoters and state officials meet on a regular basis, whether within the framework of collaboration in the delivery of public goods and services or on the occasion of NGO-sponsored events to which officials are frequently invited. The unproblematic interaction that takes place in such moments shows to what extent in normal circumstances the legally problematic status of these organisations is no obstacle to their continued operation. NGO activities are more substantially shaped by the organisations that hire them and provide the bulk of their funding. On the part of contractor

NGOs, there is a lot of self-staging and self-fashioning to meet sponsor expectations. On the part of sponsors, there is a tension between the need to work with organisations that can claim to be rooted in 'the local' and the upholding of bureaucratic procedures and managerial standards.

This monograph has approached encounters between business actors and bureaucrats as places and moments of entanglement and disentanglement. In many such encounters, such as the loading of cattle into railway freight cars or the crossing of a checkpoint by a truck, physical passage is involved. In other encounters, such as the inspection visit to certify that a public contract has been completed or the conduct of a mission to monitor the progress of an NGO project, the passage in question is less literal. Whatever the case, these encounters are occasions for those engaged in economic activities to show that they comply with the rules that are in place and for the relevant authorities to enforce those rules. I have argued that the institution of the *laissez-passer* offers a useful perspective from which to approach such encounters. With its rich resonances and deep roots in Cameroon's economic life, the *laissez-passer* is a document that, on the one hand, declares that certain conditions have been fulfilled by its possessor, and, on the other, orders the document's addressees to grant passage. The *laissez-passer* makes apparent the centrality of documents in practices of economic governance.

Some of the documents discussed in earlier chapters are explicitly conceived as *laissez-passers*. This is the case of the document traders obtain from veterinary officials when transporting cattle from Ngaoundéré to markets in southern Cameroon and the safe conduct issued by freight bureaus that is required for trucks involved in international transit. The former is evidence of an inspection confirming that the cattle being transported do not pose an animal health hazard; the latter denotes verification that the truck shipment in question observes the rules relative to the allocation of national freight quotas. The issuing of both these documents requires a payment: cattle traders pay a fee for the veterinary inspections and the safe conduct is conditional on truckers paying the freight bureau's commission on the value of the transport services rendered. But, crucially, the parties involved do not place much faith in the substance of the work that formally justifies these payments. Thus, under normal circumstances, the veterinary inspections tend to be either summary or non-existent. Similarly, the operations involved in the calculation of the national freight quotas are widely regarded with suspicion and frequently denounced for their lack of rigour and transparency; moreover, the principle that a safe conduct should free trucks from stopping at checkpoints other than the few designated in international conventions is to all intents and purposes a dead letter. Despite this, the documents are essential to secure passage for cattle at veterinary controls, as well as for trucks and their cargo at checkpoints along the road.

While no cattle or transport professionals would envisage doing without these documents, their effectiveness is not to be taken for granted.

In practice, other documents that do not have the formal rationale of affording their possessors passage may serve this function. As we have seen, in their comings and goings to cattle markets in the Ngaoundéré area, traders are often asked by police and gendarmes to show their *impôt libératoire* or business licence. Likewise, officials manning different types of checkpoints regularly take it upon themselves to verify that the person or company who owns the truck being stopped has filed a VAT return. Both proper and de facto *laissez-passers* bear out Jane Guyer's point about formality in West and Central Africa often being experienced as 'papers' rather than as 'an enduring generalizable principle' (2004: 159). Such papers are required but they do not ensure automatic passage. In extreme cases, business owners or their agents may choose to do without the relevant papers altogether and try to pay their way through controls and checkpoints, although this can hardly be an affordable, long-term option. The clearest illustrations of such dynamics can be seen at road checkpoints, where a truck, driver, and cargo in full compliance with existing rules and with all the relevant documentation can still be halted for hours. In this sort of encounter, papers can be conceived as props of various levels of effectiveness that need to be supplemented with convincing performances – and, sometimes, with additional payments. Leaving aside the obvious differences, such a situation resembles the plight of a public contractor who, having completed construction works adequately and on time, visits a treasury official to plead for as expedient a payment as possible. Successful resolutions of such conundrums may put one's charisma, skills, and pocket to the test. Much as a trucker whose charms and contacts can help minimise irregular payments at checkpoints, adept *suivistes* such as Alhadji Djibrilla can ensure that they get paid before other public contractors.

While *laissez-passer* dynamics do not exhaust the registers and practices of economic governance that I have discussed in this book, their effects are emblematic of a broader phenomenon in which economic outcomes (as basic as the circulation of people and goods) are obtained at the expense of bureaucratic rigour. The 'letting pass' involves a letting go of any aspiration to the systematic enforcement of existing rules. So, both in terms of how the relevant documents are produced and in terms of how they afford passage, *laissez-passers* are examples of the work of the law being subverted. Such situations of suspended enforcement, which are compatible with the existence of all sorts of formalities, can acquire different significance. They may be celebrated as demonstrations of what one of my interlocutors called administrative tolerance, when the procedures to comply with the rules are slow or impractical (such as the process for recognising NGO status) or when the rules in place are inconsistent, discriminatory, or otherwise problematic (as the traders argued in the case of the income tax advances paid when shipping cattle by railway). They may also be seen in a negative light as hindrances to the proper functioning of economic sectors, since they reward both unprofessional business actors and venal officials. Indeed, many of my interlocutors saw it in this way. Generalised situations of suspended or selective enforcement erode the incentives to inhabit the subject position of the law-abiding business person. Whether officials and business actors settle on a more 'predatory' or more 'permissive' approach (Nugent 2010) to these ambiguities between the presence and absence of the law, the result tends to be vulnerable economic actors poorly placed to mobilise legality in order to hold their competitors and the authorities accountable.

Bibliography

Abakar, Goni Ousman. 2010. 'Le commerce extérieur du Tchad de 1960 à nos jours'. PhD thesis, University of Strasbourg.
Abega, S.-C. 1999. *Société civile et réduction de la pauvreté*. Yaoundé: Éditions Clé.
Abubakar Sa'ad. 1977. *The Emirate of Fombina, 1809–1903*. London: Oxford University Press.
Aerts, Jean-Joël et al. 2000. *L'économie camerounaise: un espoir évanoui*. Paris: Karthala.
Amayena, Nicolas. 2003. 'Marchés publics: 50 sociétés poursuivies pour faux enregistrements', *Cameroon Tribune*, 5 March.
Amougou, Adrien D. and Agnes Lambert. 2008. *Evaluation intermédiaire du PCPA Cameroun*. Paris: IRAM.
Anders, Gerhard. 2010. *In the Shadow of Good Governance: an ethnography of civil service reform in Africa*. Boston MA: Brill.
ARMP. 2006. *Étude sur les sanctions dans le domaine des marchés publics*. Yaoundé: Agence de Régulation des Marchés Publics (ARMP).
— 2008. *Commentaire du maître d'ouvrage sur le rapport provisoire de l'audit à posteriori des marchés publics, exercise 2005*. Yaoundé: Agence de Régulation des Marchés Publics (ARMP).
Arriola, Leonardo. 2013. *Multi-ethnic Coalitions in Africa: business financing of opposition election campaigns*. Cambridge: Cambridge University Press.
Atangana, René. 2011. 'Jean Jacques Ndoudoumou dans les griffes de l'Epervier', *La Météo*, 3 November.
Azayra, Victor. 1978. *Aristocrats Facing Change: the Fulbe in Guinea, Nigeria and Cameroon*. Chicago IL: Chicago University Press.
Barrier, Eric and Jean-Marie Gugenheim. 1990. *Grands opérateurs européens du transport maritime*. Paris: Observatoire Économique et Statistique des Transports.
Batongué, Alain et al. 2004. 'PPTE, FMI . . . Le Cameroun a echoué', *Mutations*, 1 September 2004.
Batongué, Alain and Brice Mbodiam. 2011. 'Jean Jacques Ndoudoumou: les acteurs des marchés publics font front contre la corruption', *Mutations*, 2 March.
Bayart, Jean-François. 1985. *L'état au Cameroun*, 2nd edition. Paris: Presses de la Fondation Nationale des Sciences Politiques.
— 1986. 'La société politique camerounaise (1982–1986)', *Politique Africaine* 22: 5–36.
— 1993. *The State in Africa: the politics of the belly*. London: Longman

Bayie Kamanda, Cornelius. 1999. 'Cameroon: the retrenched workers of the civil service and parastatals', *Bulletin de l'APAD* 18 < https://journals.openedition.org/apad/453> (accessed 20 June 2018).

Bennafla, Karine. 2002. *Le commerce frontalier en Afrique Centrale: acteurs, espaces, pratiques*. Paris: Karthala.

Beya, Michel. 2003. 'Adamaoua: le recouvrement des taxes fait problème dans le Mbéré', *Cameroon Tribune*, 3 April.

Biakan, Jacques. 2011. *Droit des marchés publics au Cameroun: contribution à l'étude des contrats publics*. Paris: L'Harmattan.

Bidias, Jean de Dieu. 2012. 'Gouvernance: Jean Jacques Ndoudoumou limogé de l'ARMP', *Mutations*, 1 November.

Bierschenk, Thomas. 2014. 'Sedimentation, fragmentation and normative double-binds in West African public services' in T. Bierschenk and J.-P. Olivier de Sardan (eds), *States at Work: dynamics of African bureaucracies*. Leiden: Brill.

Bierschenk, Thomas and Jean-Pierre Olivier de Sardan. 2014. 'Studying the dynamics of African bureaucracies' in T. Bierschenk and J.-P. Olivier de Sardan (eds), *States at Work: dynamics of African bureaucracies*. Leiden: Brill.

Bierschenk, Thomas, Jean-Pierre Chauveau, and Jean-Pierre Olivier de Sardan. 2000. *Courtiers en développement: les villages africains en quête de projets*. Paris: Karthala.

Blanc, Aymeric and Olivier Gouirand. 2007. 'La concession du chemin de fer du Cameroun: les paradoxes d'une réussite impopulaire'. Document de travail 44. Paris: Agence Française de Développement <www.afd.fr/fr/la-concession-du-chemin-de-fer-du-cameroun-les-paradoxes-dune-reussite-impopulaire> (accessed 20 June 2018).

Bloch-Lainé, François. 1964. *A la Recherché d'une Economie Concertée*. Paris: Éditions de l'Épargne.

Blundo, Giorgio. 2001. '"Dessus-de-table": la corruption quotidienne dans la passation des marchés publics locaux au Sénégal', *Politique Africaine* 83: 79–97.

    2006 'An ordered corruption? The social world of public procurement' in G. Blundo and J.-P. Olivier de Sardan (eds), *Everyday Corruption and the State*. London: Zed Books.

Blundo, Giorgio and Joel Glassman. 2013. 'Introduction: bureaucrats in uniform', *Sociologus* 63: 1–9.

Blundo, Giorgio and Pierre-Yves LeMeur (eds). 2009. *The Governance of Daily Life in Africa: ethnographic explorations of public and collective services*. Leiden: Brill.

Bobiokono, Christophe. 2005. 'Enregistrement: les bons de commande fortement taxés', *Mutations*, 24 January.

Boutinot, Laurence. 1994. 'Le migrant et son double: migration, ethnie, religion au Nord Cameroun'. PhD thesis, University of Paris I, France.

Boutrais, Jean. 1974. 'Les conditions naturelles d l'élevage sur le plateau de l'Adamaoua (Cameroun)', *Cahiers ORSTOM Sciences Humaines* 11 (2): 145–98.

    1983. *L'élevage soudanien: des parcours de savannes aux ranchs*. Paris: ORSTOM.

    1984a. 'Les tendances de l'évolution actuelle' in J. Boutrais (ed.), *Le Nord du Cameroun*. Paris: ORSTOM.

1984b. 'Pour une histoire du développement rural' in J. Boutrais (ed.), *Le Nord du Cameroun*. Paris: ORSTOM.

1984c. *Le Nord du Cameroun*. Paris: ORSTOM.

1986. 'L'expansion des éleveurs peul dans les savanes humides du Cameroun' in M. Adamu and A. Kirk-Greene (eds), *Pastoralists of the West African Savanna*. Manchester: Manchester University Press.

1990. 'Derrière les clôtures . . . Essai d'histoire comparée de ranchs africaines', *Cahiers de Sciences Humaines* 26 (1–2): 73–95.

1991. 'Pauvreté et migrations pastorales du Diamaré vers l'Adamaoua (1920–1970)' in J. Boutrais (ed.), *Du politique à l'économique: études historiques dans le bassin du lac Tchad*. Paris: ORSTOM.

1994. 'Les Foulbé de l'Adamaoua et l'élevage: de l'idéologie pastorale à la pluri-activité', *Cahiers d'Études Africaines* 133–5 (1–3): 175–96.

1999a 'La vache et le pouvoir. Foulbé et Mbororo de l'Adamaoua' in R. Botte, J. Schmitz, and J. Boutrais (eds), *Figures Peules*. Paris: Karthala.

1999b. 'Zébus et mouches tsé-tsé' in C. Baroin and J. Boutrais (eds), *L'homme et l'animal dans le bassin du lac Tchad*. Paris: IRD.

2001. 'Du pasteur au boucher: le commerce du bétail en Afrique de l'Ouest et du Centre', *Autrepart* 19: 49–70.

2002. 'Nderkaaku: la folle jeunesse chez les Foulbé de l'Adamaoua', *Journal des Africanistes* 72 (1): 165–81.

Boutrais, Jean, Javier Herrera, and Athanase Bopda. 2002. 'Bétail, naira et franc CFA: un flux transfrontalier entre Nigeria et Cameroon'. Paris: ORSTOM <http://horizon.documentation.ird.fr> (accessed 20 June 2018).

Boyomo, Georges A. 2006. 'Corruption: comment l'argent du SIDA est détourné dans l'Adamaoua', *Mutations*, 19 December.

2007a. 'Exploitation de la bauxite/alumine dans l'Adamaoua: les populations lèvent le ton', *Le Messager*, 4 June.

2007b. 'Brouille: la société civile de l'Adamaoua vole en éclats', *Le Messager*, 12 November.

2008a. 'Maurend Mpele: "Nous sommes ouverts à toutes les contributions"', *Le Messager*, 14 January.

2008b. 'ARMP: Jean Jacques Ndoudoumou, a-t-il été manipulé?', *Le Messager*, 3 March.

2010a. 'Pèlerinage: le sous-préfet de Yaoundé II interdit une réunion', *Mutations*, 8 March.

2010b. 'Manœuvres: bal de vautours autour des ONG au Cameroun', *Mutations*, 10 March.

2012. 'Marchés publics: Abba Sadou entre défis et pressions', *Mutations*, 4 January.

Bruneau, Juliette and David Abouem. 2004. *Evaluation prospective du Programme National de Gouvernance*. Yaoundé: United Nations Development Programme (UNDP).

Burnham, Philip. 1975. '*Regroupement* and mobile societies: two Cameroon cases', *Journal of African History* 16 (4): 577–94.

1980. 'Raiders and traders in Adamawa' in J. Watson (ed.), *Asian and African Systems of Slavery*. Oxford: Blackwell.

1981. 'Notes on Gbaya history' in C. Tardits (ed.), *Contributions de la recherche ethnologique à l'histoire des civilisations du Cameroun*. Paris: CNRS.

1996a. *The Politics of Cultural Difference in Northern Cameroon*. Edinburgh: Edinburgh University Press.

1996b. 'Political relations on the eastern marches of Adamawa in the late nineteenth century' in I. Fowler and D. Zeitlyn (eds), *African Crossroads: intersections between history and anthropology in Cameroon*. Providence NJ: Berghahn Books.

Burnham, Philip and Thomas Christensen. 1983. 'Karnu's message and the "war of the hoe handle": interpreting a Central African resistance movement', *Africa* 53 (4): 3–32.

Burnham, Philip and Murray Last. 1994. 'From pastoralist to politician: the problem of a Fulbe aristocracy', *Cahiers d'Études Africaines* 133-5 (1–3): 313–57.

Burnham, Philip, E. Copet-Rougier and Philip Noss. 1986. 'Gbaya et Mkako: contribution ethno-linguistique à l'histoire de l'Est Cameroun', *Paideuma* 32: 87–128.

Çalışkan, Koray and Michel Callon. 2009. 'Economization. Part 1: Shifting attention from the economy towards processes of economization', *Economy and Society* 38 (3): 369–98.

Callon, Michel. 1998. 'Introduction: the embeddedness of economic markets in economics' in M. Callon (ed.), *The Law of the Markets*. Oxford: Blackwell.

Cameroon Tribune. 2012. 'A retenir sur les marchés publics', Editorial, 12 January.

Cantens, Thomas. 2007. 'La réforme de la douane camerounaise à l'aide d'un logiciel des Nations unies ou l'appropriation d'un outil de finances publiques', *Afrique Contemporaine* 223-4: 289–307.

Chad–Cameroon Development Project (CCDP). 2000. *Quarterly Report no. 1. 4th quarter*. N'Djaména: Esso Exploration and Production Chad Inc.

2002. *Quarterly Report no. 7. 2nd quarter*. N'Djaména: Esso Exploration and Production Chad Inc.

Chalfin, Brenda. 2010. *Neoliberal Frontiers: an ethnography of sovereignty in West Africa*. Chicago IL: University of Chicago Press.

Channon, Jean-François. 2008 'Cameroun: les marchés publics à l'épreuve de la transparence', *Le Messager*, 13 June.

Chanock, Martin. 2001. *The Making of South African Legal Culture, 1902–1936: fear, favour and prejudice*. Cambridge: Cambridge University Press.

Charlier, Florence and Charles N'Cho-Oguie. 2009. *Sustaining Reforms for Inclusive Growth in Cameroon: a development policy review*. Washington DC: World Bank.

Charreau, Paul. 1905. *Un Coin du Congo, le Cercle de Kundé*. Cherbourg: Imprimerie Le Maout.

Chendjou, Léopold. 2009. 'Le secteur du transport routier à l'agonie au Cameroun', *Le Messager*, 2 February.

Chomba, Gilbert. 2001. 'Grève de transporteurs: le carburant à nouveau disponible à Douala', *La Nouvelle Expression*, 13 July.

Clarke, Kamari M. 2009. *Fictions of Justice: the International Criminal Court and the challenge of legal pluralism in sub-Saharan Africa*. Cambridge: Cambridge University Press.

Cohen, Abner. 1969. *Custom and Politics in Urban Africa: a study of Hausa migrants in Yoruba towns*. London: Routledge and Kegan Paul.

CONAC. 2013. *Rapport sur l'état de la lutte contre la corruption au Cameroun en 2012*. Yaoundé: Commission Nationale Anti-Corruption (CONAC).

Copans, Jean. 2001. 'Afrique noire: un État sans fonctionnaires?', *Autrepart* 20: 11–26.

Courade, Georges (ed.). 2000. *Le désarroi camerounais: l'épreuve de l'économie-monde*. Paris: Karthala.

Courade, Georges and Luc Sindjoun. 1996. 'Le Cameroun dans l'entre-deux', *Politique Africaine* 62: 3–14.
Courtin, Christophe. 2011. 'Les programmes de l'Union européenne vers les sociétés civiles africaines', *Revue Tiers Monde* 205: 117–34.
CREDDA. 2008. *Rapport d'étude sur la perception du cadre Juridique actuel sur les OSC au Cameroun*. Yaoundé: Centre de Recherches pour le Développement Durable en Afrique (CREDDA).
CTMPT (Commission Technique Mixte Permanente des Transports Cameroun-Tchad) 2012. 'Procès verbal des travaux de la ivème session', Yaoundé, 15 November.
Cumming, Gordon. 2009. *French NGOs in the Global Era: a distinctive role in international development*. New York NY: Palgrave.
Dahirou, Abdoulaye. 2004. 'L'entreprise Sodea traîne le RDPC dans la boue', *L'Oeil du Sahel*, 12 April.
Davis, Kevin and Michael Kruse. 2007. 'Taking the measure of the law: the case of the *Doing Business* project', *Law and Social Inquiry* 32(4): 1095–119.
Debrie, Jean. 2001. 'Transport et espaces d'entreprise: les stratégies africaines du groupe Bolloré', *Cahiers Scientifiques du Transport* 39: 43–54.
Debrie, Jean and Sandrine De Guio. 2004. 'Interfaces portuaires et compositions spatiales: instabilités africaines', *Autrepart* 4 (32): 21–36.
De Castelnau, Pauline and Jean-François Marteau. 2009. 'Quel accompagnement des douanes par la Banque mondiale en Afrique subsaharienne?', *Afrique Contemporaine* 230: 115–34.
Deen, D. and D. Johnson. 1972. *Beef Cattle Production on the Adamawa Plateau*. Washington DC: US Peace Corps.
DeLancey, Mark D. 2012. 'Between mosque and palace: defining identity through ritual practice in Ngaoundéré, Cameroon', *Cahiers d'Études Africaines* 208: 975–98.
Delcroix, Gérard. 1937. 'Enquête sur le lahore de Ngaoundéré', *Bulletin de la Société d'Études Camerounaises* 2: 43–52.
Deleuze, Gilles and Felix Guattari. 1987. *A Thousand Plateaus: capitalism and schizophrenia*. Minneapolis MN: University of Minnesota Press.
Derrida, Jacques. 1981. *Dissemination*. Chicago IL: University of Chicago Press.
Deutchoua, Xavier Luc. 2005. 'Réforme de l'administration: Garga Haman Adji', *Mutations*, 29 December.
Dikoumé, Albert F. 1982. 'Les transports au Cameroun de 1884 à 1975'. PhD thesis, École des Hautes Études en Sciences Sociales, Paris.
Dipanda, Eugène. 2004. 'Marchés publics: les règles du jeu en fin claires', *Mutations*, 28 September.
Djarmaïla, Grégoire. 2006. 'Marchés publics: les sanctions planent', *Cameroon Tribune*, 31 March.
   2008. 'Alexandre Bodio à Bodio: "Intensifier la communication"', *Cameroon Tribune*, 17 March.
Dongmo, Jean-Louis. 1981. *Le dynamisme Bamiléké (Cameroun)*. 2 vols. Yaoundé: Centre d'Édition et de Production pour l'Enseignement et la Recherche.
Douffissa, A. 1993. *L'Élevage bovin dans le Mbéré (Adamaoua Camerounaise)*. Paris: ORSTOM.
Dronen, Thomas Sundness. 2009. *Communication and Conversion in Northern Cameroon: the Dii people and Norwegian missionaries*. Leiden: Brill.

Eboko, Fred. 1999. 'Logiques et contradictions internationales dans le champ du SIDA au Cameroun', *Autrepart* 12: 123–40.

2004. 'Chantal Biya: "Fille du peuple" et égérie nationale', *Politique Africaine* 95: 91–106.

2005. 'Le droit contre la morale? L'accès aux médicaments contre le SIDA en Afrique', *Revue Internationale des Sciences Sociales* 186: 789–98.

Eboko, Fred and Yves-Paul Mandjem. 2011. 'ONG et associations de lutte contre le SIDA en Afrique: incitations transnationales et ruptures locales au Cameroun' in F. Eboko et al. (eds), *Les Suds face au SIDA: quand la société civile se mobilise*. Marseille: IRD.

Eloundou Bidjogo, Guy-Marie. 2006. 'Adamaoua – marchés publics: le temps des sanctions', *Cameroon Tribune*, 17 April.

Elyachar, Julia. 2005. *Markets of Dispossession: NGOs, economic development and the state in Cairo*. Durham NC: Duke University Press.

Enbond, H. B. 2009. 'Transformation: le transport routier fait sa mue', *La Nouvelle Expression*, 8 December.

Engola-Oyep, Jeannot and Javier Herrera. 1997. 'Les flux transfrontaliers du bétail Camerounais et du bétail Tchadien en transit vers le Nigeria'. DIAL Document de Travail DT/97/03. Paris: IRD – Université Paris-Dauphine.

Ewick, Patricia and Susan Silbey. 1998. *The Common Place of Law: stories from everyday life*. Chicago IL: University of Chicago Press.

FAO. 2003. *Rapport national sur les ressources zoogénétiques des animaux d'élevage du Cameroun*. Yaoundé: Food and Agriculture Organization (FAO).

Ferguson, James and Akhil Gupta. 2002. 'Spatializing states: toward an ethnography of neoliberal governmentality', *American Ethnologist* 29 (4): 981–1002.

Fimigue, Victoire. 1999. 'La communauté Libanaise de la ville de Ngaoundéré de 1941 à 1998'. Master's thesis, University of Ngaoundéré.

Flegel, Eduard R. 1985 [1885]. *The Biography of Madugu Mohamman Mai Gashin Baki*. Los Angeles CA: Crossroads Press.

Fouhba, Honoré. 2012.'Ngaoundéré: des camionneurs menacent de faire grève', *La Nouvelle Expression*, 30 January.

Foute, Rousseau-Joël. 2005. 'Augustin Frédérick Kodock: "Les résultats du recensement seront fiables"', *Cameroon Tribune*, 29 November.

2013. 'Marchés publics: la réforme à l'épreuve du terrain', *Cameroon Tribune*, 13 February.

Fréchou, Hubert. 1966. *L'élevage et le commerce du bétail dans le Nord Cameroun*. Paris: ORSTOM.

Freed, Libbie. 2010. 'Networks of (colonial) power: roads in French Central Africa after World War I', *History and Technology* 26(3): 203–23.

Froelich, Jean-Claude. 1954a. 'Ngaoundéré, la vie économique d'une cité peule', *Études Camerounaises* 43–4: 5–66.

1954b. 'Le commandement et l'organisation sociale chez les Foulbé de l'Adamaoua (Cameroun)', *Études Camerounaises* 45–6: 3–91.

Gaïbaï, Dieudonné. 2009. 'Regard: nécessité de s'adapter', *Mutations*, 19 March.

Geschiere, Peter. 1986. *Village Communities and the State: changing relations among the Maka of Southeastern Cameroon since the colonial conquest*. London: Kegan Paul.

1987. 'Paysans, régime national et recherche hegemonique: l'implantation de l'U(N)C, le "Grand Parti National", dans les villages maka', *Politique Africaine* 22: 73–100.

2009. *The Perils of Belonging: autochthony, citizenship, and exclusion in Africa and Europe*. Chicago IL: University of Chicago Press.

Geschiere, Peter and Piet Konings (eds). 1993. *Itineraires d'accumulation au Cameroun*. Paris: Karthala.

Gondolo, A. 1978. '*Ngaoundéré: évolution d'une ville peule*'. PhD thesis, University of Rouen.

1986. 'Evolution du Peul urbain: Ngaoundéré' in M. Adamu and A. H. M. Kirk-Greene (eds), *Pastoralists of the West African Savanna*. Manchester: Manchester University Press.

Grémion, Pierre. 1974. 'La concertation' in M. Crozier et al. (eds), *Où Va l'Administration Française*. Paris: Éditions d'Organisation.

Gros, Jean-Germain. 1993. 'The privatization of livestock services in Cameroun: a study in the feasibility of state and market participation in economic restructuring'. PhD thesis, University of California, Berkeley.

Groupement 2AC-ACP. 2008. *Audit à Posteriori des Marchés Publics Exercice 2005: rapport final*. Yaoundé: Groupement 2AC-ACP.

2011. *Audit à Posteriori des Marchés Publics Exercice 2007: rapport final*. Yaoundé: Groupement 2AC-ACP.

Guichi, Marie Noelle. 2010. 'Les non-dits d'un recensement: des résultats très contestés', *Le Messager*, 17 May.

Guivande, Raoul. 2005. 'Ngaoundéré: un TPG derrière les barreaux', *L'Oeil du Sahel*, 13 June.

Guyer, Jane. 1987. 'Feeding Yaoundé, capital of Cameroon' in J. Guyer (ed.), *Feeding African Cities*. Manchester: Manchester University Press.

2004. *Marginal Gains: monetary transactions in Atlantic Africa*. Chicago IL: Chicago University Press.

2016. *Legacies, Logics, Logistics: essays in the anthropology of the platform economy*. Chicago IL: Chicago University Press.

Hallaire, Antoinnette. 1984. 'Les principales productions: le mil, le coton, le riz, l'arachide' in J. Boutrais (ed.), *Le Nord du Cameroun*. Paris: ORSTOM.

Hansen, Ketil F. 2000. 'The historical construction of a political culture in Ngaoundéré, Northern Cameroon'. PhD thesis, University of Oslo.

Hariou, Maurice. 1903. *Précis de droit administrative et de droit public general*. Paris: Larose & Forcel.

Hart, Keith. 1973. 'Informal income opportunities and urban employment in Ghana', *Journal of Modern African Studies* 11 (1): 61–89.

2006. 'Bureaucratic form and the informal economy' in B. Guha-Khasnobis, R. Kanbur, and E. Ostrom (eds), *Linking the Formal and Informal Economy: concepts and policies*. Oxford: Oxford University Press.

Herzfeld, Michael. 2004. *Cultural Intimacy: social poetics in the nation-state*. London: Routledge.

2005. 'Political optics and the occlusion of intimate knowledge', *American Anthropologist* 107 (3): 369–76.

2009. *Evicted from Eternity: the restructuring of modern Rome*. Chicago IL: University of Chicago Press.

Hibou, Béatrice. 2008. '"Nous ne prendrons jamais le maquis": entrepreneurs et politique en Tunisie', *Politix* 21 (84): 115–41.

2011. *Anatomie politique de la domination*. Paris: La Découverte.

Hino, Shun'ya. 1993. 'Fulbe people in African urban society: a comparative study of Cameroon and the Sudan', *SENRI Ethnological Studies* 35: 61–85.

Hugon, Philippe. 1996. 'Sortir de la récession et préparer l'après pétrole: le préalable politique', *Politique Africaine* 62: 35–44.
Hull, Matthew. 2012. *Government of Paper: the materiality of bureaucracy in urban Pakistan*. Berkeley CA: University of California Press.
Independent Evaluation Group. 2008. *Doing Business: an independent evaluation. Taking the measure of the World Bank-IFC Doing Business indicators*. Washington DC: World Bank.
INS. 2006. *Annuaire Statistique*. Yaoundé: Institut National de la Statistique (INS), Republic of Cameroon.
— 2013. *Annuaire Statistique du Cameroun*. Yaoundé: Institut National de la Statistique (INS), Republic of Cameroon.
Jiogue, Grégoire and Robert Demanou. 2015. *Étude Critique Comparative du Cadre Juridique Relatif aux Organisations de la Société Civile au Cameroun*. Yaoundé: PASC.
Johnson-Hanks, Jennifer. 2005. 'When the future decides: uncertainty and intentional action in contemporary Cameroon', *Current Anthropology* 64 (3): 363–85.
Joseph, Richard. 1977. *Radical Nationalism in Cameroon: social origins of the UPC rebellion*. Oxford: Clarendon Press.
Kaptué, Léon. 1980. 'L'administration coloniale et la circulation des indigènes au Cameroun: le laissez-passer, 1923-1946', *Afrika Zamani* 10–11: 160–84.
Karsenty, Alain et al. 2010. 'The 2008–2009 timber sector crisis in Africa and some lessons for the forest taxation regime', *International Forestry Review* 12 (2): 172–6.
Kemfang, Hervey. 1998. 'Les quartiers Baladji de Ngaoundéré: création et évolution, 1950–1997'. BA research report, University of Ngaoundéré.
— 2000. 'Des élites locales à Ngaoundéré: approche d'histoire locale'. MSc thesis, University of Ngaoundéré.
Kenmogne, B. 2002. 'La politique camerounaise en matière des ONG', *D+C* 4: 22–5.
Kimaka, Dieudonné. 2009. 'Cadre juridique des organisations non-gouvernementales au Cameroun'. Yaoundé: PASOC <https://mireilletchiako.files.wordpress.com/2015/03/cadre-juridique-des-ong-au-cameroun.pdf> (accessed 20 June 2018).
Kouete, Vincent. 2012. 'La participation des entreprises nationales aux marches publics du Cameroun', *Bulletin du GICAM* 51: 2–8.
Lacrouts, M. and J. Sarniguet. 1965. *Cheptel bovin du Cameroun: exploitation, commercialisation, perspectives d'avenir*. 2 vols. Paris: Ministère de la Coopération.
Lamissa Kaikai, Olivier. 2010. 'Adamaoua: 73 projets finances par le PNDP', *Cameroon Tribune*, 17 June.
Latour, Bruno. 1996. *Aramis or the Love of Technology*. Cambridge MA: Harvard University Press.
Latour, Bruno and Peter Weibel. 2005. *Making Things Public: atmospheres of democracy*. Cambridge MA: MIT Press.
Leblon, Anaïs. 2006. 'Le pulaaku. Bilan critique des études de l'identité peule en Afrique de l'Ouest', *RAHIA* 20: 1–84.
Ledeneva, A. 1998. *Russia's Economy of Favors: blat, networking, and informal exchange*. Cambridge: Cambridge University Press.
— 2006. *How Russia Really Works: the informal practices that shaped post-Soviet politics and business*. Ithaca NY: Cornell University Press.

Bibliography

Leonard, David K. 1993. 'Structural reform of the veterinary profession in Africa and new institutional economics', *Development and Change* 24 (2): 227–67.

Lickert, Victoria. 2011. 'Les resources minières au Cameroun: gouvernance, prise de decision et contre-expertise'. Master's research thesis, University of Paris 1 Panthéon-Sorbonne.

Lienert, Ian and Jitendra Modi. 1997. *A Decade of Civil Service Reform in Sub-Saharan Africa*. Washington DC: International Monetary Fund.

Lombard, Louisa. 2013. 'Navigational tools for Central African roadblocks', *Political and Legal Anthropology Review* 36 (1): 157–73.

Lund, Christian. 2006. 'Twilight institutions: public authority and local politics in Africa', *Development and Change* 37 (4): 685–705.

Mann, Gregory and Jane Guyer. 1999. 'Imposing a guide on the indigène: the fifty year experience of the *sociétés de prévoyance* in French West and Equatorial Africa' in E. Stiansen and J. Guyer (eds), *Credit, Currencies and Culture: African financial institutions in historical perspective*. Stockholm: Nordiska Afrikainstitutet.

Marguerat, Yves. 1984a. 'Les faiblesses de la vie sociale et économique moderne' in J. Boutrais (ed.), *Le Nord du Cameroun*. Paris: ORSTOM.

1984b. 'Le réseau urbain et la formation d'une région' in J. Boutrais (ed.), *Le Nord du Cameroun*. Paris: ORSTOM.

Maunoir, Eric. 2000. 'Camrail: une première année faste', *Inter Rail Cooperation* 5: 8–20.

Maurer, Bill. 2008. 'Re-regulating offshore finance?', *Geography Compass* 2 (1): 155–75.

Mbella, Grégoire. 2011. 'Public contracts: between good intentions and corrupt practices', *Cameroon Tribune*, 27 February.

Mbembe, Achille. 1988. *Afrique indociles: christianisme, pouvoir et État en société post-coloniale*. Paris: Karthala.

1996. *La naissance du maquis dans le Sud Cameroun (1920–1960)*. Paris: Karthala.

2001. *On the Postcolony*. Berkeley CA: University of California Press.

Mbembe, Achille and Janet Roitman. 1995. 'Figures of the subject in times of crisis', *Public Culture* 7: 323–52.

Mbog, Raoul. 2015. 'Cameroun: Biya remanie son gouvernement, qui compte 65 ministres', *Le Monde*, 5 October.

Mbonji, Edjenguélé. 1999. 'Les "deflatés" du développement: de la tradition de dépendance à la autogestion', *Bulletin de l'APAD* 18: 1–8.

Mercer, Claire and Maia Green. 2012. 'Making civil society work: contracting, cosmopolitanism and community development in Tanzania', *Geoforum* 45: 106–15.

Merry, Sally Engle, Kevin Davis, and Benedict Kingsbury. 2015. *The Quiet Power of Indicators: measuring governance, corruption and the rule of law*. Cambridge: Cambridge University Press.

Messengue Avom, Bernard. 2013. *La gouvernance des marchés publics*. Yaoundé: Éditions Le Kilimandjaro.

Messomo Ndjana, Florent. 2006. 'Étude de la distribution et de la qualité des médicaments vététerinaires au Cameroun'. PhD thesis, École Inter-États des Sciences et Médecine Vétérinaires de Dakar (EISMV), Senegal.

Meyo-Soua, Jacqueline. 1999. 'Le projet sectoriel des transports du Cameroun: bilan et réflexions' in A. Adoléhoumé (ed.), *Les projets sectoriels des transports en Afrique sub-saharienne (Actes du séminaire SITRASS 5)*. Cotonou: SITRASS.

MINEPAT. 2003. *Rapport Socio-Economique de l'Adamaoua, Exercise 2001–2002.* Ngaoundéré: Délégation Provinciale du Ministère de l'Economie, de la Planification et de l'Aménagement du Territoire (MINEPAT), Adamaoua.

Mitchell, Timothy. 1999. 'Society, economy and the state effect' in G. Steinmetz (ed.), *State/Culture: state formation after the cultural turn*. Ithaca NY: Cornell University Press.

—— 2007. 'The properties of markets' in D. Mackenzie, F. Muniesa, and L. Siu (eds), *Do Economists Make Markets? On the performativity of economics.* Princeton NJ: Princeton University Press.

Mohammadou, Eldridge. 1978. *Fulbe hooseere: les royaumes foulbe du plateau de l'Adamaoua au XIX siècle: Tibati, Tignère, Banyo, Ngaoundére.* Tokyo: ISLCAA.

—— 1983. *Peuples et royaumes du Foumbina et de l'Adamaoua.* Yaoundé: ISH.

Mokam, David. 2006. 'Les associations régionales et le nationalisme camerounais 1945–1961'. PhD thesis, University of Yaoundé I.

Monda Bakoa, Josué. 2008. 'Inertie: un mal que fait mal', *Cameroon Tribune*, 10 January.

Moore, Mick. 2009. 'Between coercion and contact: competing narratives on taxation and governance' in D. Brautigam, O.-H. Fjeldstad and M. Moore (eds), *Taxation and State Building in Developing Countries.* Cambridge: Cambridge University Press.

Mpele, Maurend. 2010. 'Exploitation de la bauxite de Minim Martap: le droit de réponse', *Dikalo*, 12 July.

Mpon Tiek, S.-M. 2004. 'Rapport préliminaire sur les ONG/associations du Cameroun'. Dakar: OSIWA.

Muller, Jean-Claude. 2006. *Les chefferies diì de l'Adamaoua.* Paris: CNRS.

Muñoz, José-Maria. 2008. 'Au nom du développement: ethnicité, autochtonie, et promotion du secteur privé au Nord-Cameroun', *Politique Africaine* 112: 67–85.

—— 2013 'The revenue imperative: Cameroon's administrative dilemmas' in T. Cantens, R. Ireland, and G. Raballand (eds), *Reform by Numbers: measurement applied to customs and tax administrations in developing and emerging countries.* Washington DC: World Bank

—— 2014. 'A breeding ground for revenue reliability?' in T. Bierschenk and J.-P. Olivier de Sardan (eds), *States at Work: dynamics of African bureaucracies.* Leiden: Brill.

Muñoz, José-Maria and P. Burnham. 2016. 'Subcontracting as corporate social responsibility in the Chad–Cameroon Pipeline Project' in C. Dolan and D. Rajak (eds), *The Anthropology of Corporate Social Responsibility.* New York NY: Berghahn Books.

Nanga, Charles. 2000. 'La reforme de l'administration territoriale au Cameroun'. Master's thesis, École Nationale d'Administration, France.

Ngabmen, Hubert. 1996. *Les transports routiers au Cameroun (1965–1995).* Yaoundé: Institut des Transports et Stratégies de Développement.

Ngayap, P. F. 1983. *Cameroun, qui gouverne?* Paris: L'Harmattan.

Ngogang, Thierry. 2004. 'Dette intérieure: des fournisseurs accusent Meva'a m'Eboutou', *Mutations*, 17 August.

Ngouo, Léon. 1997. 'Responsibility and transparency in governmental organizations in Cameroon: a review of institutional arrangements', *International Review of Administrative Sciences* 63: 475–92.

2000. 'Organizational development consulting in the context of structural adjustment in sub-Saharan Africa: role and responsibility of consultants', *International Review of Administrative Sciences* 66 (1): 105–18.

Nguele, Eric. 2010. 'Bauxite: opacité autour de la gestion du projet', *Dikalo*, 28 May.

Nkonlak, Jules R. 2008. 'Ou sont passés les résultats du recensement de 2005?', *Le Jour*, 29 May.

Nkou Songue, Felix. 2014. 'Marchés publics au Cameroun: entre recherche d'efficacité et pesanteurs systémiques'. Master's thesis, École Nationale d'Administration, University of Strasbourg.

Nouwou, David. 2011. 'Barrières de police et de gendarmerie: enquête sur les poches de résistance', *La Nouvelle Expression*, 2 February.

Ntiga, Léger. 2008. 'Marchés publics: La CUY et l'ARMP à couteaux tirés', *Mutations*, 26 November.

Ntoual, Jacques Willy. 2012. 'Réaction: Jean Jacques Ndoudoumou reste optimiste', *Le Messager*, 12 July.

Nugent, Paul. 2010. 'States and social contracts in Africa', *New Left Review* 63: 35–68.

Okalla Ahanda and Associates. 2011. *Audit à Posteriori des Marchés Publics Exercice 2008: rapport provisoire*. Yaoundé: Okalla Ahanda and Associates.

Onana, Raymond et al. 2009. 'Capitalisation des Acquis et Résultats des Actions Appuyées sur le Terrain par le Programme Concerté Pluri-Acteurs du Cameroun (PCPA-Cameroun)', *Les Cahiers du PASOC* 8: 2–56.

Otayek, R. 2004. *Les Sociétés Civiles du Sud*. Paris: Ministère des Affaires Etrangères <www.diplomatie.gouv.fr/fr/IMG/pdf/Les_societes_civiles_du_sud.pdf> (accessed 20 June 2018).

Owona Ndounda, Nicolas. 2009. 'La "vie de nuit" dans la ville de Ngaoundéré de 1952 à 2009'. Master's thesis, University of Ngaoundéré.

Pannenborg, Arnold. 2008. *How to Win a Football Match in Cameroon*. Leiden: African Studies Centre.

PASOC. 2009a. 'Capitalisation sur la mise en place des organisations relais', *Les Cahiers du PASOC* 5: 3–56.

2009b. 'Devis programme', *Les Cahiers du PASOC* 6: 7–14.

2009c. *Evaluation du travail des organisations relais du PASOC dans le dix régions du Cameroun*. Yaoundé: Programme d'Appui à la Structuration de la Société Civile (PASOC).

2010. 'Capitalisation des projets de plaidoyer du premier appel a propositions', *Les Cahiers du PASOC* 10: 8–71.

2011. *Mémorandum sur le cadre légal des organisations de la société civile camerounaise*. Yaoundé: Programme d'Appui à la Structuration de la Société Civile (PASOC).

Petry, Martin and Naygotimti Bambé. 2005. *Le pétrole du Tchad: rêve ou cauchemar pour les populations?* Paris: Karthala.

Pigeaud, Fanny. 2011. *Au Cameroun de Paul Biya*. Paris: Karthala.

Plat, Didier and Cristophe Rizet. 1989. *Politiques de réduction des coûts du camionnage en Afrique sub-saharienne: cas du Cameroun*. Lyon: Seminaire International sur les Transports en Afrique Sub-Saharienne <http://ideas.repec.org/p/hal/journl/halshs-00194057.html> (accessed 20 June 2018).

PNDP. 2004. *Manuel d'exécution*. Yaoundé: National Programme for Participatory Development (PNDP), Republic of Cameroon.

Ponel, Edouard. 1896. 'La Haute-Sangha', *Bulletin de la Société Géographique de Paris* 17: 188–211.

PRASAC (Pôle regional de recherche appliquée au développement des savanes d'Afrique Centrale). 2003. *Étude sur la commercialisation des bovines et de la viande bovine dans la région CEMAC.* N'Djaména: Commission Economique du Bétail, de la Viande, et des Ressources Halieutiques.

REM. 2006. 'Projet d'observateur indépendant au contrôle et suivi des infractions forestières au Cameroun: Rapport Trimestriel 5'. Cambridge: Resource Extraction Monitoring (REM) <www.fsc-watch.org/docs/OI_Rapport_Trimestriel_5.pdf> (accessed 20 June 2018).

Republic of Cameroon. 2003. *Poverty Reduction Strategy Paper.* Yaoundé: Republic of Cameroon.

―― 2005. *Programme National de Gouvernance, 2006–2010.* Yaoundé: Republic of Cameroon.

Republic of Chad and European Community. 2008. *Strategie de Coopération et Programme Indicatif: 9e Fonds Européen de Développement, 2001–2007.* N'Djaména: Republic of Chad and European Community <https://ec.europa.eu/europeaid/sites/devco/files/joint-annual-report-07-cooperation-eu-chad-2008_fr_1.pdf> (accessed 20 June 2018).

Riles, Annelise. 2004. 'Real time: unwinding technocratic and anthropological knowledge', *American Ethnologist* 31 (3): 392–405.

Rizet, Cristophe and Henri Gwet. 2000. 'Les surcoûts du cammionage en Afrique après la dévaluation du franc CFA', *Cahiers Scientifiques du Transport* 38: 3–18.

Roitman, Janet. 1990. 'The politics of informal markets in sub-Saharan Africa', *Journal of Modern African Studies* 28 (4): 671–96.

―― 2005. *Fiscal Disobedience: an anthropology of economic regulation in Central Africa.* Princeton NJ: Princeton University Press.

―― 2016. 'Africa otherwise' in B. Goldstone and J. Obarrio (eds), *African Futures: essays on crisis, emergence, and possibility.* Chicago IL: University of Chicago Press.

Rose, Niklas. 1999. *Powers of Freedom: reframing political thought.* Cambridge: Cambridge University Press.

Rose, Niklas, Patt O'Malley, and Mariana Valverde. 2006. 'Governmentality', *Annual Review of Law and Social Science* 2: 83–104.

Roupsard, Marcel. 1987. 'Nord-Cameroun: ouverture et développement'. PhD thesis, University of Paris X – Coutances.

―― 1991. 'Evolution des échanges entre le basin tchadien (Tchad, Nord-Cameroun) et la côte du Golfe de Guinée pendant la période coloniale' in J. Boutrais (ed.), *Du politique à l'économique: études historiques dans le bassin du lac Tchad.* Paris: ORSTOM.

Rudin, Harry. 1938. *Germans in Cameroon, 1884–1914.* New Haven CT: Yale University Press.

Saïbou Issa. 2004. 'L'embuscade sur les routes des abords sud du Lac Tchad', *Politique Africaine* 94: 82–104.

―― 2006. 'Les jeunes patrons du crime organisé et de la contestation politique aux confines du Cameroun, de la Centrafrique et du Chad'. Paper presented at the conference 'Youth and the Global South', Dakar, 13–15 October <www.ascleiden.nl/Pdf/youthconfissa.pdf> (accessed 20 June 2018).

―― 2010. *Les coupeurs de route: histoire du banditisme rural et transfrontalier dans le Basin du Lac Tchad.* Paris: Karthala.

Schler, Lynn. 2003. 'Ambiguous spaces: the struggle over African identities and urban communities in colonial Douala, 1914–45', *Journal of African History* 44: 51–72.
Schultz, Emily. 1979. 'Ethnic identity and cultural commitment: a study of the process of fulbeization in Guider, Northern Cameroon'. PhD thesis, University of Indiana.
Seh, Jacques and Jean-Baptiste Ndemen. 2013. 'Les organisations paysannes ignorantes de la nouvelle loi', *La Voix Paysanne*, 23 September.
Seignobos, Christian and Henry Tourneux. 2002. *Le Nord-Cameroun à travers ses mots*. Paris: Karthala.
Sinderud, M. 1993. 'Administrateurs coloniaux, missionnaires norvégiens et lamibé dans la subdivision de Ngaoundéré (Cameroun) entre 1945 et 1960'. Master's thesis, University of Oslo.
— 2008. 'Maccuɓe Laamiiɗo: royal slavery in Ngaoundere, northern Cameroon, c. 1900–1960'. PhD thesis, University of Oslo.
Sindjoun, Luc. 1993. 'Esquisse de théorie du droit administratif camerounais', *Penant* 813: 323–30.
— 1996a. 'Le champ social camerounais: désordre inventif, mythes simplificateurs et stabilité hégémonique de l'État', *Politique Africaine* 62: 57–67.
— 1996b. 'Le président de la République au Cameroun (1982–1996): les acteurs et leur role dans le jeu politique', *Travaux et Documents du Centre d'Étude d'Afrique Noire* 50: 1–22.
Slob, Anneke et al. 2006. *Evaluation de la coopération régionale de la Communauté Européenne en Afrique centrale*, vol. 2. Rome: Development Researchers' Network <www.oecd.org/dataoecd/38/7/38229015.pdf> (accessed 20 June 2018).
Smith, D. J. 2007. *A Culture of Corruption: everyday deception and popular discontent in Nigeria*. Princeton NJ: Princeton University Press.
Socpa, Antoine. 2006. 'Bailleurs autochtones et locataires allogènes: enjeu foncier et participation polique au Cameroun', *African Studies Review* 49 (2): 45–67.
Sojip, Michel and Bienvenu D. Nizesété. 1998. 'Jean Ndoumbé Oumar: premier maire noir au Nord Cameroun (1958–1963)', *Ngaoundéré Anthropos* III (special issue): 255–77.
Soto, Hernando de. 1989. *The Other Path*. New York NY: Basic Books.
Tadjon, Claude. 2008. 'Operation Epervier: Jean Jacques Ndoudoumou à la PJ', *Le Jour*, 27 May.
Taguem Fah, Gilbert. 1997. 'Les élites musulmanes et la politique au Cameroun de la période française à nos jours'. PhD thesis, University of Yaoundé I.
Takoua, Guy Roger. 2005. 'Meiganga: Le Préfet Scelle la Recette des Finances', *L'Oeil du Sahel*, 17 August.
Takougang, Joseph and Milton Krieger. 1998. *African State and Society in the 1990s: Cameroon's political crossroads*. Boulder CO: Westview Press.
Tamekou, Raoul. 2008. 'The National Governance Programme (2006–2010) and the modernization of the administration: Cameroon and New Public Management', *International Review of Administrative Sciences* 74 (2): 217–34.
Tchapmi, Christian. 2010. 'Réglementation: le transport routier au Cameroun fait sa mue', *Le Messager*, 14 January.
Temgoua, Albert. 2014. *Le Cameroun à l'époque des allemands*. Paris: L'Harmattan.

Teravaninthorn, Supee and Gaël Raballand. 2009. *Transport Prices and Costs in Africa: a review of the international corridors.* Washington DC: World Bank.

Terretta, Meredith. 2013. *Nation of Outlaws, State of Violence: nationalism, Grassfields tradition, and state building in Cameroon.* Athens OH: Ohio University Press.

The Economist. 2002. 'The road to hell is unpaved: trucking in Cameroon', *The Economist*, 21 December.

Topa, Giuseppe et al. 2009. *The Rainforests of Cameroon: experience and evidence from a decade of reform.* Washington DC: World Bank.

Trouillot, Michel-Rolph. 2001. 'The anthropology of the state in the age of globalization', *Current Anthropology* 42 (1): 125–38.

UNDP. 2000. *Société civile et développement: rapport proviso ire actualisé.* Yaoundé: United Nations Development Programme (UNDP).

Upetry, Kishor. 2006. *The Transit Regime for Landlocked States: international law and development perspectives.* Washington DC: World Bank.

Urry, John. 2000. *Sociology beyond Societies: mobilities for the twenty-first century.* New York NY: Routledge.

Van de Walle, Nicholas. 2001. *African Economies and the Politics of Permanent Crisis.* Cambridge: Cambridge University Press.

Vennetier, Pierre. 1991. *Les villes d'Afrique Tropicale.* Paris: Masson.

Wafo, Samuel. n.d. 'Loi regissant les ONG au Cameroun: ce qu'il faut absolument savoir' <www.repertoireong.org/association-humanitaire-cameroun .html> (accessed 20 June 2018).

Warnier, Jean-Pierre. 1993. *L'esprit d'entreprise au Cameroun.* Paris: Karthala

1994. 'La bigarrure des patrons camerounais' in J.-F. Bayart (ed.), *La réinvention du capitalisme.* Paris: Karthala.

Williams, Raymond. 1975. *The Country and the City.* New York NY: Oxford University Press.

World Bank. 2001. *Cameroon Country Assistance Evaluation.* Washington DC: World Bank.

2004. *Doing Business in 2004: understanding regulation.* Washington DC: World Bank and Oxford University Press.

2005. *Rapport analytique du système de passation des marchés publics au Cameroun.* Washington DC: World Bank.

Index

Abbo, 80, 82, 87
Abdoulaziz, 156, 158, 160, 163
Abega, Séverin-Cécile, 190
Aboubakar Gagara, 133
accounting, 121, 136, 148, 192, 194, 199
Action for Health Promotion and Environmental Protection (APROSPEN), 178–9, 184
Adamaoua Province, 20, 35, 61, 167, 171–2, 174, 177, 182, 190, 194
adashi see tontines
adjustment, structural, 12, 14, 191
African Development Bank, 171
Agence de Régulation des Marchés Publics *see* Public Contracts Regulatory Board
agrément (administrative authorisation), 58, 118, 124, 128, 177–80
Ahidjo, Ahmadou, 35, 78, 114, 135, 138, 169
Alim Pierre, 76–7, 79, 82–4, 200–1
Aliou, 80, 87
Alphonse, 166, 187, 191
Aminou, 167, 183, 187
anatomy, 7
ANCBC *see* National Association of Cattle Traders
Anders, Gerhard, 7
Arab-Choa, 46, 49
Arabo, 167, 187
Assemblée Territoriale du Cameroun (ATCAM), 27, 34
Association des Ressortissants de l'Adamaoua (ARA), 64, 84, 91
Association of Ngaoundéré Youth for the Fight against AIDS (AJLC), 173, 175, 178, 184–5, 187
association, freedom of, 64, 169, 192
associations, 176, 181
  proliferation, 169, 172

baaba saare (father of the house), 42
baaba saare (head of household), 49
Badjo, 45–50, 106–10, 112–14
Bakary Bandjou, 26, 34, 133
Bamileke, 83–4

Bandjoun, 27
Bangu, 54
Bangui, 135
Bank of Central African States (BEAC), 76, 79
banks, 39, 48, 50, 54, 60, 114, 144–5
Banque Internationale du Cameroun pour l'Épargne et le Credit (BICEC), 79
Banyo, 103–4
bappaño (paternal uncle), 41
baranda (small-scale traders), 109
Basile, 167, 180, 187
Bata, 96
Bayart, Jean-François, 4
Bélabo, 122, 135, 166, 183–4, 187
Bello, 57–62, 166, 171, 180, 187, 189, 191–2
Bennafla, Karine, 152
Benoué District, 37, 44
Bertoua, 193
Beti, 83
Biafran war, 134
Bierschenk, Thomas, 183
Biya, Paul, 2, 14, 35, 137–8, 159, 169, 197
Blundo, Giorgio, 6, 85
Bobbo, 40–2, 69–72, 87, 89–90
Bolloré, 45, 142, 152–4, 164
Boutrais, Jean, 32, 113
Brazzaville, 104, 135
brousse, la (the bush), 16–17
Bulu, 83
Bureau d'Affrètement de la Centrafrique (BARC), 146 *see also* Central African Freight Bureau
Bureau de Gestion du Fret Terrestre (BGFT) *see* Road Freight Management Bureau
Burnham, Philip, 78

Callon, Michel, 19
Calmette *see* Compagnie d'Élevage et de Cultures de Cameroun (CECC)
Camair, 45
Cameroon Cattle Farmers and Traders (ELCOBCAM), 93, 96, 107, 124

219

220   Index

Cameroon People's Democratic Movement (RDPC), 3, 36, 57, 61–2
Cameroon Tribune, 171
Camrail, 45, 93, 96, 120, 123, 142
Cantens, Thomas, 13
CARE, 173
cattle economy
   exports to Nigeria, 104, 106, 115
   insecurity, 111, 122
   markets, 32, 46, 50, 103, 107, 111, 115–17, 119, 124
   professionalisation, 111, 118, 120, 130
   repastoralisation, 32, 101
   single price system, 102
   trails, 115
   transmission of knowledge, 112
census, 10
Central African Freight Bureau (BARC), 136–7, 139, 148
Central African Republic (CAR), 135, 139, 152, 162
Chad, 131, 135, 137, 142, 152
Chad–Cameroon oil pipeline project, 2, 59, 119, 131, 142, 162, 166–7, 171, 182, 184, 189–90, 194
   regional compensation, 57, 77, 193–4
   subcontractors, 53, 57, 59–60, 143–6, 173–4, 176
Chadian business, 131, 135, 137, 143–4, 153, 158, 161, 164
Chalfin, Brenda, 7
Chamber of Commerce, 103
Chauveau, Jean-Pierre, 183
checkpoints, 57, 119, 127, 141, 157–62
Chevron, 142
Cimencam, 151
circulation, 18–19, 114–17, 120, 127, 158–62, 199, 203
civil service, 10–12, 35, 41, 43–4, 62, 78, 191–2
   General Statute, 11, 191
   politicisation, 38
   reform, 11
Civil Society Support Programme (PASC), 62
civility, 78, 91
Clarke, Kamari, 183
Cogefar, 78
Cohen, Abner, 110
Collectif des Organisations de la Société Civile de l'Adamaoua *see* Grouping of Adamaoua's Civil Society Organisations (COSCA)
Collectif, Le (the Collective), 166–8, 172–3, 180–1, 183–4, 187, 196
commandement indigène, le (native authorities), 31
common initiative groups (GICs), 59–60, 169–71, 176, 192, 196

Compagnie d'Élevage et de Cultures de Cameroun (CECC), 104–5
Compagnie Pastorale et Commerciale Africaine, 32, 101, 104–5
competition, 105, 112, 164, 168, 180, 188
concertation, la (consultation), 17, 122–4, 129, 200
Consultative Multi-Actor Programme (PCPA), 61, 174, 183, 188–9
Coopération des Transporteurs Tchadiens (CTT), 136–7, 146, 154
cooperatives, 169, 177, 192, 196
CORDAID, 193
corruption, 34, 65, 68, 84, 91, 116–17, 122, 125, 141, 159, 173, 187–8
COTCO, 57, 166, 189
   local community contacts (LCCs), 57, 189–90
Coton Sport, 36–7
Cotonou, 44
CotonTchad, 132
coupeurs de route see jargina
Credit du Sahel, 50–1
Credit Lyonnais, 50, 79
crise, la (the crisis), 2–3, 197
customs, 159, 163

Dang, 126
Danko, 154
Daoua, 55–6
Daouda, 52
de Soto, Hernando, 5
   The Other Path, 5
Deby, Idriss, 159
Deleuze, Gilles
   A Thousand Plateaus, 4
Delmas-Vieljeux, 142
descentes sur le terrain (inspection visits), 15, 122
Deschamps, Émile, 131, 146, 152, 154, 162
devaluation, of CFA franc (1994), 106, 140, 145
Development without Borders (DSF), 188
Diocesan Coordination for Development and Social Activities – Caritas (CODASC), 193
Dir, 116
Direction Génerale des Grands Travaux du Cameroun (Directorate General of Public Works, DGTC), 67
disorder, 3, 52, 137, 140
diversification, 43, 54, 110, 144, 146
Djarmaya, 154
Djerem District, 45, 49, 114
Djibrilla, 37–44, 69–73, 76, 79, 85, 88, 90, 170, 201
Doba Logistics, 143–4

Index

documentation, 119–20, 122, 128, 137, 147, 157–9, 161, 180, 182, 200, 202–3
of business transactions, 116, 199
Doing Business (World Bank), 5–6
Douala, 26, 40, 44, 84, 91, 96–7, 102–4, 131, 137, 139, 142, 154, 172, 180
Dubai, 37, 42
Dumont, René, 133

East Province, 61, 125, 190, 193
Economic and Monetary Union of Central Africa (CEMAC), 131, 156, 163
economic governance, 6, 198
'bad practices', 68, 198
interventionism, 102–3, 126
liberalisation, 52, 107, 126–7, 139–40, 148, 154
passages of, 202
tolerance, 158, 163, 203
economic interest groups (GIEs), 170, 177, 195
economy, the, 9
Éleveurs et Commerçants à Bétail de Cameroun (ELCOBCAM) *see* Cameroon Cattle Farmers and Traders
Elyachar, Julia, 190
encadrement (supervising and managing people), 15, 199
Equatorial Guinea, 46, 50
ethnicity *see* identity, ethnic
European Development Fund, 175
European Union, 62, 156, 168, 175, 177, 179, 186
Evangelical Lutheran Church of Cameroon, 169, 172
ExxonMobil, 142–3, 154, 185

facilitation, of trade, 158
Far North Province, 39, 43, 49, 61, 69, 76, 107, 171
Fonds Spécial d'Équipement et d'Intervention Intercommunale (FEICOM) *see* Special Council Support Fund for Mutual Assistance
formalities, 84, 86, 91, 160, 200–1
subversion, 200
fragmentation
of business, 95, 199
fraud, 3, 87, 200
Froelich, Jean-Claude, 26, 34, 103, 117
Fulbe, 29, 32, 35, 38, 43, 55, 78–9, 83, 103, 135

Gabon, 46, 50
Garga Haman Adji, 11, 23, 190
Garoua, 31, 35–6, 38, 41, 44, 69, 72, 78, 133–5, 151
Gbaya, 30–2, 84

gender, 82, 111
Geodis, 144, 152, 154
Geschiere, Peter, 15
ghost towns *see villes mortes*
Global Fund, The, 183
governance, 7 *see also* economic governance
good governance, 7, 13–14
National Governance Programme, 7, 13–14, 169
Goyoum, 166
Green, Maia, 168, 174
Grouping of Adamaoua's Civil Society Organisations (COSCA), 175, 183, 188–9
Guattari, Felix
A Thousand Plateaus, 4
Guider, 70, 74
Guyer, Jane, 18

haaɓe ('pagans'), 31
hadj, 38, 41–3, 47, 52, 55, 70, 82, 175, 179
Hart, Keith, 16
Hausa, 35, 40, 135
Highly Indebted Poor Countries (HIPC) initiative, 2, 76, 171
HIV/AIDS, fight against, 61, 166, 172–3, 176, 188
Hull, Matthew, 65

Ibadan, 110
identity
ethnic, 29, 40, 43, 55, 78–9, 82–4, 128, 135, 163, 176, 199
religious, 29, 43, 78–9, 82, 111, 128, 131, 199
impôt libératoire, 89, 119, 121, 123–5, 163
incivisme fiscal (fiscal disobedience), 17, 129
indeeri (naming ceremony), 69, 71
indigénat, 15
inertia, 2
informal economy, 16
informality, 16, 139, 141, 152, 201
inheritance, 38, 47, 52, 113
Integrated Project for the Support of Informal Sector Operators (PIAASI), 171
intermediaries, 103, 107, 109, 117, 119, 141, 153–4
International Financial Corporation, 5
International Monetary Fund (IMF), 2, 12, 171, 197
interventionism *see* economic governance
intimacy, 38, 81, 86, 91
Investment Funds for Agricultural and Community Micro-projects (FIMAC), 170
Islam, 43, 78, 83

Islamic Bank of Development, 170
Issa Maïgari, *laamido* (ruler) of Ngaoundéré, 35
Issa Tchiroma, 155

jargina (armed robbers), 111
Jeanne, 75, 87
joking relationships, 81

Kanuri, 35, 52, 55, 135
Kotoko, 73
Kousséri, 49, 135
kuugal laaɓdum (clean job), 92, 163

L'Oeil du Sahel (newspaper), 83
ladde (the bush), 16, 46
Lagos, 135
lahore (natron-rich natural springs), 120
laissez-passer (let pass), 18, 100, 124, 128, 159, 202–3
Laka, 30
landlockedness, 146, 158
Large Taxpayers Office (DGE), 119
League of Nations, 31
Lebanese business, 32, 133, 135, 161
legality, 6, 115, 121, 155, 176, 179, 196, 198, 203–4
  permissiveness, 199
  selective enforcement, 198
Libreville, 96, 104
licence, business, 26, 89, 103, 106, 118, 120, 122–5, 133, 135, 148, 160, 163–4, 195
literacy, 79
local government, 34, 36, 38, 68
Lombard, Louisa, 18, 162

mai gida am (my head of household) *see* patronage
Maiduguri, 135
Malabo, 96
maquis, le (scrubland), 16, 118, 139, 197, 199
Maroua, 26, 38–9, 41, 43–4, 69, 71–3, 80, 135
Martap, 174, 188
Matgénie, 70
Maurer, Bill, 195
Mayo Louti District, 70
Mbaïmboum, 46, 49, 166
Mbé, 114
Mbembe, Achille, 65
Mbéré District, 83, 116, 125
Mbororo, 32
Mbum, 29, 32
Meiganga, 47–8, 90, 103–4, 116, 125, 174
Mercer, Claire, 168, 174
microfinance, 48, 50

Minin, 174, 188
Ministry of Agriculture, 170–1
Ministry of Economic Planning and Regional Development (MINEPAT), 8
Ministry of Finance, 160, 170
Ministry of Foreign Affairs, 58
Ministry of Health, 185, 187
Ministry of Livestock, Fisheries, and Animal Industries (MINEPIA), 12, 100, 115, 117–18, 123, 129, 175, 199
Ministry of Public Contracts (MINMAP), 68, 74
Ministry of Public Works, 39, 72, 80, 159, 163
Ministry of Social Affairs, 171
Ministry of Territorial Administration and Decentralisation (MINTAD), 58, 177–8
Ministry of Transport (MINT), 3, 15, 134, 139, 147, 156–7, 164
Ministry of Water and Energy, 70
missionaries, 32, 34
Mobil, 151
Mohamadou Abbo, *laamido* (ruler) of Ngaoundéré, 27, 34
Mohamadou Wakiili, 26, 29
Mory, 134, 136
Mutuelle Communautaire de Croissance (MC2), 48

N'Djaména, 50, 131, 135, 158
Nana Hamadjoda, 27, 133
National Association of Cattle Traders (ANCBC), 93, 106, 111, 120–2, 126, 129
  Comité (Ngaoundéré chapter), 93, 96, 124
National Commission for the Hadj, 179
National Committee for the Fight against AIDS (CNLS), 166
  Central Technical Group (GTC), 167, 184–5
  local committees (CLLS), 173
  Provincial Technical Group (GTP), 166, 173
National Freight Bureau (BNF), 132, 147–8
National Implementation of Computerised Management and Logistics of State Personnel (ANTILOPE), 11
National Programme for Participatory Development (PNDP), 168, 194–5
National School of Agri-food Industries, 35
National Union for Democracy and Progress (UNDP), 36

Index

National Union of Road Transporters (SNTRC), 50, 132, 134–6, 138, 140, 144, 147–51, 159, 164
contribution syndicale (union contribution), 150
National Youth Coalition for Development (CNJD), 188
Nexus, 159, 164
Ngan'ha, 77, 91
Ngangassaou, 77, 91
Ngaoundal, 45, 47–9, 99, 106, 110, 112–13, 174, 188
Ngaoundéré, 19, 26
  Baladji (neighbourhood), 33, 35
  Grand Marché, 32, 35
  history, 29–36
  Industrial Zone (ZIN), 35
  Joli Soir (neighbourhood), 33
  Madagascar (neighbourhood), 33
  Maloumri (neighbourhood), 52
  Petit Marché, 35
  post-independence, 35–6
  Sabon Gari (neighbourhood), 33
  Tongo-Bali (neighbourhood), 175
  under French rule, 34
  under German rule, 30–2
NGO Act (1999), 58, 175, 177, 192
ngomna (government), 148
Nigeria, 96, 106, 110, 134, 183
Njobdi, Arɗo, 32
non-governmental organisations (NGOs), 78
  'donor dancing', 183
  contractualisation, 186
  hierarchies, 174, 177
  positioning, 187, 189
  profits, 195
North Province, 35, 39, 46, 61, 69–70, 73–4, 76, 174
Nouhou, 160, 162

Olivier de Sardan, Jean-Pierre, 183
Otayek, René, 190
Oumarou Dandjouma, 147
Ousmane Mey, 78

paperwork, 40–1, 69–70, 73, 76–7, 82, 87, 148
Pastorale, La *see* Compagnie Pastorale et Commerciale Africaine
patente see licence, business
patronage, 55
Peace Corps, 59
personalisation, of business, 39, 91
Petronas, 142
Pitoa, 73
plan de localisation (business location map), 73, 86–7, 120, 122
Pointe-Noire, 104, 135
Political Affairs Bureau, 26
polygamy, 38, 43, 47, 50, 52
Port Harcourt, 134
Poverty Reduction Strategy Paper, 2, 194
praise-singers, 73
prefects, 37–8, 41, 44, 86, 122, 169, 175–6, 181
press, freedom of, 169
professionalism, 92, 121, 168, 171, 174
Programme for Enhanced Revenue Reliability in Animal Husbandry and Fisheries (PSREP), 117, 129
Programme for the Support of Integrated Development (PADI), 172
Project for the Improvement of Rural Households' Income (PARFAR), 171
Project for the Preparation of the Transport Reform (PPRT), 139, 142
public contracts
  Code (2004), 66–7
  commissions (committees), 74
  fractionnement, 70, 74
  independent observers, 69
  over-invoicing, 64, 70, 92, 193
  payment, 70–1, 75, 81, 85, 88, 90
  reform, 65–9
  registration, 76, 87, 89, 200
  types, 74, 200
  World Bank's *Country Procurement Assessment Report* (CPAR), 66
Public Contracts Regulatory Board (ARMP), 67–9, 88
pulaaku (Fulbe ideals of virtue), 53, 79, 91

raiding, 30–2
railway, 35, 45, 48, 78, 93, 95–101, 105–6, 135, 142, 199
  derailment, 99
  privatisation, 45, 47, 95, 142
receveur (receiver general), 70, 77
reform, 11, 13, 198
Regifercam, 47, 136–7, 142
repertoires, of business practice, 92, 197
reports, 9
reputation, 38, 55, 152, 173, 190
respectability, 39, 42, 82, 92
rhizome, 4
Road Freight Management Bureau (BGFT), 2–5, 15, 132, 140, 147–8, 150, 154, 158, 163–4
roads
  paving, 35, 96
Roitman, Janet, 17, 65, 198
rotating savings and credit associations *see tontines*
Roumdé Adjia stadium (Garoua), 36

safe conduct, for international road transport, 1, 18–19, 147, 158–9, 161, 202
Saga, 50, 53, 138, 141–2, 154, 164
Saga-SDV, 131, 143, 145, 149, 152–3
Saïdou, 80, 82
sakaina see intermediaries
Sanda Maliki, 1, 18, 147
Sandra, 80, 82
sarkin sanu (chief of cattle), 111, 116
SCAC, 142
Schler, Lynn, 17–18
Schutztruppe (protection force), 31
SDV, 50, 142
sectors, economic, 8, 128, 199
Sehou, 78, 84
SETRACAUCAM, 52
Simé, Pierre, 147
single party, 149, 169
Smith, Daniel Jordan, 190
Soaem, 134, 136
sociétés de prévoyance (SPs), 102, 169
SOCOOPEDs (cooperative societies for production and development), 169
Socopao, 134, 136
Sodecoton, 36, 141, 151, 164
Sogetrans, 134, 136–9, 141, 145, 148, 164
Sokoto caliphate, 20, 29
South West Province, 172
Special Council Support Fund for Mutual Assistance (FEICOM), 70, 72
specialisation, 182
statistics, 2–3, 10, 116, 148
straddling, 11–12, 62, 75, 81, 191
suivisme, le, 78–80, 82, 84–5, 91
Support Programme for Decentralised Capacity Building for Urban Development (PACDDU), 186
Support Programme for the Structuring of Civil Society (PASOC), 175, 179–81, 184, 188, 193
Synergies de Développement (Sydev), 176, 178, 181, 184

tasa ginnaaji (station run by jinns), 52
taxation, 73, 86–91, 100–1, 114, 160–1, 190, 195, 200
 audits, 89
 direction par objectifs (management by objectives), 87, 119
 General Manager of Taxes (DGI), 86, 120
 sécurisation des recettes (enhancing revenue reliability), 117, 120

Tax Code, 192
taxpayer base, 88, 120
taxpayer categories, 89–90, 119, 125
Tchad-Cameroun Logistique (TCL), 145
Tello, 107
Tibati, 103–4
tokkal see tokke (plural)
tokke (sets of followers), 30, 34, 112
tontines, 75, 83, 114
Total Oil, 134, 151
tour de rôle (order of loading), 149, 164
Transport Bureau, 27
transport corridors, 135, 144
treasury, 41, 70–2, 75–6, 80, 83, 86–8, 90, 200
trésorier-payeur général (paymaster general, TPG), 71–2, 76, 79, 81–3, 201
trucking, international
 quotas, 132, 137, 139, 146–8, 202
tutelle, la (trusteeship), 14–15, 127, 199

uncertainty, 96, 155, 198
UNICEF, 171–2
Union du Peuple Camerounais (UPC), 16
United Nations Development Programme (UNDP), 11
United Transport Africa, 141, 151
University of Ngaoundéré, 20, 35–8, 49, 57, 59

value-added tax (VAT), 90, 157, 160
veterinary controls, 103–4, 111, 114, 116, 202
 fees, 100–1, 127
villes mortes, les (ghost towns), 2, 13, 36, 139–40, 198
Vina District, 49, 85, 114, 118, 176

Warnier, Jean-Pierre, 27–8
waybill, international, 147
West Province, 75, 80
Williams, Raymond
 The Country and the City, 17
World Bank, 3, 12, 65–6, 139, 142–3, 147, 166, 170–1, 174, 185, 194
World Food Programme, 61
World War One, 31

Yaoundé, 26, 44, 46, 48–9, 58, 60–1, 68, 71, 93, 96–7, 99, 102–4, 110, 112, 167, 172–3, 179–80, 195
Yero, 50–60, 149, 152–3, 161–4
Yola, 29, 31

Titles in the series

59. LIZ GUNNER *Radio Soundings: South Africa and the Black Modern*
58. JESSICA JOHNSON *In Search of Gender Justice: Rights and Relationships in Matrilineal Malawi*
57. JASON SUMICH *The Middle Class in Mozambique: The State and the Politics of Transformation in Southern Africa*
56. JOSÉ-MARÍA MUÑOZ *Doing Business in Cameroon: An Anatomy of Economic Governance*
55. JENNIFER DIGGINS *Coastal Sierra Leone: Materiality and the Unseen in Maritime West Africa*
54. HANNAH HOECHNER *Quranic Schools in Northern Nigeria: Everyday Experiences of Youth, Faith, and Poverty*
53. HOLLY PORTER *After Rape: Violence, Justice, and Social Harmony in Uganda*
52. ALEXANDER THURSTON *Salafism in Nigeria: Islam, Preaching, and Politics*
51. ANDREW BANK *Pioneers of the Field: South Africa's Women Anthropologists*
50. MAXIM BOLT *Zimbabwe's Migrants and South Africa's Border Farms: The Roots of Impermanence*
49. MEERA VENKATACHALAM *Slavery, Memory and Religion in Southeastern Ghana, c.1850–Present*
48. DEREK PETERSON, KODZO GAVUA, AND CIRAJ RASSOOL (EDS) *The Politics of Heritage in Africa: Economies, Histories and Infrastructures*
47. ILANA VAN WYK *The Universal Church of the Kingdom of God in South Africa: A Church of Strangers*
46. JOEL CABRITA *Text and Authority in the South African Nazaretha Church*
45. MARLOES JANSON *Islam, Youth, and Modernity in the Gambia: The Tablighi Jama'at*
44. ANDREW BANK AND LESLIE J. BANK (EDS) *Inside African Anthropology: Monica Wilson and her Interpreters*
43. ISAK NIEHAUS *Witchcraft and a Life in the New South Africa*
42. FRASER G. MCNEILL *AIDS, Politics, and Music in South Africa*
41. KRIJN PETERS *War and the Crisis of Youth in Sierra Leone*
40. INSA NOLTE *Obafemi Awolowo and the Making of Remo: The Local Politics of a Nigerian Nationalist*
39. BEN JONES *Beyond the State in Rural Uganda*
38. RAMON SARRÓ *The Politics of Religious Change on the Upper Guinea Coast: Iconoclasm Done and Undone*
37. CHARLES GORE *Art, Performance and Ritual in Benin City*
36. FERDINAND DE JONG *Masquerades of Modernity: Power and Secrecy in Casamance, Senegal*
35. KAI KRESSE *Philosophising in Mombasa: Knowledge, Islam and Intellectual Practice on the Swahili Coast*
34. DAVID PRATTEN *The Man-Leopard Murders: History and Society in Colonial Nigeria*
33. CAROLA LENTZ *Ethnicity and the Making of History in Northern Ghana*
32. BENJAMIN F. SOARES *Islam and the Prayer Economy: History and Authority in a Malian Town*

31. COLIN MURRAY AND PETER SANDERS *Medicine Murder in Colonial Lesotho: The Anatomy of a Moral Crisis*
30. ROY M. DILLEY *Islamic and Caste Knowledge Practices among Haalpulaar'en in Senegal: Between Mosque and Termite Mound*
29. BELINDA BOZZOLI *Theatres of Struggle and the End of Apartheid*
28. ELISHA RENNE *Population and Progress in a Yoruba Town*
27. ANTHONY SIMPSON *'Half-London' in Zambia: Contested Identities in a Catholic Mission School*
26. HARRI ENGLUND *From War to Peace on the Mozambique–Malawi Borderland*
25. T. C. MCCASKIE *Asante Identities: History and Modernity in an African Village 1850–1950*
24. JANET BUJRA *Serving Class: Masculinity and the Feminisation of Domestic Service in Tanzania*
23. CHRISTOPHER O. DAVIS *Death in Abeyance: Illness and Therapy among the Tabwa of Central Africa*
22. DEBORAH JAMES *Songs of the Women Migrants: Performance and Identity in South Africa*
21. BIRGIT MEYER *Translating the Devil: Religion and Modernity among the Ewe in Ghana*
20. DAVID MAXWELL *Christians and Chiefs in Zimbabwe: A Social History of the Hwesa People c.1870s–1990s*
19. FIONA D. MACKENZIE *Land, Ecology and Resistance in Kenya, 1880–1952*
18. JANE I. GUYER *An African Niche Economy: Farming to Feed Ibadan, 1968–88*
17. PHILIP BURNHAM *The Politics of Cultural Difference in Northern Cameroon*
16. GRAHAM FURNISS *Poetry, Prose and Popular Culture in Hausa*
15. C. BAWA YAMBA *Permanent Pilgrims: The Role of Pilgrimage in the Lives of West African Muslims in Sudan*
14. TOM FORREST *The Advance of African Capital: The Growth of Nigerian Private Enterprise*
13. MELISSA LEACH *Rainforest Relations: Gender and Resource Use among the Mende of Gola, Sierra Leone*
12. ISAAC NCUBE MAZONDE *Ranching and Enterprise in Eastern Botswana: A Case Study of Black and White Farmers*
11. G. S. EADES *Strangers and Traders: Yoruba Migrants, Markets and the State in Northern Ghana*
10. COLIN MURRAY *Black Mountain: Land, Class and Power in the Eastern Orange Free State, 1880s to 1980s*
9. RICHARD WERBNER *Tears of the Dead: The Social Biography of an African Family*
8. RICHARD FARDON *Between God, the Dead and the Wild: Chamba Interpretations of Religion and Ritual*
7. KARIN BARBER *I Could Speak Until Tomorrow:* Oriki, *Women and the Past in a Yoruba Town*
6. SUZETTE HEALD *Controlling Anger: The Sociology of Gisu Violence*
5. GUNTHER SCHLEE *Identities on the Move: Clanship and Pastoralism in Northern Kenya*

4. JOHAN POTTIER *Migrants No More: Settlement and Survival in Mambwe Villages, Zambia*
3. PAUL SPENCER *The Maasai of Matapato: A Study of Rituals of Rebellion*
2. JANE I. GUYER (ED.) *Feeding African Cities: Essays in Social History*
1. SANDRA T. BARNES *Patrons and Power: Creating a Political Community in Metropolitan Lagos*